ACKNOWLEDGEMENTS

This book should have been written and published before the British Brexit Referendum of June 2016. Although my 'research' that went into this book—in other words, the reading and pondering—began with my undergraduate degree in History at the University of London 1978–1981, my full teaching load did not give me the time to write this book. It took a lecture series as incumbent of the Vincent Wright Chair at Sciences Po' in the first semester of 2018 to force me into further reading and pondering, and a grant from the Smith Richardson Foundation (administered by the Foreign Policy Research Institute) to finance research leave that enabled me to get down to writing. I also owe many thanks to my colleagues at the 'Laboratory of Excellence' (Labex) 'Writing a new History of Europe', run from the Sorbonne in Paris, to my colleagues at Sciences Po' Paris and Reims and to my colleagues at the University Paris II Assas with whom I had many very helpful exchanges on this and related subjects. Finally, I want to express my gratitude to the University of Glasgow that hired me in 2017 yet immediately let me get away for research leave. I also owe thanks to the German Historical Institute in Paris under Thomas Maissen and Stefan Martens with its splendid library, its support for the Labex and its generous hospitality towards visiting researchers like myself.

ACKNOWLEDGEMENTS

Several colleagues who are experts on periods I am brazenly summarizing here have kindly guided me to avoid at least some howlers. Deserving of my warmest thanks for this are due especially to Professor Andrew Knapp, who patiently combed through the entire manuscript spotting many an error and making invaluable corrections, but also to Professors John Gillingham, Hans van Wees, Joachim Whaley, Janet Nelson and Anne Deighton as well as Drs Andreas Osiander Cian O'Driscoll and Emma Aston. All remaining errors are exclusively my own.

As always, I must thank my forbearing husband and daughter for putting up with me when I cut back on our time together to juggle the commitments of my work. They have long learnt that holidays are times when I tap away frantically on my computer, hide in libraries, or wander about museums or historical sites with a dazed look collecting material for my next argument. At least it takes them to interesting places!

INTRODUCTION

THE DIALECTIC OF EMPIRE, SOVEREIGNTY, AND CO-OPERATIVE SYNTHESES

This book explains Brexit—the British movement to secede from the European Union (EU)—in the context of centuries of struggle about the European order. From the beginning of European integration after the Second World War, Britain has famously played a special role in it, often one of being the odd one out. Yet it was British politicians who were the first to propose, indeed to initiate, European integration, including the devolution of a key part of sovereignty—the freedom to decide to use armed force.

The decision of 51.9% of the British voters in the referendum of 23 June 2016 in favour of Britain's leaving the European Union (EU) would have come as no surprise to Winston Churchill, who first urged the European states to move towards integration in a speech made in 1946, but who by 1950 claimed that he had never seen Britain as part of this. It would not have surprised Charles de Gaulle, the French President at the time when the United Kingdom belatedly in 1961 and 1967 made bids to join the European Communities which had been created, without British participation, in the 1950s. De Gaulle later vetoed both British attempts to accede to the European Communities by explaining that, in his view, Britain's true loyalties lay elsewhere: in her special relationships with the Commonwealth and above all with the USA (see Chapter 11). The British electorate's decision of June 2016 was welcomed by Russian President Putin and by US President Trump, men who both put sovereignty and 'nation-states' above multilateralism and international co-operation.

The objections voiced in Britain in the run-up to the 2016 referendum—the loss of sovereign control, being dictated to by a larger entity dominating the continent, rejection of any higher authority than that of the government of Britain—have a long pedigree of precedents. It is inspired by ideas articulated by the Greek city states in their resistance to Persian hegemony in the fifth century BC, and it is a direct copy of the repudiation by French monarchs since the twelfth century of any deference to the Holy Roman Emperor. It was French rulers who, for seven centuries, did all within their power to counter-balance, thwart, form alliances against and even go to war against successive empires in Europe (unless France provided the emperor). In this, English rulers eagerly copied the French.

Yet it was from France, and then also from some other European states including England, that proposals emanated for the creation of a European state system as an alternative to either domination by the Holy Roman Empire, or complete anarchy in which sovereign states would freely compete and go to war with one another. From the fourteenth century onwards, a series of political philosophers—many with government experience—proposed some sort of federation or confederation of states that should co-operate to settle conflicts among them peacefully and deal with other issues of common concern (especially external threats to Europe). Thus not only the concept of sovereignty has been present and has been fiercely defended for centuries, but also the concern that sovereign states would wage war with one another too easily if not restrained in some way. Moreover, time and again, the sovereign states of Europe, all following their own narrow interests, failed to put up a successful common defence against Islamic expansionism, first by Arabs and Berbers, later by Turks. To remedy this, proposals aiming at the creation of a more robustly pacific European system, a European order, a European league or even a European Union—a term already used by the Abbé de Saint-Pierre in the early eighteenth century—have thus also been put forward for centuries, albeit not applied before the nineteenth century.

This book aims to sketch the pedigree of the sovereigntist, independentist stance embodied in the 2016 Brexit referendum vote in the United Kingdom (UK), as well as its antithesis in the form of a universal empire or monarchy, and of proposals for a third way: that of bringing the polities of Europe together in a European system or European Union to let them settle their differences peacefully, tackle common problems jointly, and to mount an effective common defence against external threats. A fourth option was also implemented: the great-power oligarchy that took various forms, and which we still find in the Pentarchy of the Permanent Five Members of the United Nations (UN) Security Council.

State Systems: Neglected Dimension of International Relations Theory

Apart from tracing the origins of ideas underlying British Euroscepticism, this book also aims to make an academic contribution to International Relations as a discipline. It sketches the evolution of theory and practice of relations between states and other state-like entities (organised societies with the capacity of policy-making). It is concerned with their origins, mainly in Europe and in the area where Europe was born, the Eastern Mediterranean and its Middle Eastern littoral states.

We will identify patterns of inter-state relations which originated in Antiquity so as to emphasise theories about them that have been handed down to us. These theories were analytical (explaining how the relations between polities worked) or prescriptive (explaining how they should work, increasingly with the aim of limiting or eliminating war), sometimes both.

As we shall see, the behaviour of entities would at several stages in European history crystallise into patterns, and even into systems. Systems of states have been defined by Heinz Duchhardt as consisting of 'multiple political organisms that are linked by manifold cultural, economic and political linkages [*Verflechtungen*] ... the ... interaction of which is intended to last and is not primarily aimed to destroy [one or more] partners and thus the System itself'.[1] A pattern of inter-state behaviour can emerge for periods of variable length; it has a degree of predictability, so that if one entity does one thing, another is likely to do another. A system—and that is the way the term is used here—contains an element of deliberate design on the part of a number of entities (in modern European history, states) forming the system, with the intention, to paraphrase Duchhardt, that the pattern of interaction is intended to last, as is the system. We shall see that the aim of creating such systems was to bring about peaceful inter-state relations. Given these intentions and these designs, theories about the interaction of states underlay the conscious formation of such state systems. Together with an analysis of the actual patterns of relations between states or less developed polities, theories of inter-polity or 'International' relations are thus also discussed in this book.

With some notable exceptions, the theorists who will be introduced wrote mainly from the fourteenth century onwards, but with a background knowledge and cultural heritage of ideas

4

taken from the Hebrew Bible and from classical Antiquity (hence the inclusion of the Eastern Mediterranean) as well as from Medieval European theories and practice. These need to be explained before we can focus on the theorists themselves, as does the fact that they assumed certain characteristics of polities and human society particular to their own times which were not always present in human history. It is necessary also to highlight alternative structures of polities and patterns of inter-polity relations to show that theorists were and are often limited by their own knowledge of the world and of history. Yet some produced theories of how states should relate to each other that were thought utopian and radical in their own age (and even today).

Theory was always to some extent informed by what was known to theorists of (mainly European and Middle Eastern) history, and by what they had witnessed in their own lifetime or what catastrophes or other major events had occurred within living memory. Rarely in the short term, but sometimes in the long term, prescriptions made by theorists would in turn have an impact on the shaping of new systems or orders of inter-polity relations. Some prescriptions still seem unworkable or were applied but failed miserably. Some ideas derided as utopian in their own time have later been turned into policy-guiding principles or structures that we now live with today. Dozens of thinkers since the fourteenth century prescribed converging remedies for the war-proneness of Europe, variations of which have been put into practice in the world and in Europe since the early nineteenth century (see Chapter 6). The Congress System of the nineteenth century, and in the twentieth century, the League of Nations, the UN and the European Union (EU), the Organisation for Security and Cooperation in Europe (OSCE) and many other International Organisations are the children of these theories.

This branch of the theories of International Relations that deals with the patterns and systems of inter-polity relations and looks at how conducive such systems have been to war or to peace offers both huge insights, and crucial thoughts for our future. It is wrongly relegated to the margins of the discipline by the excessive emphasis in research and teaching on other, arguably less important patterns of interpretation.[2]

The principal reason for this is the deliberate blindness to change of most theories of International Relations. This begins with the very entities the relations between which are studied in this discipline, as we shall see. Polities—i.e. organised human societies—have always come in all shapes and sizes, from the tiny Republic of San Marino to the Kingdom of Sweden, as have polities made up of distinct entities, from the Delian League or the quasi-state of the Hanse to the Roman Empire, or the Austro-Hungarian Empire, the European Union (EU) or the Russian Federation. As we shall see, it is difficult to find terms broad enough to encompass all of these and the complex patterns of their relations. It is thus easier to pretend that 'International Relations' can be reduced to the dynamics of billiard balls, all of a same size and weight, bouncing off one another. Yet this simplistic simile does not help us deal with let alone resolve the security problems of the real world.

2

INTER-'NATIONAL' RELATIONS?

PROBLEMS OF TERMINOLOGY
AND BASIC ASSUMPTIONS

The Evolution of Words and Ideas

Before moving on to the main subject of this book, we need to preface it with a few short explorations of some key terms widely used in literature dealing with International Relations, and their underlying assumptions. As we shall see, many of them are extremely misleading or at least lend themselves to confusion and misinterpretation, obstructing, rather than helping, our understanding of the subject. These terms include 'international', 'state', 'nation', 'realism', 'liberalism' and 'liberty', 'republic', 'democracy', sovereignty and *imperium*/empire. This is important as we are all too often blinkered by terms we use vaguely and inaccurately, which may distort realities to the point of obstructing understanding. Some terms such as 'nation-state', supposedly the basic building block of inter-'national' relations, are used wrongly most of the time when applied to Europe, derailing attempts to analyse reality. Moreover, experts from different disciplines often engage in a dialogue of the deaf as different disciplines use the same word differently, sometimes in blatant disregard of how those words are commonly used by the rest of the population.

'International Relations' is a fundamentally flawed term, as Donald Cameron Watt noted.[1] The invention of the term 'international' in the context of 'international law' is attributed to Jeremy Bentham, writing just after the Americans had won their independence from the United Kingdom in a war that turned British settlers into a new *nation*, when the French Revolution was stirring up Europe, with a *nation* shaking off the rule of an elite—monarchy, aristocracy, nobility—to rule itself. In the ensuing wars which pitted huge French conscript armies against neighbouring countries, including Bentham's own, one could see why Bentham used this term. In law, the previous terms had included the *ius inter gentes*, between peoples, and the difference between the terms 'people' and 'nation', in Bentham's times and in wider use since, was the latter's definition as the population of a state (rather than a tribe or an ethnic group without its own state). So the term 'international law' stuck and is here to stay.

The term has been applied more recently to the study of relations between states; in this context, it is misleading. It conjures up the idea of actual encounters between these nations, perhaps through mass tourism or visits by huge crowds of international football fans, or school exchanges, or more fatally, through mass conscript armies clashing on battlefields. But it is not the encounter of common people in peace or war that International Relations studies.[2] Instead, this hybrid discipline with roots throughout diplomatic history and political theory studies the relations between governments which may lead to throwing mass armies against each other in bloody wars, but for long stretches of time simply consists of diplomatic exchanges, treaties, negotiations, dynastic alliances forged by marriages, against a background of trade—important though this is—and other relations between private citizens and companies.

More properly, therefore, we should be talking, not about international relations when studying systems, but inter-state relations. We have already touched on the word 'state'. Crucially, the obsession of Political Science and International Relations (IR) Theory with the 'state' suggests that it is an immutable basic social formation, more important and lasting than cities or sub-state regions or supra-state organisations, and that entities that are not States will not endure. By assuming and preaching that States are the main actors in politics, vast parts of Political Science and IR Theory condition the minds of students and a greater public beyond to subscribe to this self-fulfilling prophecy.

Let us consider, for a moment, the origins of the word 'state'. It is derived from Latin *status*, meaning what we still encounter in the expression 'the state of affairs' or the US President's annual 'state-of-the-Nation' speech. In the Middle Ages it came to denote the Estates—a class system—and on from that, by the seventeenth century, in the context of the Netherlands the components of the Dutch Republic (referred to as the Estates-General). From there it spread to denote 'state' in the sense of a polity with a population, a territory, a government, in many ways the modern equivalent of the *res publica*, especially when it comes to state-owned (i.e. public) institutions such as schools, libraries or public record offices. For these, English has no adjective other than 'public' or indeed 'national' where German would use *staatlich*, or Russians, *gosudarstvenniy*—of the state, belonging to the state. Moreover, American political scientists use the term 'national' as the synonym for 'federal' to differentiate the level of Washington DC's policies or legislation from those of the State of, say, Texas. They will refer to the USA as a 'nation-state' to make this distinction, but as we shall see, the term rarely fits European contexts.

Pedants will object to the very use even of the term 'state' for medieval monarchies. A state, they will say, surely needs more than a monarch who has commandeered a number of priests, monks and bishops to help run a primitive kingdom in which hardly anybody outside the clergy could read or write. A state would have an apparatus of government: civil servants, a standing army, regular tax revenues, a judiciary and penitential system. To use Max Weber's definition of the state, a state would surely have and not just ineffectively claim a monopoly of the use of force, as medieval monarchs did progressively. Today we would call a state that is torn apart by civil wars and mafia-style feuds a 'failed' state, a reason for foreign powers to intervene and take over government functions. Therefore, ignoring the city-states of ancient times and of some parts of Europe in the Middle Ages (Italy, Flanders, the cities of the Hanse) and several empires of Antiquity with their fairly large and effective bureaucratic apparatus, many scholars insist that there were no 'proper' states before 'modern' times. So a study of 'inter-state' relations, narrowly defined, would have to leave out the kingdoms of the Middle Ages, a period of roughly 1,000 years of diplomacy, treaties, wars, trade and above all politics. But all these entities—and here is an acceptable word that could be applied to Greek city-states as much to the kingdom of the Franks or sixteenth-century Spain—had relations worth studying. To stress the structured policy making of these entities, it is perhaps best to turn to the Greek word polity, denoting an organised society that has the structures to make politics. And this is the term we will use here, and with it, inter-polity relations, to be able to cover such a long span of European history with its many variations in political structures.

There are further terms that need explanation because of their problematic or even inappropriate usage. Theorists of international relations have come to use the noun 'realism' (along with the adjective 'realist', as opposed to 'realistic') in an odd way. To them it does not mean the attitude with which the Scot or the Englishwoman takes her umbrella along regardless of whether the sky is blue or grey. Instead they take 'realist' to label a particular sort of blind, narrow selfishness with which some leaders in history furthered their own, or their dynasty's or their country's or their 'race's' supposed interests at the expense of everybody else's (only to find that at some stage, everybody else has had enough, fights back, and more often than not leaves the 'realists' with a very bloody nose and much worse off than before). Such a hijacking of common language often leads to confusion and even serious misunderstandings, and one should avoid it.

Equally, one should not assume that a word like 'freedom' or 'liberty' meant more or less the same thing at various stages in European history, and in different languages.[3] Far from it. If ancient Greeks fought for *eleutheria*, that freedom did not stop where the freedom of another began, but included the freedom to rule over others. In several conflicts such as the Peloponnesian War, the wars of Alexander III of Macedon and the wars following his death, parties on both sides claimed to be fighting for liberty. Meanwhile, they saw no contradiction between their own quest for freedom and their practice of keeping slaves.[4] 'Liberties' were the banner under which medieval barons and nobles opposed the interference by their own or a foreign king in their government of their own country in which there were slaves, serfs, and where 95% or more of the population had no say in government. The word 'liberty' was used in the *Magna Carta* of 1215, imposed by rebellious barons on King John of England, and in the Scottish Declaration of Arbroath of 1320, stating the Scottish barons' determination to protect their 'freedom' (*pro nostra libertate*) against English encroachments. When fourteenth- or fifteenth-century townsfolks in the Holy Roman Empire staged a revolt, the *freyheiten* (liberties) they claimed to defend tended to be the local rights and privileges they felt had

11

been encroached upon, such as the right to hold a market, charge merchants for the right to sell their goods at this market, brew beer, try, sentence and hang criminals, or, for their patricians to elect a mayor from among their number. When in the fourteenth to sixteenth centuries peasants rose up in France and England, their call for liberty was usually directed against unbearably high taxation; elsewhere it was against forms of serfdom and was not a demand for the vote. In the Early Modern period, Protestants throughout Europe used the term to mean freedom of conscience and freedom of religious practice. By contrast 'Liberals' of the eighteenth and nineteenth centuries wanted constitutions that would restrict the rule of the monarchies in which they lived; they sought an *État de droit* or *Rechtsstaat* (a state upholding the laws, how strange that there isn't an English term for this). English Liberals wanted freedom from arbitrary arrest while revolutionary Frenchmen wanted the freedom to vote—thus each could claim that the other was threatening liberty. This is why supposed 'Liberals' like Edmund Burke and Immanuel Kant scorned 'democracy' (by which they meant the democracy of Revolutionary France with its attendant *terreur*). 'Liberals' tended to want fewer restrictions on trade or even free (sic!) trade, but some simultaneously defended colonialism along with slavery, as did the German Liberals of the nineteenth century who were mostly interested in reaping the benefits of capitalism for themselves.

Today 'Liberal' parties in most European countries want lower taxes and a reduction of state power, while in the USA 'Liberal' is associated with the wish for a stronger central government and thus for higher taxation. While some 'Liberals' might seek to promote human rights abroad, to fight for the rights of oppressed peoples elsewhere in the world (which since the early nineteenth century was referred to as 'liberal interventionism'), other 'Liberals' might argue that all cultures and practices should be free to flourish and Westerners should not impose their values, shrugging off the concept of universal human rights: everybody should be free to choose their own laws and customs. After all, there are women in Europe who explain their wearing of the burka as part of their freedom to choose what they wear, and others who campaign to 'free the nipple'. So 'liberty', 'Liberal' or 'Liberalism' can mean many different things, and it is puzzling how any 'Liberal theory of International Relations' could be constructed around this exceptionally imprecise term.

Intimately linked to the demand for freedom is that of sovereignty. As we shall see, the concept of sovereignty was built on the principle that any ruler should be free to do within his or her realm what he or she saw fit, without foreign interference—a principle of international relations so strong that in the 1930s, it did not occur to anyone in Britain, France or the US to interfere with the systematic discrimination and imprisonment of hundreds of thousands of German citizens because they were Communist or merely Social Democrats, Freemasons, Jehovah's witnesses, wholly or partly by descent Jewish, or homosexual. Even after World War II was well underway, the stopping of the systematic murder of these groups was never a war aim for the Allies, although they clearly knew that it was taking place. Only after the Second World War with the International Charter on Human Rights of 1948, indeed perhaps only with the Helsinki Final Agreement of 1975, did a consensus emerge that the sovereignty of a state, protected by the UN Charter, should not allow a government grossly to violate the human rights of its own populations, and that committing acts of genocide and the like would warrant international intervention.

That words change their meaning over time applies to many other terms as well. The *res publica* (originally meaning: the public thing, what concerns the public—as opposed to just one clan or family) of ancient Rome would mean many things to many different societies in due course. Even when Roman Emperor Augustus founded what became a largely hereditary monarchy, when the consultation and work of the Senate were generally subjected to the decisions of the emperor, and the *plebs* no longer had an input into policy-making, the term was still used to designate public affairs.[5] Medieval Italian oligarchies like Venice called themselves 'republic'. In its English translation—'commonwealth'—the word could designate Oliver Cromwell's authoritarian government as well as a loose confederation of former British colonies linking them to the motherland by elite nostalgia. As we shall see, the Prussian philosopher Immanuel Kant, but also before him some of the French *Lumières*, defined a 'republic' not as a state in which every man (let alone woman) had the vote, but a state governed in the interest of the nation as a whole, not just of the monarch or ruling dynasty.

Particularly confusingly, the Latin word *imperium*, meaning originally rule (over an area), power over and control of, morphed several times over the centuries. Originally it applied to a Roman consul's or a provincial governor's powers but came to denote the whole area under Rome's direct rule, the Roman Empire. In the Middle Ages, there was the assumption that all of Christendom, or at least Latin Christendom, continued to form one *respublica Christiana*, one Christian commonwealth, under the spiritual authority of the Pope. The word *imperium* usually referred to the Holy Roman Empire, that federal entity encompassing many sub-entities including a kingdom, several duchies, free cities and many other statelets stretching from the North of Germany to Italy, which saw itself as successor state of the Roman Empire at least in the West and was governed by the emperor, with increasing internal checks and balances coming into being from the electors among whom he was chosen, and the other entities that made up this Empire. Until the eighteenth century, when somebody referred to 'the Empire' in English, it was the Holy Roman Empire that was meant.[6]

But as *imperium* implied that no outside secular authority had a say in this realm, the word would in medieval times be used to designate the powers of monarchs, the Latin rendering of a word denoting the supreme ruler, the *soverano*, which made its way from Italian to French *souverain* and to English *sovereign*. So in the later Middle Ages, from the twelfth century onwards, monarchs whose lands had been left outside the Holy Roman *Empire* (France, Spain, England...) would claim *imperium*/sovereignty for themselves, a power no outside force must interfere with. From the sixteenth century onwards, the word *imperium* when employed by these monarchs outside the Holy Roman Empire was occasionally used to denote their overseas' possessions. From the nineteenth century, it came to mean 'colonial empire' for Britain. If you mention 'the Empire' to Britons today, they will think with nostalgia of Queen Victoria and India, not of Rome, Charlemagne, the Ottos or the Habsburgs.

Prescriptions for Inter-Polity Relations

Ever since medieval thinkers honed their intellectual skills on the question of how to contain wars and settle quarrels between polities, a range of different theories has been developed, either trying to explain how polities actually relate to each other, or seeking to prescribe a new order or system that would allow entities to resolve conflicts without resorting to war or with minimal force. While the ancient Greek philosophers did not dwell on this question directly, some of their pronouncements inspired later thinkers, as we shall see. While Romans devoted whole rituals to ensuring that their wars were 'just', no one treatise deals fully with inter-polity relations. Some medieval authors came closer by addressing the relationship between the Holy Roman Empire and monarchs outside it, or the relations between the cities and other polities within the Holy Roman

Empire and its head, the emperor. Others were more concerned about the problems that arose from the structural paradox built into the European Christian order: it was bicephalous (i.e. it had two heads), a secular head, the emperor, and a religious head, the pope. In theory they were supposed to work together closely and complementarily, but in practice they often collided not least because their respective competences overlapped. Matters got worse when the Reformation led a large proportion of Europeans to deny the pope's authority, and to question or reject the authority of the emperors who at that stage were solidly aligned with the popes and the Church of Rome. From this emerged new proposals for a European system that should help resolve conflicts. They all turned on federal or confederative structures that would include the Holy Roman Empire as just one among several states, a council of state representatives and/or a parliament to discuss and resolve any problems concerning several or all the polities represented. Prescriptive rather than descriptive, these concepts (which we shall discuss below) had their roots in medieval schemes to further peace among Christian entities. Often drawn from the authors' own experiences of ecclesiastical councils, or mediations, or peace negotiations, they are the earliest form of International Relations Theory. This type of proposals continued to be put forward throughout the nineteenth and well into the twentieth century, since when they have generally morphed into more limited proposals for the reform of existing international organisations or new multilateral agreements.

With some early forerunners in the nineteenth century, but mainly since the First World War, we find a growing number of works analysing the behavioural patterns between states, often with less, sometimes with no concern for lessons to be drawn for the real world. We have already alluded to the labels of two schools that emerged, that of 'realism', that of 'liberalism'. A further school overlapping with that of 'liberalism' is referred to as 'idealism', implying either that its members are closer to the prescriptive than the analytical genre, or else that they take ideological motivations into account and should properly be called ideationists. More recently, writing subsumed under the title 'constructivism' has emerged as a strong competitor to the other schools. Its strength lies in its greater complexity, and above all in its sensitivity to the fact that people in different periods, cultures, contexts saw the world in different ways, projecting different world views and assumptions upon reality which in turn influenced and formed reality.

Without denying the explanatory power of 'realism' and 'idealism' (indeed we shall see examples of people with 'realist' and 'idealist' mindsets and behaviour interacting in war and peace) this book delves further into the relations between polities as *additional* means of analysis. Building on constructivism, we must note that the inter-polity relations as practised—behaviour of social entities towards one another—both are a function of people's expectations, and in turn condition the evolution of assumptions about such relations. A long period of peace will lead people to assume that peace is the norm; wars in short succession will lead to the assumption that war is inevitable; wars limited in scope and destructiveness will lead to the assumption that future wars will follow the same pattern unless conscious efforts are made to break out of this pattern, and so on.

But before turning to my main theme, two other hugely important dimensions of inter-polity relations need to be explored: space and populations. Discussing them in slightly greater detail, in historical perspective and underscoring change and variety, will challenge standard assumptions found in much International Relations literature about what constitutes polities, states, nations and thus the relations between them. It will help eschew misleading categorisations blinding us to the understanding of the complex world we live in and to what the future might hold—there is no reason to suppose that change occurred only in the past.

Geography, Geopolitics and Geostrategy

A further approach to the analysis of 'International Relations' focuses on geography. There can be no doubt that there are features of geography which enduringly condition the relations between peoples and governments—oceans and seas, coastlines and rivers, mountains, fertile areas and steppes and deserts. But on the one hand, the interplay between geography and the evolution of technology has produced change, as has the change of geography through natural or man-made influences on the other.

For long stretches of history, communication and commerce were easier to effect by sea than by land. This was true before the development of Roman roads, and in the dark centuries after 476 in the West and during and after the progressive reduction of the territories of the East Roman territories, when they were left to decay by subsequent invading or indigenous populations that had lost the high standards of Roman engineering and state organisation, and before the renewed efforts to build roads and then railway lines in modern times. Even the Roman Empire was more developed along its coastlines and main rivers than in the inland depths of its provinces. The result of this relative ease of communication by boat and water made it easier for populations to spread and settle along rivers and coasts, and yet remain in touch with each other. Consequently, just as Indian and Chinese civilisation sprang up along the great rivers of Asia, and as the Egyptian state developed in a narrow band of land along the Nile, a number of other civilisations developed along rivers: the Celtic peoples lived mainly along the Danube, and a millennium later, the

Norsemen (Vikings or Varangians) moved along the Neva, Volga and Don to settle in what is now Russia and Ukraine.

Networks of polities also established themselves along sea shores: the Phoenicians and their Carthaginian heirs, along the Mediterranean littoral; Greek city states colonies by the Aegean and others in Sicily, Southern Italy and as far as South-Eastern France and Spain. In the first millennium, it is pointless to try to trace Norwegian, Danish or Swedish 'national' history as the Scandinavian countries were inhabited by peoples mainly living on the coasts and forming a polity that had the North and Baltic Seas as their main corridors of communication, soon to include also the occupation of a substantial part of the British Isles. In these polities, nobody would have seen a consolidated landmass as the prerequisite for collective identity in the way in which in the nineteenth- and twentieth-century nationalists postulated for the 'nation-state'.

Well into modern times, the quasi-state that was the Hanse consisted of a collection of cities scattered along the coasts of (mainly northern) Europe; in any of these, people would have been accustomed to their neighbours in the hinterland speaking quite different languages. Burghers from Danzig (now Gdansk) or Königsberg (now Kaliningrad) would have intermarried more easily with those from Stockholm, Hamburg, or Groningen, rather than with the populations who lived only a few miles inland from them. The last Venetian client-cities on the North-Eastern shores of the Adriatic such as Ragusa (Dubrovnik) and Zadar only lost their Italian-speaking populations with the end of the Second World War, when Yugoslavia took her revenge for the Italian occupation and sought to constitute herself as a homogeneous (ethnic) nation-state. Previously, they had been part of an Italian cultural space. Vestiges of the Venetian and Genoese trading empires can still be found both in architectural remnants and occasionally in human minorities in towns and cities in the Aegean and Ionian seas, all the way to Kostantiniyye (as the Ottomans called Constantinople), where Italian merchants stayed on after the fall of the Byzantine Empire in 1453 trading happily with the new Turkish occupiers.

People living along coasts are (obviously) more likely to develop seafaring skills and economies than people living inland—and indeed we can find differences in such traditions very long-lived. The linguistic difference between Flemish- (or Dutch-) speakers and French-speakers in North-Western France, Belgium and the Netherlands goes together with a historic difference between seafaring coastal people and inland farmers with no interest in the sea. Yet there is no 1:1 equation of coastal people and seafaring, let alone naval-empire building. Theorists of 'geopolitics' or 'geostrategy', extrapolated from Britain's location that she was predestined to become a great naval power and construct an overseas' empire. But much the same geography in the centuries before the Meiji restoration should have made Japan a power with huge naval and imperial expansionist ambitions, or one of the tribes of the Philippines should, by this logic, have sought domination over all others and then begun to expand, perhaps towards Indonesia. None of them did, so there must be other factors turning geo-location into expansion by sea or even empire-building.

The peoples of the great Eurasian steppes, once they had discovered horses, tended to take advantage of easy terrain and invade and pillage surrounding areas—a pattern seen from the Scythians and Sarmatians to the Huns, the Mongols, Magyars and Turks. Not all of them settled, however, or tried to create an 'empire' for themselves: Scythians and Sarmatians disappeared altogether from Europe and from history. The Mongol empire, larger than any the world had seen as it stretched from China to Central Europe, and relying on an impressive communications network ensured by horsemen in the absence of roads, collapsed at the end of the thirteenth century on the death of Kublai Khan.

Until the seventeenth century, the ideal of a 'territorial state' with the shortest possible borders around a consolidated territory containing no enclosures belonging to other polities, and without possessing enclaves elsewhere, was not only unrealistic but not even dreamt of by theorists. Several other forms of geographic configuration existed before this. Throughout most of Europe, it was at some stage more usual than unusual for people to live in villages, towns or cities next to neighbours speaking a different language, but with kinship, language and cultural bonds with settlements once or twice removed, than to find people of their own language for hundreds of miles around them. The latter case existed, for example in the Roman Empire, but the common language was for many a second language, a *lingua franca*, which they spoke in addition to their own. A study of European place-names shows not only the successive settlement of different peoples in identical key locations (Paris for example going from Celtic settlement to Roman and then to Frankish town) but also the implantation of groups of newcomers in new settlements between already existing ones (such as, in the Thames Valley in Oxfordshire, the Celtic hillfort next to the Astons, Roman Dorchester, and Saxon Wallingford, all built half-a-dozen miles from one another).

Among the scholars who have focused on geography to create explanatory patterns for the history of war and peace, some have been able to predict little, such as Sir Halford Mackinder, who conceived a pattern of a heartland (centring on Russia) and a rimland (a semi-circle stretching from Europe through the Middle East, the Indian subcontinent to South-East Asia and China). He claimed that 'Who rules Central and Eastern Europe commands the Heartland. Who rules the Heartland commands the World-Island [Asia + Europe]. Who rules the World-Island commands the world.' Fortunately, so far he has not been proved right although these ideas fuelled fears about German and Russian/Soviet domination of the world. Others have used geographic factors as arguments for aggressive expansion. One was Karl Haushofer, one of Hitler's main inspirations, who wrote, in 1928: 'Geopolitics is the scientific foundation of the art of political action in the states organs' fight for life and death for *Lebensraum* (vital space).'[7] Another was Carl Schmitt with his obsession of creating a *Grossraum* or sphere of influence for Germany in Europe, similar to that claimed by the USA in the Western Hemisphere with the Monroe Doctrine.[8]

Early geopolitical theories tend to dwell on geographic constants. Yet even in its purest, most physical sense, the earth is ever-changing, with rivers and ports silting up, coastlines modified rising or falling sea levels, deforestation, soil exhaustion and other natural or man-made changes modifying the importance or accessibility of areas to humans. Even where geography has remained constant, technology has changed its importance in some contexts. The invention of the compass and of ships that could sail the oceans or later of the railways made it possible to overcome ever greater distances at ever greater speed. The telegraph and the telephone made it possible to co-ordinate business transactions but also military operations from afar, at lightning speed. When during the Napoleonic Wars Admiral John Jervis, first Earl St Vincent quipped that he never claimed that Napoleon couldn't invade Britain, only that he couldn't come by sea, his contemporaries had a good chuckle. But a mere half-century later, British Foreign Secretary and subsequently Prime Minister, Lord Palmerston, worried that steam ships had 'thrown a steam bridge across the Channel', making an invasion of the United Kingdom more likely.[9] Another half-century later again, in January 1907, the British Foreign Secretary Sir Eyre Crowe in a famous memorandum still expanded on the 'the immutable conditions of [Britain's] geographical situation on the ocean flank of Europe as an island state with vast oversea colonies and dependencies'. But already two months earlier, the press baron Lord Northcliffe recognised the signs of change with the arrival of aircraft. 'England is no longer an island', he wrote. The 'aerial chariots of a foe' could now descend 'on British soil if war comes.' In other words, 'The isolation of the United Kingdom may disappear.'[10] During the First World War, Britain's Committee of Imperial Defence echoed this insight, noting that henceforth, British territory was directly vulnerable to bombing from the air, and the Channel was no longer a 'moat defensive' against all attacks.[11] Geography may in large parts be immutable, but technology can change the entire strategic equation.

England had long taken an interest in Flanders and the Low Countries as the most likely area from which an invasion of England might take place; by the 1930s these areas were identified as most likely launch-pads for bomber raids. As future Prime Minister Stanley Baldwin told Parliament in mid-1934, 'When you think of the defence of England you no longer think of the chalk cliffs of Dover; you think of the Rhine. That is where our frontier lies.'[12] With the increasing range of bombers, however, Belgium and the Netherlands became irrelevant as potential base areas for air raids against the United Kingdom, and since the 1970s, Britain has been in the range of Soviet and now Russian Intermediate-Range Ballistic Missiles which would reach their targets a few minutes after being fired. Technology has much reduced the importance that the Channel once had.

Equally, technology has from time to time changed the importance of certain land areas. With the invention of the coal-fuelled steam engine, coal suddenly became an extremely sought-after commodity, and the Franco-Prussian and two world wars were fought over the coalfields of Southern Belgium, Northern France, Lorraine, the Saar and the Ruhr areas. When fuel oil began to replace coal, the discovery of oil fields leapt to the top of the agenda of many scientific expeditions and suddenly turned poor Middle Eastern areas into highly desirable colonies or protectorates, and later into rich states. The discovery of North Sea oil and gas gave Britain, set on a path of economic decline, a temporary boost propping up her status as a great (second-tier) power for several decades. Hopes of finding ways to access further oil and gas fields under the Arctic Ice or in Antarctica explain international interest in these inhospitable areas of the globe.

Of course huge aspects of geography have remained unchanged despite technological advances. Earthquakes still occur in areas where tectonic plates collide, usually mountainous areas, and when they strike, the very terrain always makes it particularly difficult to bring help to the afflicted. Earthquake-induced tsunamis, tidal waves and floods tend to recur in the same parts of the globe, and nothing has so far been devised to prevent them. Areas prone to disaster are areas of political instability and prone to create refugee movements affecting surrounding areas. Mountains remain hostile terrain in which to operate. When NATO in 1998/1999 considered how to stop the clashes of Serbs and Kosovar Albanians in Kosovo, then still a part of Serb-dominated Yugoslavia, the option of staging a land-intervention from Albanian territory was discarded because then as today, this mountainous region would have provided a poor base, challenging to cross to supply forces on the other side. Amazing feats can be accomplished occasionally, such as the Berlin airlift of 1948/49 in which, apart from food and fuel, the components of an entire power station were flown into Berlin across hundreds of miles of blocked land routes. But the cost of such operations is still such that the political gains must be very high to make them worth implementing.

On the whole, there is little about geopolitics that cannot be worked out by a student with some good maps and a thoughtful mind. Where complications arise, they tend to be a function not of geology, habitats and climate, but of the humans operating in each environment. And this in turn depends very much on the humans, their culture, and their social organisation, as the American geostrategist and naval historian Alfred Thayer Mahan explained: to be a sea power, one needed not only long coastlines but also 'a society with an aptitude for the sea and commercial enterprise; and a government with the influence and inclination to dominate the sea.'[13] This would explain the difference in the history of the Philippines, the Indonesian isles, or Japan before it began to start imitating the West in the late nineteenth century on the one hand, and the Cretans, or later Genoa, Venice, and England/Britain, on the other. It would explain the seafaring culture of the Norsemen, even though they seem to have spread out among the European coasts and the Russian rivers without much of a systematic government-sponsored plan. In short, and unsurprisingly, the relationship between geography and inter-polity relations depends on what people make of it. And people have always been on the move—first it took them generations to move a mere 100 miles, but over time, the speed of their movement picked up so that fewer and fewer people still live where their grandparents were born. But then, the idea of autochthonous inhabitants who have always lived in a particular part of Europe, of *Ureinwohner*, is largely a figment of the imaginations of nineteenth- and twentieth-century nationalism. Unfortunately, this fantasy is experiencing a revival in our own times.

Demography and Identities

It is indeed a fantasy, for all Europeans are immigrants. Or at least, descendants of immigrants.[14] The first humans to have settled in Europe were the Neanderthals (*homo neanderthalensis*), who died out, suspiciously, after *homo sapiens* had arrived, despite having survived several Ice Ages and other huge challenges. Moreover, most Europeans today speak an Indo-European language, imported by people who came after, mixed with and/or displaced an earlier population of *homo sapiens* of whom only small groups remain—the Basques are the only population in Europe still speaking a pre-Indo-European language. Within historical times—eras of which we have written evidence— Minoans and Etruscans constituted such populations before being absorbed by later migrants moving into Crete and the Italian peninsula respectively. Picts probably lived in Scotland before the arrival of Indo-European tribes. In most cases we do not know what languages these populations spoke. In the case of the Picts, all we know is that the Romans called them *picti*, the painted ones, but we have no idea what they called themselves. Nor do we know what to call the people who built Stonehenge or those who put up the standing stones of Carnac in Brittany; all we can be certain of is that they preceded the Indo-European Celts who settled across Europe, especially along the Danube, and later immigrated to Britain.

Most European population movements have taken place within historically and/or archaeologically documented times. According to their descendants, the people who founded Rome came to the Italic peninsula in the eighth century BC, and indeed, the first settlements within the boundaries of modern Rome can be archaeologically dated to that century. The Romans themselves later recorded the spread of Celtic peoples in Europe; in 390 BC, one Celtic tribe moved south within the Italic peninsula and sacked Rome. In the following centuries, the Romans gradually turned the tables on them, by and by defeating some tribes, winning some as allies against other Celts, and finally occupying just about all the areas inhabited by Gauls, including the Iberian Peninsula, modern France, Belgium and the Netherlands, and most of Britain, but also modern Austria, Hungary, Romania and

Bulgaria. Intermittently, non-Indo-European tribes invaded Europe from the East, but there were also other Indo-Europeans (Germanic tribes) which started to move across Europe in waves, staging raids into the Roman Empire and gradually establishing themselves within it, until they brought down (and partly took over) the Roman Empire in the West late in the 5th century.

These invasions by nomadic peoples who rustled cattle and sheep and raided the stocks of grain gathered by the peasants of the Roman Empire form part of a structural conflict between nomads and settled peoples the world over. In recent years, we have still seen this type of conflict between nomads and settled populations in Darfur (Sudan). Usually, the agriculturalists draw the short straw in such conflicts, as by definition the mobile raiders can withdraw beyond the reach of any revenge or punitive action by the farmers.

A recurrent pattern of human settlement in Europe is one in which a first wave of settlers establishes villages that are sometimes at a considerable distance from one another, in advantageous spots, near a fresh-water source, perhaps on an easily defensible promontory where they could secure themselves against nomadic raiders. The villages were likely to be separated by forests or wooded areas. The villagers may have engaged in agriculture and in hunting. A second wave of migrants might have arrived later (as with the Celts and Vikings), perhaps by boat along a river, establishing themselves along that river and along subsidiary streams. They, too, might have been farmers, but perhaps more skilled at fishing than hunting, and they would have stayed in touch with kinsfolk living a long way upriver or downriver from them. They would have traded with the hunters, but they would probably have spoken a different language and not intermarried much. Such patterns of settlement could still leave space for further peaceful settlement when migrants from other areas arrived (in Europe, usually from the East or North-

East), driven out of their homes by famine, drought or raiders, or forcibly moved by a government. (East and West Roman emperors, and following their example Charlemagne, as well as later Russian emperors, and Stalin after them, transferred whole populations over hundreds and thousands of miles, inserting them in new settlements between those of loyal subjects. The relocation of the conquered Saxons by Charlemagne can still be illustrated by villages or towns containing the name 'Sachsen' are dotted all over Western and Southern Germany.) Often such settlements required further forest clearances, again reflected in place names. The result would be a chequer-board of settlements in which neighbouring villages belonged to different ethnic groups, while entertaining bonds through kinship and inter-marriage with more distant villages, patterns that can still be discerned in many parts of Europe: the pattern of Celtic, Roman, Saxon, Viking and sometimes Norman place names across Britain is evidence of this.

Such ethnic and customary differences would not pose a prob-lem as long as the soil was sufficiently fertile, game and fish plentiful, and there was enough space for everybody. Indeed they could be mutually very advantageous: the river people could bring in trade from afar which the forest-farmers would otherwise not have access to, and all sides could have benefitted from the trans-fer of skills, of technically more advanced ways of working met-als, firing pots, or tilling the soil. Problems would only arise when times of scarcity produced competition for resources, and populations formed competing groups on the basis of kinship and cultural affinity, pitting the river people against the moun-tain farmers, or perhaps both against the most recent settlers. But even such conflicts might die down.

Thus ethnic minorities have existed over centuries within many states of Europe. This is true not just where one ethnic group came to lord it over another, such as the Anglo-Saxons over the

Celtic peoples of the British Isles, or the French over the Bretons, Basques and Corsicans, or the Poles over the Kashubians. Not only did rulers on occasion carry out punitive population transfers. Some also invited large groups of foreigners into their own realms if these satisfied particular economic needs, from the skilled craftsmen from German-speaking Central Europe who were invited to settle in Transylvania (*Siebenbürgen*) in the twelfth century, or in Russia in the eighteenth at the invitation of Empress Catherine the Great, to the Protestants mainly from Scotland settled in Northern Ireland in the wake of the Cromwellian Act of Settlement, to the Poles who came to work in French and Belgian coal mining and steel-making areas in the late nineteenth century and the 'guest-workers' (*Gastarbeiter*) from Italy, then also from Yugoslavia, Greece, and Turkey who were invited to Germany, Austria, later also the Netherlands and several other European countries in the second half of the twentieth century. While among the latter, the Italians, Greeks and Yugoslavs usually assimilated within a generation, Turkish and Kurdish (Muslim) guest workers and their families who tended to follow them later often continued to live in a bubble, to preserve their own religion, culture, language and social structures and to defy assimilation into the local population.

For centuries, this co-existence of economic migrants and their descendants forming ethnic minorities, and earlier populations and their descendants, in parallel societies, could work well. Friction would only occur when one ethnic group found itself backed by a government that tried to impose its religion, or else its language, customs and laws on all the others with the aim of achieving homogeneity, and of constructing a single ethnically-defined 'nation', in a single, ethnically defined 'nation-state'. This was inevitably problematic as all territorial states that emerged from the huge population movements of the first millennium and the Middle Ages contained linguistic minorities.

While in France the Southern French dialect was suppressed, Breton in Brittany and a Germanic dialect in Alsace and Lorraine are tolerated to some extent and remain so to this day. The Holy Roman Empire was multi-ethnic, including Northern Italy, Bohemia, Frisia and a variety of Slav peoples of whom the last remnants, the Sorbs, can still be found in Eastern Germany. In the United Kingdom, pockets of Gaelic-speaking Scots and Welsh-speakers survive, even if Cornish died out in the early twentieth century; the Griko, last remnants of Greek-speakers who are believed to have settled in Calabria in Southern Italy from the eighth century BC, still exist today but are disappearing into the Italian-speaking majority culture.

Linguistic differences between rulers and some of the ruled, or between neighbouring settlements mattered little for populations who were used to their superiors speaking another language, and to the use of interpreters when they had to deal with law courts or other parts of officialdom. The larger part of the European populations continued to be illiterate, and well into the seventeenth century, only the richer strata could afford to give their sons schooling. Consequently, it did not matter to most people if books were printed in a different language from theirs, or whether important business was transacted in Latin or in another language of which they had no or little knowledge. As long as they had the same religious confession it was only when states through their officials insisted on interacting with their populations in one sole state language that minorities began to stand out as different.

To sum up, for two millennia of recorded history, compact territorial states with an ethnically homogeneous population, clear frontiers and a centralised, sovereign governments did not exist. Indeed, even now, after the multiple genocides and forced population transfers of the Second World War and its immediate aftermaths, ethnically homogeneous 'nation-states' do not exist in Europe due to the new immigration from former colonies, then of guest workers, and lately of other economic migrants and refugees. Consequently, no theories of inter-polity relations that assume such ethnically homogeneous 'nation-states' as main building blocks of Europe or the world make sense. The term 'nation-state', ethnically defined, only makes sense as a political programme: to unite all people of one ethnicity in one state (invariably implying either the elimination by murder, assimilation or expulsion of minorities from different ethnicities, and/or the conquest of neighbouring territories where pockets of one's own ethnic group live). It is most appropriately used to describe the political programmes of elites of ethnic groups divided by state frontiers, by ethnic minorities within a state who want or wanted to secede from it and form their own 'nation-state', like Slovaks, Slovenes, Croats and Bosniaks in the 1990s and the Catalans today. If they succeeeded, the result of a new state-formation, in most cases is objectively not a full ethnic 'nation-state' in that it does not comprise all members of that ethnic group: the Yugoslav Wars of the 1990s were particularly pro-tracted where pockets of one ethnic group ended up in a differ-ent state, such as the Croats in Bosnia, with newly-independent Croatia trying to prize that strip of land away from Bosnia. Kosovo, inhabited mainly by Albanians, is now independent from Belgrade, but it is not a 'nation-state' in that it does not contain all Albanians: Albanians also reside in neighbouring Albania, and in Macedonia.

But one is easily confused: Otto von Bismarck, the Prussian Chancellor, used pan-German nationalism as a force to weld together the Second German *Reich* or Empire of 1871, and claimed Alsace and Lorraine from France partly on the grounds that they were populated by German-speakers (and had previ-ously belonged to the Holy Roman Empire). He thus claimed that he was constructing a 'nation-state'. In reality he followed a very different logic by excluding Austria with her German-speaking population from the 1871 *Reich*—only thus could he ensure Prussia's, not Austria's (or the Hohenzollerns', not the Habsburgs') predominance within it. He fooled most of the German speakers whose support he won for his unification project—no wonder this confuses students to this day.

No state in Europe has as yet fully succeeded with a programme of building an ethnic 'nation-state', even though Hitler made it his key ambition to bring all German-speakers into his 'Third *Reich*' and to eliminate all those who were not. Being Austrian himself, unlike Bismarck, he included Austria in his Reich, but also aimed to bring 'home' all the other pockets of German-speakers, scattered as they were all over Eastern Europe, such as the Transylvanian Saxons. Hitler's grand strategy of 'Germanizing' Eastern Europe comprised turning non-Germanic populations into slave labour or massacring them in the millions. Against the background of Hitler's horrendous attempt to create the perfect German nation-state (not the scaled-down version of Bismarck), it is chilling in the extreme to hear President Putin bemoan the loss of 25 million Russians who were left 'outside' Russia when the Soviet Union collapsed. The Slav countries' reaction to the Hitler's nation-state project was quite logical, although also tragic: the expulsion of the German-speaking populations from Poland and Czechoslovakia in the immediate aftermath of the Second World War led to at least one in ten dying on the way.[15]

Britain is a particularly odd case. A host of institutions suggest that the United Kingdom contains several nations: there is a Welsh National Opera as well as an English National Opera, a Scottish National Gallery and an English National Theatre, and of course separate Scottish and English national school curricula. The French periodically complain that with a similar-size population as that of France, the United Kingdom is allowed to field several national rugby and football teams in inter-national matches. Yet the National Records Office in Kew, outside London, contains the public records of governments of the whole of the United Kingdom, not just those of England, as the name might suggest. Citizens of Northern Ireland are, under the Good Friday Agreement of 1998, given the choice of calling themselves 'British' or 'Irish' or both. In short, the jury is still out on whether the British constitute one nation or four, and that makes it difficult to call the United Kingdom a 'nation-state' in an ethnic sense. The term 'nation-state', ethnically defined, should thus be used with great caution, if at all, in a European context.

Alternatively, 'nation-state' as used in the sense of the French Revolution (or the United States of America) is a shorthand for saying that the nation, not a king or oligarchy, is sovereign.[16] If used in this political sense, half the states in Europe, that is, the monarchies from Spain and the United Kingdom under its 'sovereign lady the Queen Elizabeth' to the Netherlands, Norway, Denmark and Sweden, are of course not 'nation-states'. So again, the term is problematic when applied to Europe. In short, the term 'nation-state' does not reflect European realities unless it is used in the narrow senses of either democratic republic, or the political programme of ethnic state-building described above. Most IR literature uses it in neither sense, thus being based on false premises and thoroughly misleading: no wonder its readers are brainwashed into a skewed and unrealistic vision of the world, however much they proclaim themselves to be 'realists'.

Nor is it sensible to assume that relations between organised societies of the future will continue to be dominated by territorial states with clearly defined state boundaries, or that the states of Europe will all become ethnically homogeneous in due course. Identity and identities fluctuate. Feelings of collective identity—'we-ness'—can crystallise around several concepts: common ancestors, real or imagined, a common language, a common

religion, a common tradition of seafaring and trading, loyalty to
a particular dynasty, to a particular ruler, to an ideology, to a
physically visible polity like a city or an imagined community
such as a nation or to a joint project for a common future. Early
forms of nationalism, as we shall see, emerged among elites in
several European countries a few times even before the French
Revolution, but it could also cede priority to other identifiers
such as religion or loyalty to a particular leader or party, an
ideology or a cause.

A social configuration that has long offered an implicit challenge to 'national' states has been the existence of ethnic networks
transcending state boundaries. These go back long before the
'nation-state' was conceived, with the networks of city-states
along coastlines, either under a dominating polity such as Athens,
Carthage or later Venice, or as associations such as the Hanse.
Trading networks cutting across polity boundaries existed also
between ethnic minorities operating from many different cities,
such as the Armenians, who, initially pushed south out of their
homeland by the Turks in the eleventh century, later fled to Persia
and modern-day Ukraine. By the seventeenth/eighteenth centuries, they had trading posts and communities in cities from
Amsterdam to Madras, from Arkhangelsk to Addis Ababa.
Similarly, stretching all over the Middle East and Europe until
their extermination there by the Germans in the Second World
War were Jewish networks, although Jews had previously been
expelled at various points from individual countries (England in
1290, France in 1182, 1306, 1394; Spain in 1492) or subjected to
deadly persecutions (or both). In the late nineteenth and twentieth centuries, Greek shipping companies and merchant networks
played a substantial role in the Mediterranean, building on networks between Greek communities which had endured the fall of
the Byzantine Empire and would survive that of the Ottoman
Empire. Jewish, Armenian and Greek diaspora networks spanned

the globe. For centuries, migrant skilled craftsmen, musicians, artists and scholars moved to wherever their skills were needed and appreciated. New patterns of diaspora merchant networks have become established in the twentieth century, for example among Indians, Pakistanis, and Chinese, entertaining family and also commercial links that encompass the globe. The guest workers even when settled more permanently have retained strong links with their country of origin (and even its politics); the same applies to many Frenchmen of North African Muslim origin, and British citizens of Asian and Caribbean origin, made possible by the revolution in cheap air travel.[17]

For centuries, while many people were part of ethnic networks stretching way beyond territorial states, often across seas, their principal allegiance tended to be to a city. Cities can create strong feelings of identity not least because they are actual communities, not 'imagined communities' like nations,[18] 'Christendom', or the Umma of Islam, or other huge human groups most of whom the individual member will never encounter. Cities have concrete problems that affect most of their inhabitants, such as failings in transport or refuse collection, power cuts or poor public school education. The rhythm of city life dictated by school holidays, or the upsurge of activity during an annual fair or a major sporting event, a local scandal or a crime will unite citizens in their experience, in their criticism or praise for the mayor. In short, they will be more aware than in many 'imagined communities' that they really inhabit a common polity.

While city-dwellers are thus in part united by their common experiences of such cities, there are also polarisations and parallel societies within cities. As of 2018, forty-seven cities around the globe have grown to encompass more than 10 million inhabitants. In Europe, Moscow, London and Paris belong to this category. Several of these megacities or conglomerates outside Europe are developing unmanageable slum areas with high crime rates, big pockets of poverty and unemployment, and massive discontent. But most bigger European cities have long had areas of high crime, high unemployment and social exclusion, with quarters verging on ghettos predominantly inhabited by particular ethnic minorities. The 'inner cities' of Britain have their equivalent in the French 'banlieues', and patterns of connections between Islamist terrorists and particular quarters of big cities such as Molenbeek in Brussels are telling signs of distinctive communities living side by side, barely tolerating each other.

Identities are forever shifting, but some collective cultural 'memories', clichés about identity passed on from generation to generation, are amazingly impervious to change, and about as useful for coping with our world as are the behavioural patterns which psychologists tell us were hard-wired into us in hundreds of thousands of years of prehistory. Thus many European nations from France, Spain, Portugal, Italy, Austria, Croatia, Serbia, Greece, Hungary, Poland, to Romania and Bulgaria believe they (alone) were the last bastion against the expansion of Islam, or the main victims of Muslim occupation. This in part explains attitudes towards the influx of Muslim refugees, especially if there have been few Muslims in these countries in recent times (this applies particularly to Poland, Hungary, Rumania, Bulgaria, Slovakia and the Czech Republic). But it is certainly not true that any of them were the only people in the past either to hold out against conquering Islam or to be defeated and occupied by it. Or take the example of Poland, which was several times divided and occupied by countries to its East, West, and South, and one should add the North, as Sweden long held the southern coast of the Baltic. If Poles today are convinced that the Germans and the Russians are out to get them, they are seeing the present through the lens of the past, which—whatever else might be true of the policies of Berlin and Moscow—skews the picture. While Britons insist on their special connection to the sea, many of them only get to see it when at the Costa Brava or the resorts of Greece, Cyprus or Turkey, or from a ferry—romantically preferred to the Eurotunnel—*en route* to another Continental holiday, the very occasional Sunday outing to the local beach notwithstanding. Other Britons might only see it from the air, on their hard-earned biennial holiday to visit relations in Pakistan, India or the Caribbean.

Looking back at the history of Europe over the last two millennia, what stands out is that cultural diversity and parallel ethnic societies became a problem when an ideology (an intolerant strand of Christianity or ethnic nationalism) posited that religious or linguistic-ethnic minorities could not be tolerated within a polity or when the polity moved towards democracy, drawing all adults into a political discourse that needed to be conducted in a common language. Religious intolerance lies at the origins of the many persecutions of Jews since the Middle Ages, culminating, of course, in the Holocaust. They were also the source of Europe's confessional wars which started, if one does not count the Albigensian Crusade (1209–1229), with the Hussite Wars in Bohemia in the early fifteenth century and in a new permutation persisted until the Yugoslav wars of the 1990s. Religious intolerance tended to merge with ethnic discrimination: English-Irish conflicts from the sixteenth century were both ethnically and religiously motivated, as was the Eighty-Years War between the (Protestant) Netherlands and their (Catholic) Spanish masters. Mutual massacres carried out between (Muslim) Turkish and (Christian) Bulgarian villages in the late nineteenth and early twentieth centuries equally combined the two strands of constructed antagonisms.

While Central Europe—in the wake of the genocide perpetrated by the Nazis and the subsequent population displacements after the Second World War—had by the mid-twentieth century become more ethnically homogeneous within state borders than ever before, since the 1960s we have seen a new multi-ethnicity emerging, particularly in Europe's big cities. We may in future be moving closer to a pattern where large proportions of the populations of big cities identify with that city, and beyond that with a network of ethnically related groups elsewhere in the world, rather than with the nation of the hinterland of their city. Cultural and economic elites, too, will be more at home in a set of other big cities in other countries than in declining formerly industrial towns of their own country, let alone in its agricultural hinterland. With reduced populations—a trend which started with the Industrial Revolution and has not stopped—agricultural areas but also former mining villages are neglected by centralised governments. Whole sectors of the population feel they have been forgotten and left out: rural populations in Romania and Bulgaria; but also in France's less attractive areas; unemployed workers in Belgium's formerly coal and steel producing south; East Germans in minor towns far from Berlin; Greeks and Spaniards with summer jobs in tourist resorts far from home facing unemployment every winter.

In previous centuries, this might well have led to the large-scale intra-state migration of these populations. We still see some of this, while a lack of initiative and minimal, albeit often inadequate, social welfare keeps many of them in place today. By contrast initiative and greater desperation has led to new waves of immigration into Europe, this time across the Mediterranean and from the Middle East—reinforcing the pattern we identified. In some cases—Muslim and African refugees in Italy, Roma in Transylvania—they are settled by governments in depopulated villages, recreating the chequer-board pattern of pre-twentieth-century settlements. Elsewhere, they cluster among their own people in town and city quarters where housing is cheapest, living in their own bubble, often with newspapers, radio and above all television programmes in their own language. As mutual religious intolerance, xenophobia and nationalism are again on the rise in Europe, history would indicate that this is a very dangerous configuration.

Such parallel societies, cultural bubbles existing side by side and even ghettos, were not necessarily a problem politically and legally in medieval Spain or in the nineteenth-century Austro-Hungarian Empire. They are at odds, however, with all modern political structures requiring the government's ability to communicate directly with its citizenry, and citizens to communicate widely with one another, and with the principle of legislation being equally applicable to all citizens. In polities where all adult citizens have the vote and can participate in politics, not sharing a single language in which to conduct the political discourse poses a huge problem, as the case of Belgium shows, even without recent immigration. State-provided compulsory education encounters difficulties when children do not speak a common language properly, or when they come from minority cultures (including long-established indigenous cultures) which do not value formal education. Moreover, unless company is parted with the belief that laws should apply to everybody, that the Universal Declaration on Human Rights, or the European Charter of Human Rights, apply to everyone, the secular states of Europe cannot tolerate the practice of different laws on their soil. They cannot accept that one convicted thief is protected from having his hand cut off and another is not, that one fourteen-year old is protected from an arranged marriage and another is not, that one woman is protected against her husband's bigamy and another is not, according to whether they live under state law or Sharia Law. The existence, side by side, of separate communities, of parallel societies that would only interact in the market place, which in the past made multi-ethnic but non-assimilated cohabitation possible in the villages of forest-hunters, river-fishermen and the new settlers in between, in the religiously tolerant

Empire of Persian King Cyrus or the Ottoman Empire in its more clement times, or in the Habsburg lands, cannot be married to modern democracy or our fundamental value of the equality of all before the law.

We have seen that migration within Europe and to Europe is nothing new. Given the gap between living standards of most of Europe and most of Africa, and the instability of parts of the Middle East, there is no reason to believe that the desire of people in Africa and the Middle East to move to Europe will diminish.[19] Europe is thus returning to patterns of multi-ethnicity resembling pre-twentieth century configurations. Against this evolution, the revival of nationalism and religious fanaticism is already leading to internal tensions and could lead to ghastly clashes not dissimilar from persecutions witnessed in previous centuries. These would largely be intra-state clashes, but possibly not confined to any one state or taking place in parallel in different states, along similar patterns.

All this was worth spelling out to illustrate that the terms so commonly used in the literature about 'Inter-national Relations', especially the term 'nation-state' and the assumption that all states are 'territorial states' without large diasporas abroad, and the assumption that sovereign states are the pinnacle and end-state of human development, are unlikely in the twenty-first century to be helpful in understanding the needs and problems of the populations of Europe and beyond. It is plain that to deal adequately with these transnational issues, states need to be at once checked (if they infringe their citizens' human rights), supported and complemented by supra-state legislation and institutions, and for Europe, that is above all the EU. The situation in Northern Ireland and its complex relationship with both the Republic of Ireland and the United Kingdom is just one case in question. Politicians constantly conjuring up the interests of their own 'nation' or the independence of their 'nation-state' are demagogues blinding their voters to the interconnectedness, the complex identities and the demographic mix of the world in which we live.

We have also seen that simplistic equations of 'Liberalism' and 'Democracy' or 'Liberalism' and 'Internationalism' are not helpful representations of reality past, present, or future. In using them, we cannot strip them of mistaken assumptions, and we blind ourselves to engaging with a much more complex world than much literature on International Relations Theory allows for, especially where it emphasises inter-state relations, inter-state security and eclipses intra-state and trans-border dynamics. In sum, much literature on International Relations is guilty of misrepresenting the key terms by attributing simple and unvarying meanings to them. Such over-simplification leads to false claims about supposedly unvarying patterns of inter-polity relations. Worse still, they make us blind to solutions that require us to overcome nineteenth-century ideas of state and nation.

In the following, we shall try as much as possible to disentangle the shifting meanings of terms over time, while sketching how some basic ideas—often captured by different terms in their own time—have returned periodically, forming four themes. One is the balance-of-powers theme, a term invented in the early eighteenth century for which precedents can be found in many earlier configurations. A second is that subsumed by the medieval expression 'universal monarchy', inspired by the Roman Empire's provision of internal peace (the *Pax Romana*) and the late Roman Empire's identification with Christendom, and later connected to the Holy Roman Empire, or any other great power attempting to assume its place. In the Middle Ages and in modern history, these two themes formed a dialectic, aspiring to 'universal monarchy' or predominance or hegemony within Europe on the one hand, and a pushing back in the form of a balance-of-power politics on the other by insisting on the sovereignty and freedom of action of other polities, which periodically joined up to check a power set on expansion. A third and fourth theme that emerged are the syntheses of this dialectic. The third is the attempt to regulate European (or later: world) affairs largely through voluntary co-operation among (usually five) great powers. The fourth consists of many proposals which converge in the idea that all European polities, and not just the great powers, should come together voluntarily to form a confederation with set norms and rules to settle disputes and take common action on common problems. The proposals were largely inspired by the inner workings of the Holy Roman Empire, even if the main purpose of the proposals was to replace it with a more egalitarian structure including all the polities of Europe, in which there would be no one head, no emperor, no one dominating power.

3

IDEAS INHERITED FROM ANTIQUITY

Theories of Inter-'national' relations, just like any political theories, are in good part conditioned by ideas generated in the past. When exploring inter-polity relations in European history, we must begin with the ideas inherited from ancient civilisations. The idea of the centralised state, perhaps with a range of different subject peoples, goes back to Middle Eastern mega-polities—Empires *before the word*—that far predate anything comparable in Europe. Babylonians and Egyptians for example were known to the Europeans only indirectly through the heritage of the Hebrew Bible; they were seen (through the eyes of the Israelites) as wicked adversaries. Similarly, the Persians were regarded through the prism of many Greeks (and Macedonians), themselves part of the second great ancestral culture of the Europeans, as sprawling imperialists against whose encroachment the plucky, liberty-loving little Greek city states stood up repeatedly.

Outside Europe but with considerable influence on the Mediterranean region of their day, Babylonians, Egyptians, Persians and Hittites not only went to war but also engaged in diplomatic relations and concluded treaties with other polities.

The oldest known peace treaty in this region is that of 1276 BC concluded between the Egyptians and Hittites after the Battle of Kadesh. It is inscribed on a stele, in which the Hittites promised to come to the aid of Egypt if the latter were attacked by a third party. Alliance politics are also documented in the Hebrew Bible, where we find examples of war, exaction and cheque-book diplomacy;[1] of alliances, vassalage and hegemony.[2] Inter-polity relations were thus complex and well-developed even in these very ancient times, and precedents of this kind were available for later generations to read about as the Hebrew Bible was translated, first into Greek, later into Latin and then into vernacular languages. Through the Old Testament, Israelite examples, sanctified by God, could thus influence the politics of Christian polities and have continued to play this role until the present. For Christians saw themselves as God's new Chosen People, and looked to the Hebrew Bible for guidance.

One People, One God: the Israelites

Christians above all internalised this trope from the Hebrew Bible: that they were a special, unique people, chosen by the only 'real' God (or the only 'good' God—compared with ogres like Moloch), which found itself in almost perpetual contest with hostile neighbours. While Israelite history, as recorded in the Bible, was one of multiple kingdoms and rival kings, the simplified version of this complex history concentrated on an early king-less period when the Israelites were guided by their prophets, followed by the periods of kings of all of Israel whom God had chosen. Those remembered were above all Saul, David and Solomon, who created the model for kingship throughout later Christian Europe. The French, especially, saw themselves as the new and better Israelites, with their monarchs consciously emulating these great biblical kings. The kingdom of David and his dynasty—supposedly ancestral to Jesus—also furnished the blue-print for the structure of society: one people, one king, but with a caste of priests (in Christians times, the Church) as advisers and intermediaries with God, the supreme authority. This would later constitute an important root of the Western just war tradition which demanded a legitimate authority (for the Israelites: God) that alone could authorise warfare. From the Christianisation of the Roman Empire until the Reformation, the just war tradition demanded the sanctioning of war by the Church (even if in practice, wars, especially at the level of feuding barons, or punitive actions by lords against disobedient vassals, were often enough waged without such authorisation).

This selective reading of the Hebrew Bible also bequeathed a tradition to Europe which was one of extreme intolerance of enemies, and indeed of all intermarriage with peoples of different faiths. The Jahve of the early Israelites might have been benevolent towards them (when they were in an obedient phase), but not towards enemies they had vanquished in war. Here is but one of several similar examples of instructions he passed on through his prophets:

The Lord said to Moses, 'Take vengeance on the Midianites for the Israelites. ...'

...So twelve thousand men armed for battle ....

They fought against Midian, as the Lord commanded Moses, and killed every man. ...The Israelites captured the Midianite women and children and took all the Midianite herds, flocks and goods as plunder. They burned all the towns where the Midianites had settled, as well as all their camps. They took all the plunder and spoils, including the people and animals, and brought the captives, spoils and plunder to Moses and Eleazar the priest and the Israelite assembly at their camp on the plains of Moab, by the Jordan across from Jericho.[3]

While other occasions of such gender segregation are recorded in the Hebrew Bible, on this occasion Moses ordered the killing of all male children and all women who were not virgins, as women had supposedly 'enticed the Israelites to be unfaithful to the Lord'.[4]

Such patterns of merciless behaviour towards defeated enemies, not uncommon in the ancient world,[5] would be eagerly copied by Christians on many later occasions, sometimes directly citing the Hebrew precedent, especially in contexts of religious wars: they were used to excuse repeated atrocities committed by Christians against 'heretics' and Jews, by the Crusaders during their sack of Jerusalem in 1099 and of Constantinople of 1204, and then during the confessional wars of the fourteenth to seventeenth centuries.

Fighting for Liberty, and Rival Autarkic Polities: Ancient Greece

Ancient Greece had similar practices: normally, victors in a war would spare women and children from death but enslave them. More importantly, Ancient Greece in turn bequeathed its own patterns of inter-polity relations to posterity which would inspire political theorists and rulers when these ancient texts became available to the Latin West in translations of the Middle Ages and the Renaissance. For while ancient Greece had no actual theorist dealing explicitly and fully with the relations between polities, enough could be gleaned from the writings of its philosophers to form a picture of inter-polity relations.

The Greek polities or city states had a strong and powerful neighbour: Achaemenid Persia, the hegemon in the Near East which dominated most of Asia Minor up to the Aegean Sea. Here, many Greek and other polities had come to an arrangement with the Persians or Medes, they had 'Medized', and existed as quasi-client states of the Persian Empire. Other Greek polities of Asia Minor in 499 BC staged a revolt against the

Persians which led to the long draw-out Greco-Persian Wars of that century, drawing in polities in (what is today) the Greek mainland, including Athens and Sparta. Herodotus, our main source, gave equally complex explanations for this, including individual Greek leaders' attempts in turn to conquer and dominate other Greek polities. But the main argument that would stick in people's memory was one of a dialogue between an envoy of Persia and the Athenians, offering a peace treaty and reminding the Athenians of the great strengths of the Persians, to which the Athenians answered thus:

> We know very well that the Persian forces are many times more numerous than ours; so that there is no need for you do the reckoning for us. Nevertheless, because we long for liberty we shall defend ourselves as best we can...[6]

From this point onwards, the Athenians portrayed themselves and were portrayed as the great defenders of the 'liberty' of the Greeks against oppression by the Persians, even though a closer look reveals that Greek city states at times oppressed others more so than did the Persians. Athens owed its leadership role or hegemony among the Greek polities to having taken the lead in opposing the Persians. Yet the Delian League, the anti-Persian alliance which Athens led, turned into a quasi-empire within a generation.

Even without the Persian interference, inter-polity relations were not peaceful in ancient Greece. Plato in his *Laws* attributed the opinion that peace is 'only a fiction' to one of his speakers, as 'all states by nature are fighting an undeclared war against every other state.'[7] Plato himself argued, by contrast, that 'one must legislate in military matters for the sake of peace rather than legislate in peace for the sake of war',[8] which has been interpreted[9] as anticipating Aristotle's more explicit tenet that:

> ...*we make war in order that we may live in peace*. Now the exercise of the practical virtues takes place in politics or in warfare, and these

professions seem to have no place for leisure. That is certainly true of the military profession, for *nobody chooses to make war or provokes it for the sake of making war.*[10] [my emphasis]

This idea—that only a better peace as its outcome could possibly justify any war—would be echoed in and thus spread through the writings of Cicero to whom we owe the first approximate summary of Roman (pre-Christian) criteria for a just war;[11] it would become a central tenet of the just war tradition that is still with us today.[12]

Not a political theorist as such, but a general, eyewitness and historian, Thucydides with his account of the Peloponnesian War arguably had the most important Greek influence on European theories about inter-polity relations. His history of that war was translated into Western vernacular languages from the late fifteenth century, and thus he bequeathed to posterity the view of a world divided into rival polities with their allies and dependencies, competing for power and suspicious of the growth of the power of their competitors. To the question of why the Spartans began this war against Athens in the century following the Persian Wars, Thucydides answered that 'The truest cause I consider to be ...: the growth of the power of Athens, and the alarm which this inspired in Sparta, made war inevitable.'[13]

Here we find the first of the two great themes that would henceforth run through inter-polity relations in Europe, a dialectic which remains with us till today. Athens and Sparta found themselves in a competitive relationship, with the growth of one being checked by the other out of fear that it would lead to an unacceptable domination by the former. Translated into vernacular languages, Thucydides' writings would influence theoreticians from Lorenzo Valla and Francesco Guiccardini, Thomas Hobbes and David Hume to twentieth-century 'realist' theorists of International Relations like Morgenthau and Kenneth Waltz. Two millennia after his death, his works would be used as evidence that competition, rivalry and counter-balancing ('balance-of-power') strategies eternally dominated the relations between polities, to the exclusion of other factors. As generations of students from the Renaissance onwards were raised on Thucydides, this competitive approach to inter-entity relations, and distrust of any strong and especially growing power, seen as dangerous by definition—regardless of whether it was actually hostile—diffused throughout Europe. Indeed, this excused the preventive recourse to war before the opponent would have become too strong. Absent Thucydides, an atavistic sense of competition rather than consultative cooperation was apparently hard-wired into many—especially the more primitive—political cultures and, more importantly, their leaders. But Thucydides gave them the words to express this in terms of 'power' relations.

It must be emphasised that the Peloponnesian War between Athens, Sparta and their respective allies was perceived by Greeks as a civil war, and thus more regrettable than defence against foreign aggression. Thucydides tells us that there were supporters of Athens and Sparta in most Greek city-states, with different political factions lining up behind each: the popular factions with Athens, the oligarchic factions with Sparta:

> The whole Hellenic world was convulsed; struggles being every-where made by the popular chiefs to bring in the Athenians, and by the oligarchs to introduce the Spartans. In peace there would have been neither the pretext nor the wish to make such an invitation; but in war, with an alliance always at the command of either faction for the hurt of their adversaries and their own corresponding advantage, opportunities for bringing in the foreigner were never wanting to the revolutionary parties.[14]

No wonder later readers saw parallels with the confessional wars of the sixteenth century where supporters of both confessions were found in most European states, or in the Cold War. Echoing this differentiation between civil war and external war that can be traced back to Homer, Plato later distinguished two types of war: *polemos* between Greeks and foreign foes, and *stasis* between Greek polities.[15] Taken up by Saint Augustine, this translated, in European medieval thinking, into the distinction between 'hostile' or inter-polity war and civil war.[16] This has led to a (largely unhelpful) long-lasting distinction in the West between legitimate war (war against outside powers) and civil war or illegitimate insurgencies against state governments. The latter were seen by default as illegitimate by other governments. They always contain an element of rebellion against a government claiming legitimacy, hence all civil war presents a challenge not only to the one, but to all governments. Only since the Second World War has civil war begun to be regulated by international law which is why we now speak of the Laws of 'Armed Conflict' rather than the laws of 'war'.

In addition to identifying the competition for power as a cause of war, Thucydides furnished a brilliant, and brilliantly short, analysis of the three 'strongest motivations' governing inter-polity relations that can be widely applied: 'fear, honour, and interest'.[17] He did not suggest these were the only ones, but modern Europeans would recognise these three in particular in their own experience.

It has been much debated what Thucydides himself thought about the conduct of the war as he described it. At any rate it was gruesome. Thucydides summed up a position which would later be central to the 'realist' theory of International Relations, namely that the powerful would do what they can, and the weak would suffer what they must. He illustrated this with reference to the case of Melos, an island which wished to remain beyond the Spartan-Athenian conflagration, but was forced to choose sides by Athens. When the Melians refused to opt for the Athenians, the latter 'put to death all the grown men whom they took, and sold the women and children for slaves, and subsequently sent out five hundred colonists and inhabited the place themselves.'[18] (While in theory, Greeks were supposed to behave more humanly towards other Greeks, in practice they rarely did).[19]

The ongoing rivalry among the Greek polities led to the formation of alliances which would later be reflected upon by IR theorists. What was not understood by the later 'realist' theorists of International Relations is that alliances in ancient Greece came in several forms: with cities and colonies related through kinship, an alliance was called *syngeneia*, and would be expected to last indefinitely, creating an element of stability in this otherwise quite fluid environment. This also applied to an alliance founded on long-term friendship or *philia*, which presupposed shared values and shared cultures. Again, this was expected to last for long. Then there was the short-term alliance stemming from a temporary convergence of interest, concluded in order to defeat a common enemy, the *symmachia*. A purely defensive alliance, the *epimachia* could also be of short duration. It is misleading to translate all these by the same term of 'alliance', but this is what we find in most translations of Thucydides into English.[20] 'Realists' have concluded that the frequent changes of alliances among European princes in the Modern Era were a timeless phenomenon, but this is to misrepresent inter-polity relations in Ancient Greece, which contained alliances of long duration and greater loyalty as well as short-term balance-of-power line-ups.[21]

Aristotle provided the Western world with another key ideas about war and the relations between polities: the ideal of the autarkic sovereign state with the *kurios* or rule in which no other power had any right to interfere.[22] In reality, this was an elusive ideal for most of the many small polities of the Greek world, as alliances could turn into hegemonic pseudo-empires, in which one polity, the hegemon, dominated all others, as with Athens in the Delian League. Thus rivalling blocks formed, seeking to keep each other in check through war, which was welcomed, it seems, particularly by the poorer people who in many Greek polities survived on pay for military service and doles dealt out by the government. Writers belonging to the Athenian elite went as far as suggesting that democracies were more liable to go prosecute war than oligarchies who tended to argue in favour of peace as they would benefit from the commerce it facilitated.[23]

Alexander's Empire: Liberator or Tyrant?

The rivalry between the main Greek city-states and their allies and dependent states (not all states were fiercely independent-minded, and some that were, like Melos, were unable to defend their independence) was not the only model of inter-polity relations which the ancient Greeks bequeathed to Europe. For over two millennia, people have marvelled at the achievement of one young Macedonian, King Alexander III, in creating an (admittedly ephemeral) empire that reached from Greece to India. But the reasons for his foreign adventures and his aims were disputed, even in antiquity.

Alexander made much of two reasons for embarking on his extraordinary campaign to bring Persia to heel. He claimed, on the one hand, 'that the freedom of the Greeks was the object for which he had taken upon himself the war against the Persians',[24] that is, that he fought to free the Greeks from Persian tyranny. Indeed, many Greek polities had become client states of Persia, but some found the arrangement mutually profitable. In the process of 'freeing' the Greeks (particularly those who had not been under Persian influence), Alexander threw his weight about to the point where the Thebans encouraged the other Greeks to join them 'in freeing the Greeks and destroying the tyrant of Greece', by which they meant Alexander. The latter vented his anger at this insult by destroying Thebes in 335 BC.[25]

On the other hand, Alexander (like his father before him) claimed to avenge the injuries done by Persia to Greece.[26] The

Persians in the fifth century BC had burnt the Parthenon in Athens, the temple of Athena. Alexander did indeed, after the battle of Granicus in which he beat the Persian army, send, '[a]s an offering to the goddess Athena, ... to Athens 300 full suits of Persian armour, with the following inscription: Alexander, son of Philip, and the Greeks (except the Spartans) dedicate these spoils, taken from the Persians who dwell in Asia.'[27] (The Spartans were not keen on Alexander either.) Also, when Alexander's victorious armies reached Persepolis, 'He burnt the palace of the Persian Kings' although advised against this 'because the Asians would ... be less willing to support him if he seemed bent merely on passing through their country as a conqueror rather than upon ruling it securely as a king.' Alexander explained 'that he wished to punish the Persians for their invasion of Greece; his present act was retribution for the destruction of Athens, the burning of the temples, and all the other crimes they had committed against the Greeks.'[28]

Alexander made himself ruler of Persia and all other areas he had conquered. As far as his motivations are concerned, we have ample evidence that they changed over time, and that he kept moving forward wherever the going was good. In this he had much in common with Attila the Hun, with Genghis Khan, with Napoleon and with Hitler. When Alexander died just short of the age of thirty-three, his huge empire collapsed as his companions and friends parcelled out his conquests among themselves. Eventually, the kingdoms of Alexander's successors were absorbed into the Roman Empire, and under the Sasanians, Persia rose again as the main adversary of the polities of the Mediterranean world. Had it not been for his early death, who knows what Alexander would have been tempted to do: supposedly he wanted to turn West for further conquests, which would have led him to clash with Rome.[29]

Rome: Imperium *becomes Empire and* Pax Romana

Rome according to her own legend was founded by refugees from the Trojan War and also began its existence as a small city state. She gradually eliminated her competitors on the Italian peninsula one by one, usually integrating not only the lands but also the subjected tribes into her orbit. Rome, too, concluded several alliances *(foedera)*, which enjoined both sides to come to each other's aid if necessary and apparently there was no assumption that they would only be of short duration. Rome bestowed a range of titles upon her allies: *foederati*, if they were linked by a formal treaty for specific defensive purposes, or *amici et socii populi romani*—allies and friends of Rome, if there was no immediate common enemy to contend with. It was a principle of Roman policy that *pacta sunt servanda*, treaties have to be observed, so that if her ally was attacked, Rome was obliged to come to his defence and expected as much from her allies. The obligation to come to the defence of an ally (an alliance of course usually being or containing a mutual defence engagement) was a Roman bequest to all following centuries of European history.

There is a big debate about the question as to whether Rome's expansion was largely or mostly defensive, as Romans liked to argue.[30] At least the concept of a just war, which included earlier Greek ideas but was developed further by the Romans, presupposes that only a defensive war is just, and a just authority was needed to determine that this description fitted the case at hand.[31]

But the city-state Rome behaved very differently from the city-state Athens or the city-state Sparta in its interaction with neighbouring polities. The Romans were surrounded by peoples of thoroughly different cultures, who spoke quite different languages (like the Etruscans). They eschewed the Greek idea that they were surrounded by polities which were essentially the same as them, and violent conflicts from cattle raiding or the abduction of women to full-fledged war were not seen as different from (or more regrettable than) wars with powerful invaders (such as the Gallic Senones in the early fourth century or the Carthaginians in the Punic Wars). Therefore the Romans not only exercised *imperium* or control—that is, government—over vanquished enemies, but turned conquered territories, at ever further distances from their original city-state Rome (the *urbs*), into part of Rome (the *imperium Romanum*), complete with Roman garrisons, Roman colonists, and Roman towns. By the time Virgil wrote the *Aeneid* in the reign of emperor Augustus, this could be turned into an imperial 'mission'. In Virgil's words:

> Roman, remember that it is for you to rule over the peoples.
>
> For this purpose you have the art to impose peace through (rules of) good conduct, to spare the vanquished and through war to defeat the proud.[32]

Two aspects of this would be a crucial bequest to later generations: one was the gradual transformation of the defeated populations in the annexed territories from subject peoples into Roman citizens, beginning with their elites. This was something that did not happen overnight but haltingly, over centuries: there were times when Rome tried to stop the intermarriage of Roman citizens with occupied populations, and others when generously large numbers of non-Romans were made citizens.[33] Already Emperor Augustus had prided himself on turning 500,000 prisoners of war into Roman citizens, to have allowed them to return to their country, to have given them land to till or to have recruited them into the army as paid soldiers.[34] In 212 Emperor Caracalla extended Roman citizenship to virtually all free-born inhabitants of the Empire, but this number would expand as all freed slaves would also become Roman citizens. Towards the end of the Roman Empire in the West, inhabitants of the Roman Empire who were not slaves were usually Roman citizens. Most would speak Latin or Greek, albeit often as a second language, and where it was widely spoken, Latin gradually developed local dialects and later separate Romance languages, while the Eastern half of the Empire dropped Latin in favour of Greek in the seventh century. But Rome was the focal point of this Empire, its customs, laws and culture, the point of reference in everything. Even when the Empire was subdivided into two or four parts to facilitate its administration, with administrative centres at times in Trier, Milan or Aquileia, Nicomedia, Thessaloniki or Antioch and Constantinople, there was still a sense of belonging to one huge state with a dominant language, a single legal code that applied everywhere, a single currency, and armed forces that could be deployed anywhere in the Empire. The latter was also united by its state religion with multiple gods who were added to liberally when a new people were incorporated into it with its own deities.

Only the Jews and the Christians presented the Roman Empire with a lasting problem as they staunchly refused to tolerate these multiple gods, and the emperor-worship (as the emperors were regarded as divine) that went along with it. This intolerance on their part led to intolerance on the part of the Roman state and explains the clashes and persecutions that resulted.

The other, closely related, bequest of ancient Rome is that of the Empire as a zone of peace, referred to as *Pax Romana* or, after Augustus who imposed peace after the Civil Wars, as the *Pax Augusti*. This is how Augustus wanted to be commemorated: that after having pacified Spain and Gaul, 'the Senate voted to consecrate the altar of August Peace in the field of Mars for my return, on which it ordered ... annual sacrifices.' It had been an old tradition for the temple of Janus 'to be closed when throughout all the *imperium* of the Roman people, by land and sea, peace had been secured through victory. Before my birth it had been closed twice in all in recorded memory from the founding of the city; the senate voted three times in my Principate that it be closed.'[35] Since Augustus' ended the civil wars, it was considered as the norm that peace and the rule of law prevailed within the Empire, while war and chaos came from the outside, from Barbarian incursions or the continuation of the competitive relationship with the Persians which the Greeks had known so well.

The idea of the single ruler ruling over a zone of peace is also reflected in emperor Caracalla's dedicatory inscription left in Egypt, where he is referred to as '*kosmokrator*', ruler over the (ordered) universe or cosmos. And to make his point, he suppressed an insurgency in Alexandria with bloody massacres.[36] Chaos is not part of cosmos. The problem of the Roman order was that, depending on who was emperor, it could so easily turn into tyranny.

The Israelite model of one-God, one-people, one-ruler, became fused with the Empire as zone of peace when the Roman Empire embraced Christianity in several steps (from tolerance to making it state religion) in the fourth century. The zone of peace, the singular political entity stretching from Pictish Caledonia to the Black Sea, from Iberia to Egypt, under a single emperor and a single pope, was now largely coterminous with Christendom. In the words of the late Roman Christian poet Aurelius Prudentius Clemens (384-c.413):

> What is the secret of Rome's historical destiny? It is that God wills the unity of mankind, since the religion of Christ demands a social foundation of peace and international amity. Hitherto the whole earth from east to west had been rent asunder by continual strife. To curb this madness God has taught the nations to be obedient to the same laws and all to become Romans. Now we see mankind living as citizens of one city and members of a common household. Men come from distant lands across the seas to one common forum, the peoples are united by commerce and intermarriage. From the intermingling of peoples a single race is born. This is the meaning of all

the victories and triumphs of the Roman Empire: the Roman peace has prepared the road for the coming of Christ.[37]

The reality of multiple emperors—four under Diocletian's Tetrarchy, two when the East-West division of the Empire became more permanent in the late fourth century—and of multiple patriarchs—who were ignored and down-graded by the Roman *curia* which unilaterally elevated the patriarch of Rome to the position of sole primate of the Catholic Church, without any consultative process—was blotted out in this simplified world view. But in this model—one universal (Roman) Empire, with one law, a zone of peace (the *Pax Romana*), coterminous with one God, one Christian Church under one emperor and one pope—would form a crucial part of Europe's political memory and make-up. It even found its echo in Islam which copied so many ideas from Judaism and Christianity: Islam defines the world as divided into two zones, the zone where Islam prevails, the *Dar al Islam*, and the zone of war, the *Dar al Harb*.

Admittedly, no empire had ever ruled over all the world, not the Chinese, not the Persian, not Alexander's and not the Roman. But from the perspective of those within the Roman Empire, it was the only one, the universe, the cosmos, the realm of order where outside there was war and chaos. This perception, too, would be passed on through the ages, the ideal of a single universal empire, the *imperium universalis* or a universal monarchy. This is the second theme, the second pole of the great dialectic of European systems that would dominate inter-polity relations in Europe, the West, and at times the world, until our days.

4

THE MIDDLE AGES

THE CHRISTIAN UNIVERSE

The long period from the fall of the old Rome in the West in 476 AD to the fall of the Second Rome (Constantinople) in the East in 1453 saw the emergence of a rules-based system of relations between multiple polities in Europe, even if the rules were broken at times. The rules and assumptions were: first, although Rome had ceased to be the *caput mundi*, the secular head of the world, the Roman world had survived as *Christianitas* (Christendom)— referred to in the Latin West by many different terms such as *universitas Christianorum* (Christian universe), *res publica Christiana* (Christian commonwealth)[1]—with the pope, still in Rome, as its spiritual leader. Secondly, within Christendom, Christian monarchs should not go to war with one another. A third rule was posited but highly contested: that the successor state to the West Roman Empire, the Holy Roman Empire, and the emperor as its secular head, could claim pre-eminence among polities. Christian Europe presented an alternative to a system of sovereign states and yet was no longer the universal monarchy of Augustus' Roman Empire.

The prohibition of resorting to the use of force to settle quarrels in theory applied to all Christians: had not Jesus told them to 'turn the other cheek' when struck? This approach clashed fundamentally with the bellicose traditions of the (barely) Christianised barbaric tribes in Europe, however, and both the Church and kings had difficulties restraining their nobles and barons from feuding endlessly among themselves. Yet major wars—and formal battles—among Christian polities were rarer and waged on a smaller scale than they would be once the Reformation destroyed this unity of outlook and the fiscal-military state came into being.[2]

After the fall of Rome, West Europeans were well aware that the Empire had not disappeared but that what was left free from barbarian, mainly pagan, occupation was governed now exclusively from Constantinople. About twenty years after the fall of Rome, Clovis, the leader of the Germanic Franks who had settled in Gaul made a vow that he would become a Christian if he prevailed in battle against the Alemanni, another Germanic tribe, whom he wanted to turn into tributaries. When he won the battle of Tolbiac against them in c. 496, he fulfilled his promise and had himself baptised in Reims by the local Christian bishop, Rémi. At this point all other Christian chiefs and kings in Western Europe were seen by the pope as heretics as they had embraced a teaching at odds with that agreed by the Church Councils. (After Christianity became the Roman state religion in the fourth century, the Christians in turn showed great intolerance—not just of pagans, but also of varying interpretations of Christianity deemed 'heterodox' as opposed to the 'orthodox' interpretations endorsed by the patriarchs). At the time, this made Clovis the only Christian king of whom the pope and indeed the emperor in Constantinople, Anastasius I, approved. As a sign of this, Anastasius sent Clovis a letter bestowing upon him the title 'consul'. For good measure, Clovis appropriated the title of 'Augustus', while the title 'emperor' was still reserved for Anastasius alone. But *Francia* and the French Church would henceforth claim to be 'the oldest daughter' of the Catholic Church, and France would claim precedence over all other West European polities and their rulers.[3] To this day we see echoes of this French claim to pre-eminence in Europe.

The Restoration of the Roman Empire and Peace through Universal Empire

For another three centuries Western Europe remained the backwater that it had become with the fall of Rome. The centre of power continued to lie in the East, in Constantinople. From there, in the sixth century, Emperor Justinian not only produced the collection of Roman laws which still constitutes the foundation of civil law in Europe today, but also despatched his armies to Italy and Spain to free them from the new barbarian rulers and bring about the *Restauratio Imperii*, the restoration of the Empire. Neither his own reconquest of large parts of the West Roman Empire, nor those of his successor Heraclius in the seventh century, lasted for long. Both Justinian and Heraclius still struggled to contain Persian expansionism just as the Greeks had done for centuries. No sooner had the Persian Empire finally ceased to push to the West, however, when a new and even more successful expansionist force was unleashed by Mohammed in the Arabian desert in the 620s. In the astonishingly short span of forty years, the Arabs under the green banner of the Prophet of Islam conquered most of the East Roman provinces, leaving only Asia Minor and the European parts of the East Roman Empire under the control of Constantinople. The Christian intolerance of deviant Christian interpretations of the Gospel would later help the Arab conquests of the Middle-Eastern and North-African parts of the Roman Empire which were condemned as heterodox and heretical by Constantinople, and experienced greater tolerance under the early Muslim rulers than within the Empire.

Less than a century after Mohammed had begun the Islamic war of expansion, Muslims had replaced the Christian kingdoms of Spain and in 732 stood battle against the Franks in the middle of France, near the Atlantic Coast, between Tours and Poitiers. Even though the armies of Constantinople were not strong enough to defend Christendom in all these places, it was still recognised throughout Europe and beyond as the place in which the legitimate succession of Rome was invested, and as the political centre of the Christian universe. The Roman Empire's continued existence was acknowledged for many centuries after the fall of Rome, despite the anarchy on the Italian peninsula. It was only when the excuse was found that there was no legitimate emperor in the East that the pope in Rome and a successor of Clovis saw it fit to take action—and recreate the Roman Empire in the West. In the late eighth century, the Annals of the monastery of Lorsch recorded,

> as the title of Emperor had then come to an end among the Greeks, who were [= because they were] under the rule of a woman, it seemed to Pope Leo himself and to all the holy fathers present at the council, as well as to the rest of the Christian people, that they ought to give the rank of emperor to Charles, King of the Franks, who held Rome itself, where the Caesars had ever been wont to dwell, as well as other places in Italy, Gaul and Germany. Since almighty God had put all these places in his power, it seemed to them but right that, in accordance with the demand of the whole Christian people, he should have the title also. This demand King Charles would not refuse; but, submitting in all humility to God, at the prayer of the clergy and of the whole Christian people, he received the title of Emperor together with consecration from Pope Leo.[4]

Thus Charles, ruler of one of the many kingdoms that had sprung up in Europe within and beyond the confines of the defunct Western part of the Roman Empire, was crowned *Imperator Romanorum*, and his seal proclaimed that his aim, much like that of East Roman emperor Justinian's before him, was to restore the Roman Empire (*renovatio romani imperii*). His counsellors wanted him ideally to be not merely *primus inter pares* among the rulers in Europe, but a ruler with universal aspirations. As a text written by his entourage put it, 'King is who [rules] over one people or many. The emperor is who [rules] over the entire world or excels in it.'[5]

Less educated than his clerical counsellors, Charles often acted more in the tradition of Germanic kings than of Roman emperors. At his death, he divided his realm among his three sons rather than assuring the integrity of the newly recreated Empire. For several generations, his territories were periodically reunited when only one of several sons survived, but as this was not always the case, the ultimate result was the separation of Charlemagne's Empire into three parts—till this day reflected in the separation into France in the West (which would thenceforth remain outside the medieval Empire); the middle area which would ultimately crystallise into the Netherlands, Belgium, Switzerland and Northern Italy plus the long-fought-over areas of Burgundy, Alsace and Lorraine; and Germany in the East. Charlemagne's Empire was thus partitioned. His heritage would in the long term engender a sibling rivalry between the two main successor polities, the West Frankish kingdom and the East Frankish kingdom, which respectively became France and the Holy Roman Empire and which would for centuries wage war over who was to dominate the lands in between, and ultimately, Europe. This sibling rivalry between France and 'Germany'— actually, many different entities: the multi-ethnic Holy Roman Empire, then the Habsburg dynasty in Austria and Spain, then Prussia, then the German Reich of 1871–1918, then Nazi Germany—was to polarise Europe for eleven centuries and repeatedly drag it into bloody wars. It would be resolved only from the 1950s with European integration, initially coterminous with the successor states of Charlemagne's Empire: France, Germany, the Netherlands, Belgium, Luxemburg, and Italy.

The title of emperor continued to be bestowed upon successive descendants of Charlemagne until the early tenth century, after which, for a few decades, no one king had a firm enough position to claim it. Power within the Germanic East (*regnum francorum orientalium*, the Kingdom of the East Franks) shifted further East still to Saxony, which had only been conquered by Charles a century-and-a-half earlier. The Duke of the Saxons, Henry the Fowler, managed to have himself crowned King of the East Franks. Both he and his son Otto bolstered their position greatly by fending off invading Magyars, who after the Battle of the Lechfield in Bavaria in 955 stopped their drive to the West and settled in the plains to the South of the Danube-valley where Alps and Carpathians meet. Henry had broken with the tradition of dividing his lands between his sons. After his victory over the Magyars, Otto had such prestige that he could revive the imperial title, getting himself crowned emperor in Rome in 962, largely copying the Byzantine model. His fawning biographer, Widukind of Corvey, called Otto '*totius orbis caput*', the head of the entire world.[6]

Otto himself was aware that he was not, and that the rulers of Constantinople had the older and better claim to this title. Consequently, he arranged a marriage between a Byzantine princess and his eponymous son. The issue of this marriage, a third Otto, was like father and grandfather crowned Roman Emperor (*Romanorum imperator augustus*). Espousing pure Roman-Byzantine iconography, this third Otto had himself depicted in a precious illuminated Bible he commissioned, as world ruler, holding an orb signifying the globe in his hand, the earliest precedent of the depiction of monarchs in this fashion.[7] On the page opposite we see the four parts of Europe that he dominated bearing him their gifts: Roma, Gallia, Germania and Sclavinia—as Otto encouraged the Christianisation of the Slavs.[8]

Like his grandfather and father before him, Otto III sought to legitimate his position even further by yet another Byzantine match. In the absence of male heirs in Constantinople, Zoë, the princess he had chosen, would later become East Roman empress in her own right. Tragically, when she arrived in Italy in 1002 to marry the young West Roman emperor, he had just succumbed to cholera, leaving his hopes of a dynastic merger of the Byzantine East and West Roman Empires, the planned culmination of his political programme of the *'renovation imperii Romanorum'*, unfulfilled. Yet the idea of Empire and emperor was now fully re-established in medieval minds. The Holy Roman Empire as created by the Ottos would exist uninterrupted until 1806.

With it was established, with the Ottonians at the latest, the aspiration to universal rule, *imperium universalis*. The power base of the medieval (West) Roman emperors consisted of several duchies, kingdoms and ecclesiastical states to the north of the Alps plus the pope and the North Italian kingdom of Lombardy or, later, several North Italian city states. A number of emperors like Otto I managed to secure the emperorship temporarily for their dynasty, often by having a son crowned as co-ruler and emperor-elect in their own lifetime. But this involved an election (at least in theory until 1806) by a small number of electors, themselves heads of the chief polities of the Empire. Any one of these could turn against a candidate, which led to repeated power struggles within the Empire. Popes could try to intervene in the imperial election process, or claim the right to depose emperors or at least excommunicate them. In turn emperors could try to influence the elections of popes. Again, this could lead to clashes, with pope and emperor lining up princes or city states within the empire on their respective sides, such as the line-up between Guelfs and Ghibellines. Monarchs outside the empire took an active interest, with the French kings in particular claiming their say as representatives of *Francia* as the 'oldest daughter of the

Church'. French political theorists emphasised that Charlemagne had been king of the Franks before he was crowned emperor, which made them equal to the Holy Roman emperors.[9] Counter-emperors and counter-popes were elected from time to time, with the entire papal court under French influence being transported from Rome to Avignon between 1309 and 1376. The papacy regained its relative freedom from French domination upon its return to Rome, and entered another period of strength and influence in the fifteenth century.

Relations between the Christian monarchies outside the Empire and the Empire were always ill-defined. They accepted the Empire as in some form pre-eminent, at least as first among equals, and they might ask the emperor (or the pope) to mediate in their quarrels—medieval princes resorted to war among themselves less frequently than their feuding barons. But it was the pope, not the emperor, who claimed to be supreme spiritual leader of all of Christendom on earth—all of it, thus downgrading the patriarchs of Constantinople, Antioch, Jerusalem, and Alexandria, to which Rome had originally merely been an equal. They also tried to upstage the emperors of West and East, by claiming authority not only over the constituent parts of the Holy Roman Empire, but also, beyond it, the Iberian Peninsula, France, the British Isles, Scandinavia, and vast territories to the East populated by Slavs and Magyars.

Thus the pope was also regarded as the true lord over all lands that had once formed part of the (Christian) Roman Empire, including those now ruled by Muslims. Writing in the late four-teenth century, the French political theorist Honoré Bovet opined that the pope could not order the conversion of Jews or Saracens by the sword as no-one must be brought to the faith of Jesus by force. Nor could the pope legitimately order a war to conquer 'Saracen'-held (that is, Muslim-held) territory which had never previously been Christian. By contrast, he had every right to order wars against the Saracens to liberate Jerusalem or anything else that was previously Christian territory ruled over by the '*prince de Romme*' (the Roman emperor).[10] It was thus the pope, and not an emperor, who could call for a war to liberate the oppressed Christians in the East from Muslim rule. And this is what Pope Urban II did in 1095.

Arguably, Pope Urban was the most influential prescriptive theorist of inter-polity relations of the Middle Ages. When Turks had replaced previous more tolerant Muslim rulers in the Middle East with a regime of terror, extortion and forced conversion, Urban called what would later be dubbed the First Crusade. By ingeniously transforming the old institution of pilgrimage to the Holy Land, now blocked by the Turks, into an armed pilgrimage (which is what the crusades were originally called) to the Middle East, he succeeded in channelling outward the nobility's love for war and physical fighting, and the ambitions of younger sons left without an inheritance, simultaneously creating a reason to impose temporary truces and more lasting peace within Latin Christendom.[11]

With this, Urban introduced a new pattern into European inter-polity relations, a new rule of the game. Already previously, it had been a rule in Christendom that a pilgrim's property must not be interfered with in his or her absence. Now at least in theory, once anybody declared that he had embarked upon a crusade, he and his lands and other possessions must not be attacked by rivals at home, as they stood under the protection of the Church. Thus Urban tried to restore to Europe the internal *Pax Romana*, now often referred to a *Pax Dei* or *Pax Christiana*.

Three Forms of War vs Pax Dei and Landfrieden

Barbarian incursions into Christian lands had not ceased with the fall of Rome in 476 AD and the Christianisation of the earlier invaders—the Avars, Goths, Burgundians, and later Magyars, Norsemen and Slavs. While earlier Christian authors had taken all war to be unjustifiable, St Augustine of Hippo, around 400 in the midst of pagan invasions of the Christian Empire, fell back on the pagan Greek and Roman definition of defensive war as justifiable and just. While he largely followed the pagan Roman tradition with this, it laid the foundation for the Roman Catholic just war tradition, making a *'guerre mortelle'* or 'Roman war' in defence of Christian lands against non-Christian aggressors by definition just, even without special dispensation from the pope.[12]

The Roman Empire in the West after its espousal of Christianity had not seen large-scale civil wars, but then it had come to an end only a century after Christianity became its state religion. In theory it was an anomaly that Christian princes should go to war with one another, but in practice they did so from time to time, normally over succession disputes. The medieval theory was that to seek legitimacy, they should turn to the pope for adjudication or a blessing of their cause. War between Christian princes was referred to as *'bellum hostilum'*.[13]

Most common was a third form of war, 'private war' within kingdoms or the Empire among barons, over a host of different reasons. Much disapproved of by the Church, this third category of wars was sometimes referred to as *'guerre couverte'*, and more usually as feud, *faide* (French) or *Fehde* (German). From the tenth century, the Church tried to contain this form of warfare by reminding all sides that Christians were not supposed to go to war with one another, and that the ideal for all of Christendom was that it should be a zone of peace, in the tradition of the *Pax Romana*. In a series of Church Councils which spread from South-Western France, the lesser nobility in particular were urged to abstain from war during periods called the Truce of God (*Treuga Dei*) in honour of the periods of fasting before major feasts (Lent before Easter, Advent before Christmas), but then also Sunday as the Day of the Lord, Friday as the day of the crucifixion, and then the entire weekend. As the Church was unable to stop war among Christians entirely, at least it tried to establish small periods of peace. Such 'truces' were promoted alongside the *Pax Dei* which obtained when individual kingdoms or all of Christendom were engaged in legitimate external wars.

It was the *Pax Dei* which Pope Urban II in 1095 linked with the call for an armed pilgrimage or crusade. Henceforth, the idea of the fight against Muslims as a Christian service to God and one's fellow-Christians and the obligation for those staying behind to keep the peace domestically would be linked. The Crusaders should be able to go forth without fearing that others would take advantage of their absence to appropriate their possessions. Eventually, in 1495, the Holy Roman Empire proclaimed a perpetual domestic peace that would be known as *Landfrieden* so that it could better defend itself against the Turks who had now consolidated their grip on South-Eastern Europe and were pushing further West. The equivalent of the *Pax Romana* was thus formally re-established, albeit only within the Holy Roman Empire. Here conflicts between the barons, princes, cities and other Estates were henceforth to be settled by arbitration, by a Court of Justice created for this purpose in 1495, and not by war. It was unforeseeable that this admirable super-state would be shattered, less than a century later, by the confessional wars triggered by the Reformation.

The Outsiders' Bid for Independence: Sovereignty and Competition

There were a number of medieval political philosophers who thought the Holy Roman Empire, and the emperor as its head, was a monarchy with universal jurisdiction throughout Christendom and should have the monopoly of use of force and impose universal peace. This is what historian Bruno Arcidiacono has called 'peace by hegemony'.[14] They argued that he, not the pope, should decide which war was just and which was not. Among them was the Cologne canon lawyer Alexander von Roes (c.1225-before 1330), who was reacting specifically to French monarchs' claims to be sovereign equals of the emperors: he specifically defined the Holy Roman Empire as the direct continuity of the (Christian) Roman Empire of late Antiquity.[15] A similar approach was taken by the Styrian Abbot Engelbert of Admont (c.1250–1313), who argued that all temporal rulers should be subject to the emperor;[16] Lupold von Bebenburg (1297–1363), Bishop of Bamberg, who sided with emperor Louis IV against several popes and was temporarily excommunicated;[17] the English Franciscan philosopher William of Ockham (1290–1349), who in his *Dialogue on the Power of the Pope and the Emperor* argued that the pope should keep out of worldly politics,[18] and the Italian jurist Bartolo da Sassoferato (1313–1357), who was a counsellor to Emperor Charles IV. Bartolo declared that all worldly power stemmed from the Roman Empire, even if emperors had occasionally granted rulers and polities (such as the Italian city states that had revolted against the emperor in the twelfth century) the right to live according to their own laws.[19] Following Bartolo, the Bologna lawyer Giovanni da Legnano (1320–1383) deduced from this that no prince had the right to go to war without the authorisation of the emperor, rather than the pope.[20] Probably the most popularly famous defender of the rights of the emperor was the Florentine poet Dante Alighieri (1265–1321) who in his treatise on monarchy, written in 1310–1313, argued that the (Holy) Roman Emperor held his authority from God directly and need not bow to the pope, and that as direct successor to the Roman emperors, he rightly had *imperium* over all humanity.[21]

The methodology used by all of these fourteenth-century philosophers and lawyers was to deduce the rights of the emperors from texts describing the powers of the Roman emperors, and from passages of the Bible. These authoritative texts were taken to spell out the will of God, and given Christian beliefs, this genealogy of authority was the most important to these authors. They cared neither to analyse the actual relationship of forces or needs in the world in which they were living, nor to prescribe improvements on existing arrangements, such as compromises that might have smoothed over the structural problems of the emperor-pope bicephaly, or the position of monarchs outside the Empire. Courtiers surrounding the Habsburg emperors in the late fifteenth and in the sixteenth centuries continued to make the argument that the Holy Roman Emperor was the monarch of the universe, generally reproducing the arguments of the authors cited above.[22]

Within polities outside the Holy Roman Empire, especially France and England, princes also tried to monopolize the use of force, this time not under pope or emperor, but for themselves as against their barons and nobles, the latter often their brothers, uncles, cousins, sons, or related by marriage. In this, the king of the French and also the princes of the realm from the twelfth century competed not only with the emperor but were also up against the Church's *Pax Dei* movement.[23] In 1155 King Louis VII of France assembled a Council of nobles and clergy at Soissons where he proclaimed that for ten years, all possessions of the Church, all peasants and their property, all travellers should be under his protection, and he made both nobles and clergymen swear to respect this and to help the king enforce this temporary peace among them.[24] This was also the time when the political philosopher Étienne de Tournai formulated the principle that the French king was 'emperor in his realm', rejecting any superiority or right to intervene on the part of emperor or pope.[25] One century later, French kings clashed with popes over the appointments of bishops in France, asserting the royal prerogative to have the final say in this, a position that would be referred to as Gallicanism. (Two centuries later, Henry VIII of England would be copying this approach but in a more radical fashion when breaking with the Roman Catholic Church to impose himself as head of his English—Anglican—Church. Henry thus sought to remove his realm from the Christian Universe. This first English withdrawal from Europe was seen as a forerunner of Brexit by the "Historians for Britain" who put Henry VIII's portrait on the home page of their website in the Brexit campaign of 2016.)

In England, already Anglo-Saxon kings had tried to impose the 'King's Peace', which their Norman successors emulated. In the second half of the twelfth century, King Henry II (r 1154–1189), son of a French count and the heiress of King Henry I, widow of a Holy Roman Emperor-elect, copied this French defiance of pope and emperor. A seal shows him on one side enthroned holding the sword of justice—symbolic of the domestic monopoly of the use of force—and on the other, on horseback, wielding the sword in defence of his kingdom—the monopoly of the right to go to war. These would of two key markers of sovereignty: the monopoly of the use of force, both internally, and externally in inter-polity relations.

With his reign coming after a prolonged civil war over the succession to the crown of England, Henry II did not just try to monopolize the use of force or of legislation with regard to his own subjects. Like French monarchs a century later, Henry II also tried to gain greater control of the Church within his realm. This misfired and famously led to a fatal quarrel between him and his Archbishop of Canterbury (the primate of England), Thomas Becket. The quarrel ended with the assassination and subsequent canonisation of the latter, and the grovelling submission to the Church by Henry.

Before these dramatic events, in the earlier part of Henry's reign, the English political philosopher John of Salisbury was defining the polity with all its components. Drawing on the Graeco-Roman Plutarch, he described a *res publica* or commonwealth as a living body, with a soul to worship God:

> And therefore those who preside over the practice of religion should be looked up to and venerated as the soul of the body. ... Furthermore, since the soul is, as it were, the prince of the body, and has rulership over the whole thereof, so those whom our author calls the prefects of religion preside over the entire body. ...

> The place of the head in the body of the commonwealth is filled by the prince, who is subject only to God and to those who exercise His office and represent Him on earth, even as in the human body the head is quickened and governed by the soul. The place of the heart is filled by the Senate, from which proceeds the initiation of good works and ill. The duties of eyes, ears, and tongue are claimed by the judges and the governors of provinces. Officials and soldiers correspond to the hands. Those who always attend upon the prince are likened to the sides. Financial officers and keepers ... of the privy chest may be compared with the stomach and intestines, which, if they become congested through excessive avidity, and retain too tenaciously their accumulations, generate innumerable and incurable diseases, so that through their ailment the whole body is threatened with destruction. The husbandmen correspond to the feet, which ... need the ... care and foresight of the head... Take away the support of the feet from the strongest body, and it cannot move forward by its own power...[26]

While thus trying to maintain that the Church should stand above the secular ruler (John would become the chief hagiographer of Thomas Becket), John at the same time promoted the idea of the individual polity as perfect and distinct entity, free of any outside interference or point of reference other than God. No Empire or *universitas Christianorum*, no emperor, no pope had a place in this self-contained entity. Plutarch had of course described the Roman Empire, but in applying Plutarch's ideas to any polity, John arguably pioneered the idea of the sovereign state.

From the twelfth and thirteenth centuries onwards, we see the return of an approach to inter-polity relations which considered (at least some) polities (notably France, but England, Spain and Scotland would soon make the same claim) to be independent of any other political authority and sovereign. This tendency to underscore the completeness of each individual polity, to play down the unity of Christendom, the role of the pope and the emperor was strengthened further by the rediscovery of Aristotle's *Politics* in the thirteenth century, with the emphasis on the self-sufficient (autarkic) polity with exclusive rule over itself, that is, self-determination devoid of any outside interference. Kings and other rulers outside the Holy Roman Empire began to claim the sovereign right to go to war and rejected the notion that they needed anybody else's blessing.

Even within the Empire, polities at times resisted the papal or imperial demand that they should settle conflicts peacefully. Italy in particular sprouted polities that much resembled the city-states of ancient Greece, and in part consciously modelled themselves on them. In the fifteenth century, Thucydides was being translated into Western vernacular languages and began to have an impact on how contemporary authors perceived war. In 1440 Lorenzo Valla wrote that wars are embarked upon 'for a desire of glory', 'for the hope of booty', 'for fear of incurring disaster later, if the strength of others is allowed to increase'— echoing the very words of Thucydides' explanations of the origins of the Peloponnesian Wars. Valla added the reason most frequently put forward by the Romans reason for going to war, 'for avenging a wrong and defending friends'.[27] The historian J.R. Hale from this point onwards identified many examples of wars fought to check the rise of another power.[28] Indeed, Europe at the beginning of the Renaissance was so full of Thucydidean rivalries that the Burgundian diplomat Philippe de Commynes (1447–1511) thought God's creation to be a system of forces and counter-forces:

It seems to me that God has created nothing in this world, neither men nor beasts, to which he has not made something opposed, so as to keep it in fear and humility. ... For to the Kingdom of France, He has given, as opposite, the English, and to the English, the Scots. To the Kingdom of Spain, Portugal. ... To the princes of Italy ... God has given as opposites the city-republics [*les villes de communauté*], which are in the same country of Italy, like Venice, Florence, Genoa, sometimes Bologna, Sienna, Pisa, Lucca and others, which in many ways are opposite to the Lords and the Lords to them: each has his eye on it that his counterpart does not grow. And ... to the House of Aragon He has given the House of Anjou as opposite; to that of the Sforza, usurping the place of the Visconti in the Duchy of Milan, the Duchy of Orleans ... To the Venetians, the Lords of Italy, ... and more still the Florentines. To the Florentines, those of Sienna and Pisa, their neighbours, and the Genoese. ... As regards Germany [*Alemaigne*] you always have the Houses of Austria and Bavaria opposing one another ...[29]

While Commynes did not use the term 'balance of power', here was the full recognition of the rivalries and competition which set these powers against one another, even within the Holy Roman Empire. With similarities to the Peloponnesian War as described by Thucydides, we see the emergence of a system of counter-balances in which each polity followed its own interests, checked only by external forces (except for the Holy Roman Empire with its internal checks and balances). Not surprisingly, we also find this described as a mechanism of counter-weights (*contrapeso*) or balancing each other (*fare contrapeso*) to create, ideally, a system off counterbalances (*contrapesati*) which could be perfectly balanced (*bilanciate*) in the *History of Italy* written by Francesco Guicciardini (1483–1540) in the early sixteenth century. Implicitly, Guicciardini described Italian inter-city politics of the fifteenth century as a delicately balanced mechanism which was upset by the invasion of French Charles VIII in 1494, ushering in a series of Italian Wars.[30]

In such a complex balancing mechanism, individual rulers could play a game of lending their support to whichever side they chose, thus tipping the balance in its favour. The first to conduct inter-polity relations in this way in early modern times was Lorenzo de' Medici, the *ago della bilancia* ('the tongue of the balance'). Popes, the Republic of Venice, but also other rulers sought and gained this reputation. To Henry VIII of England was attributed the motto *cui adhaero praeest*—he to whom I adhere prevails. A lost or possibly apocryphal portrait is supposed to have shown Henry holding a pair of scales in one hand with symbols representing France and Spain in the two bowls, and in the other a weight which he would throw in on one side or the other, as he pleased.[31] Two centuries later, Frederick II of Prussia was keen to play this balancing game. While 'the tradition of England as holding the balance has taken on almost mythical proportions' (historian Moorhead Wright), it was in fact an Italian recipe followed by a number of rulers and polities.[32]

If princes and other regimes saw no need to put their cause before any higher authority such as pope or emperor, or lay it out before a council of peers, it was enough that they claimed to have a just cause. In the sixteenth century, the Spanish Dominican and jurist lecturing at the University of Salamanca, Francisco de Vitoria, revolutionised the theory of international law by postulating that:

> It is not incompatible with reason, indeed, when there is right on one side and ignorance on the other, that a war may be just on both. For instance, the French hold Burgundy in the mistaken ... belief that it belongs to them. Now our Emperor Charles V has a certain right to that province and may seek to recover it by war; but the French may defend it.[33]

Vitoria thus argued that one should no longer focus on who was right and who was wrong (the issue of the just war or the *ius ad bellum*), but on how to limit the damages caused by war, that is, the *ius in bello*.[34] Thus began a long period of European history in which the just war tradition was relegated to the sidelines as sovereigns claimed the absolute right to go to war, unhindered by any higher external authority.[35] While they tended to produce justifications for their actions, effectively, no higher authority could pass judgement on them. This state of affairs was to last until the First World War.

Arbitration and Mediation

In the absence of a court of justice, the verdict of battle decided the quarrels between princes as it had done in the past. War thus fulfilled the function of a tribunal, as Francisco Suárez recognised in the early seventeenth century.[36] A little later, Samuel von Pufendorf wrote in his *Laws of Nature and Nations*:

> [W]hoever resolved to take up war against another when he could have settled the controversy by peaceful negotiations, is understood to have left the decision of the issue to the *dice of Mars*, and it is, therefore, idle for him to complain of any terms which the fortunes of war have meted out to him. ...

Thus practically all formal wars pre-suppose an agreement that he upon whose side the fortune of war has rested can impose his entire will upon the conquered.[37]

Alternatives to war existed even in the absence of a European supreme court of justice. Before the Reformation, one was to call upon the pope to mediate in disputes between princes. Pope Innocent III was called upon in 1200–1201 to judge the rival claims to the imperial throne by Philip of Swabia and Otto of Brunswick. Pope Boniface VIII tried to arbitrate a peace between the kings of France and England/Aquitaine in 1294, as did his successors in the fourteenth century.[38] While the rulers of polities outside the Holy Roman Empire fiercely denied the emperor any powers over them, some emperors had the moral standing and reputation of wisdom as individuals that would lead other princes to call upon them to mediate. But this also applied to other monarchs of particularly high standing. Thus Alfonso VIII, king of Castile and Sancho VI, king of Navarre in 1176 asked King Henry II of England to settle a dispute over border towns between them; one of them was the son-in-law of King Henry, which might have loaded the die in his favour, but apparently both Iberian monarchs were content with the settlement.[39] In the following century, King Louis IX of France (reigned 1226–1270) was one of those monarchs upon whom other Christian princes called to mediate among them, as he was known as a peacemaker, a *'faiseur de paix'*. For example, he was asked to arbitrate by the competing dukes of Luxembourg, Champagne and Bar.[40] This activity was evoked as arguments for his canonisation, effected by Pope Boniface VIII in 1297.[41] King Philip VI of France (reigned 1328–1350) was invited to mediate a quarrel between Brabant and Luxembourg. His grandson Charles V (reigned 1364–1380), known as 'the Wise', was another monarch whose mediation was sought several times by other princes. King Louis XI was asked, in 1475, to arbitrate between Tyrol and the Swiss.

Rather than calling upon a single arbiter, there was the option of seeking arbitration in a larger circle. This rarely happened before princes with clashing interests resorted to war, but in modern times would become the standard procedure by which wars were ended and peace established. The only prescription we know of for such a form of pre-war mediation comes from Christine de Pizan, who in her *Book of Deeds of Arms and of Chivalry* had suggested that to resolve a conflict that might otherwise lead to war, a monarch should assemble:

> A great council of wise men in his parliament, or in that of his sovereign if he is a subject, and not only will he assemble those of his own realm, but in order that there be no suspicion of favour, he will also call upon some from foreign countries that are known not to take

sides, elder statesmen as well as legal advisors and others; he will set out or have [somebody else] set out the whole matter in full without holding anything back, ... In short, in this way the affair will be put in order, clearly seen and discussed, and if through such a process it appears that his cause is just, he will summon his adversary to demand of him restitution and amends for his injuries and the wrong done to him. Now if ... the adversary in question puts up a defence and tries to contradict what has been said, let him be heard fully without special favour, but also without wilfulness or spite. If these things are duly carried out, as the law requires, then the just prince may surely undertake war, which on no account should be called vengeance but rather the complete carrying out of due justice.[42]

Perhaps under the influence of Christine de Pizan's suggestion, an international congress designed, admittedly not to prevent war, but to bring about peace, including the belligerents and mediators, took place at Arras in 1435. This has been described as the first of its kind by historian Jean-Pierre Bois. It broke the alliance between England and Burgundy by establishing a peace between France and Burgundy: the Duke of Burgundy recognised Charles VII as King of France but did not have to pay him homage. The English King Henry VI did not want to sign up to this so the Congress did not lead to lasting peace between France and England, but it set the precedent for future peace congresses.[43]

Comparable congresses were held in the following centuries, albeit very irregularly, and normally to negotiate a peace at the end of a war, rather than as an alternative to war. They included the 1570 Peace Congress at Stettin, convened by Emperor Maximilian II to mediate between Sweden and Denmark who had fought each other for seven years. The actual host was Duke Johann Friedrich of Pomerania-Stettin; Augustus Elector of Saxony attended in person, and France and Poland sent emissaries. Then there were the peace congresses of Münster and Osnabrück 1644–1648, designed to end the Thirty Years' War, followed by the Congresses of Nijmegen 1678, Rijswijk 1697 and Utrecht 1712–1713. Each of these attempted not only to set in stone the outcome of the war and who now had the dominion of which territory, but also to lay down a set of rules of mutual respect for future conduct. All were designed to bring about a *'paix universelle et perpétuelle'*, as it said in the Treaty of Rijswijk.[44] While these hopes were regularly foiled, the congresses inspired some observers to formulate ideas on how a permanent congress might create a lastingly peaceful state system. But let us turn first to the reasons why these peace congresses and treaties did not bring perpetual peace.

Dynastic Ambitions and Proto-Nationalism

We have seen that, from the twelfth century onwards, the kings of France and England, and later also of the states that emerged in the post-*Reconquista* Iberian Peninsula, claimed sovereign independence from and equality with the emperor. This meant that whatever promises they or their predecessors had made in peace treaties, they had no wish to forgo the right to use force. Meanwhile, their political theorists and poets developed an early form of nationalism which other parts of Europe would not espouse until the nineteenth century.

The narrative of France as the oldest daughter of the Church and of the Franks as Europe's lead nation was already fully established when, in 1095, Pope Urban II travelled to Clermont to call upon the French to take the lead in the First Crusade. French kings did indeed follow Urban's call, and the default configuration was that the kings of France would lead Crusades, with or without the English king and the Holy Roman Emperor. Indeed, an anonymous account of the First Crusade would be headed, *The Deeds of the Franks*, another, by the Abbot of Nogent, *The Deeds of God through the Franks*.[45]

The kings of the Spanish peninsula were preoccupied with their own particular form of the crusade: the reconquest of the lands taken by the Muslims, the *Reconquista*. Its completion, after more than two centuries of sluggish progress, was achieved when the main kingdoms of Castile and Aragon were united through the marriage of their monarchs, Isabella and Ferdinand. With great religious fervour they ousted the last Arab ruler from Granada, expelled the Jews from Spain and gave rise to a Spanish proto-nationalism that would inspire the elites for a long time to come. In the Spanish case, this was intimately entwined with Catholic zeal, deployed, first, against the Muslims, and later in the Inquisition and Counter-Reformation. As the heiress of Isabella and Ferdinand's thrones married the heir to the Habsburgs lands, their descendants in Spain and in Austria inherited this goal and saw themselves as chief defenders of Catholicism.

In Austria, it was the pretensions of the Habsburg family rather than an elite-supported proto-nationalism which would fuel the dynastic rivalries with other leading European families. The enigmatic family motto A.E.I.O.U., adopted by Frederick III, the first Habsburg to be crowned Holy Roman Emperor[46] was interpreted to be the abbreviation of '*Austriae est imperare orbi universo*', it is for Austria to rule the universal globe, or in its German version, all the earth is subject to Austria. That this motto was taken up by his descendants who with their fruitful marriage politics would unite to Austria's possessions and to the Empire the lands of Burgundy and Spain made this an implicit bid for universal rule beyond the confines of the Empire, and an implicit challenge to other sovereign rulers.

English kings also claimed the role of leaders within Christendom, particularly as they saw themselves as legitimate pretenders to the French throne (the issue over which the Hundred-Years' War was fought). Proto-nationalism, already found in England in the thirteenth century, waxed strong in the late sixteenth and was closely coupled with England's Protestantism which pitted it especially against Philip II, the Catholic Habsburg ruler of Spain. With the precocious English development of high seas navigation and the loss of the continental possessions of English monarchs, this led to the invention of English separateness: some could now see the Channel not as waterway connecting the lands on either side through trade and personal union of inheritance, but as 'a moat defensive', as Shakespeare famously put it. Others, however, feared that 'the tail of these storms'—the religious wars—'which are so bitter and boisterous in other countries may reach us also before they are ended', as the Chancellor of the Exchequer, Sir Walter Mildmay, said to the House of Commons in 1576; arguing that against such storms, the Channel is no barrier.[47] In addition, King Philip II's Spain with her staunch defence of Catholicism, her brutal repression of Protestantism in the Netherlands, with the Inquisition and with her designs to bring England back into the Catholic fold by marriage or war was cast as perfect bully and antithesis to a flourishing polity that would defend its freedom of religion. Here is how one of Queen Elizabeth's courtiers, the Earl of Essex, leader of the anti-Spanish party who wanted the queen to launch a decisive military campaign against Philip of Spain, described this antagonism in 1596,

> You two are like two mighty champions entered into the lists to fight for the two great general quarrels of Christendom: Religion and Liberty; [Philip] forcing all to worship the Beast, your Majesty standing for God and his truth, [Philip] affirming to an universal monarchy, your Majesty relieving all the oppressed, and showing that you are powerful enough to make him feed within his tether.[48]

Two years later, Essex told the Queen's Council that Philip's ambition was to 'establish... a *Spanish* universal monarchy'.[49]

We see that in all of this internal family rivalries, first between Valois and Plantagenet, later between Valois and Habsburg, and between Protestant Tudor England and Catholic Habsburg Spain, were conflated into a larger pattern, pitting sovereigns and their states against the real or supposed bid for universal monarchy on the part of the Habsburgs.

How Europe Came to Rule the World

While Catholic theologians conceded that not even the pope had the right to order a war to conquer territories that had not previously been under Christian rule and that were now owned by Muslims (or other peoples), the papacy, established once more in Rome from 1376 began to see this otherwise. In 1452, Pope Nicholas V issued the bull *Dum Diversas*, to the king Portugal, which read, 'We grant you'—as though he had the authority to do so—'full and free permission to invade, search out, capture, and subjugate the Saracens and pagans and any other unbelievers and enemies of Christ wherever they might be, as well as their kingdoms, duchies, counties, principalities, and other property ... and to reduce their persons into perpetual slavery.' Only one year later, however, the practical impossibility of such an expansionist agenda vis-à-vis the Muslims was fully demonstrated when the Ottoman Turks once more besieged and finally conquered the last remnants of the Byzantine Empire, the golden city of Constantinople itself. Nor was Turkish expansion stopped. It would continue to be the curse of South-Eastern Europe for three centuries to come.

The discovery of the Americas led Europeans to pose a different (and quite disingenuous) question: what if territory belonged to nobody? This is where the papacy in its most conceited period, at the prodding of European rulers who saw their own ambitions limited by the fully attributed lands of Europe and the defences of their neighbours, claimed the authority to apportion such *terra nullius* to the monarchs it favoured: the kings of Spain and Portugal. In 1493 Pope Alexander VI, born as the Spaniard Rodrigo Borgia, felt it to be within his rights to decree with his bull *Inter Caetera*, that lands discovered 100 leagues to the West of the Azores and the Cape Verde islands should belong to Spain. The Portuguese King John II, also engaged in financing naval expeditions to access new markets and find a new passage to India, demurred. He persuaded the monarchs of Spain to agree on a division leaving the lands discovered or yet to be discovered from what would later be called Brazil to Macao East of China to Portugal. Only new discoveries on the other side of the globe—the lands stretching from West of Portugal to what would become known as the Philippines in honour of King Philip II of Spain—should go to Spain.

This bull and this extraordinary bilateral treaty mark the turning point after which European explorers felt they could lay claim to any previously 'undiscovered' territories—arguing that they belonged to no-one, discounting local populations who were dismissed as not having proper political structures and thus not constituting proper polities. In vain did the Spanish jurist Francisco de Vitoria in the following century defend the rights of the indigenous populations: the voyages of discovery of Christopher Columbus and other seafarers unleashed the era of European colonialism. This was an attractive business above all for monarchies that had remained outside the Holy Roman Empire: through their colonies and trade, they could aspire to compete with it for wealth, power and prestige. Thus Queen Elizabeth of England would send out her enterprising sea captains—whom the Spanish called 'pirates', and they had a point— 'to discover, search, finde out, and view such remote, heathen and barbarous lands, countries, and territories, not actually possessed of any Christian Prince, nor inhabited by Christian People ... so to bee possessed and inhabited ... with our Realmes of Englande and Ireland'.[50]

Thus European dynastic competition, encouraged by enterprising merchants and captains, went global.

The Medieval System

To sum up, the period 476 until 1453 fits badly with any 'realist' or 'liberal' interpretations of International Relations. The earlier centuries following the disintegration of the *Pax Romana* in Western Europe saw waves of invading pagan tribes both impose themselves by sheer force, and yet find themselves greatly impressed by the social structures they encountered. These latter were a mix of Roman and Judaeo-Christian structures and customs which the pagan rulers could adopt to their advantage to enhance their standing within their own tribes. In return they owed deference to the Church which could by and by impose a view of a community of Christendom which Islam would copy with its notion of the umma.

For several centuries, the Occident showed deference to the East Roman emperors as primary or at least co-equal secular heads of Christendom, until in 1204 greed deviated a crusade from its true aim of liberating Jerusalem to sacking Constantinople, a deed condemned by the Pope. Here and in many other contexts, the Church's teaching that war among Christians was in principle to be avoided was cast aside as Germanic traditions of the feud took centuries to yield to attempts to recreate states with a monopoly of the use of force. But in principle, there was the notional unity of Christendom, whether or not one accepted the concrete pre-eminence of the Holy Roman Empire. Wars among Christians were recognized as ethically problematic and at the very least subject to limitations. It was not accepted that a sovereign ruler could go to war as he or she wished, but a just cause had to be demonstrated and the support of a higher authority—pope or emperor—sought.

5

EARLY MODERN HISTORY

Just as European dynastic rivalries went global, the medieval limitations on warfare painstakingly established by the Catholic Church began to crumble. The Reformation delegitimised these stops on fierce inter-state competition reminiscent of Thucydides' world, but with the admixture of a religious zeal that often stifled compassion and reason. The old constraints—the primacy of the Pope as spiritual leader, the Catholic Church's disapproval of war between Christian monarchs, the primacy of the emperor in secular matters, the just war criteria, *Treuga Dei* and *Pax Dei*—were challenged and then cast aside. Moreover, the Confessional Wars, starting with the Hussite Wars (1419–1439) and ending roughly with the Thirty Years War (1618–1648)—with some stragglers such as the Jacobite Rebellions (1688–1746) in the British Isles—added a Europe-wide religious confrontation between Protestants of various sorts and Catholics on the older and enduring pattern of wars of dynastic competition. It is no coincidence that the War of the Three Kingdoms which includes the English Civil War (1639–1651) overlapped with the catastrophic Thirty Years' War—similar ideological-political

issues (including not only confessional strife but also the distribution of power within states) and socio-political dynamics are
found in both.

The Reformation

The Protestant Reformation came into full swing during Charles
V's reign, but it had its antecedents: already in 1381, the Peasants'
Revolt in England had been influenced by ideas that were revolutionary both in the secular and in the religious sphere. The
trigger was economic—taxes raised by the crown—but the inspi-
ration was politico-religious, with a radical cleric by the name of
John Ball preaching 'Lollardism'[1]—from a sect following John
Wycliffe who first had the Bible translated into English. It was
no innocent question to ask, as did John Ball in an open-air
sermon, 'Whan Adam dalf [=delved] and Eve span, who was
thanne a gentilman?' John Ball went on to argue that 'From the
beginning all men were created equal by nature, [while] servitude had been introduced by the unjust oppression of men,
against the will of God; for, if it had pleased Him to create serfs,
surely in the beginning of the world would have laid down who
should in future be a serf and who a lord.' Ball encouraged his
audience to consider that the time had come, appointed by God,
that they should cast off the yoke of servitude and rejoice in
newly found liberty. In words that could have come from the
French Revolution, he incited peasants and townsfolk to 'uproot
the tares that generally destroy the grain' by, 'first, killing the
great lords of the realm, then letting perish the lawyers, justices
and jurors, and finally removing from the earth everyone whom
they knew in future to be harmful to the community.'[2]
Unsurprisingly, John Ball was captured, hung, drawn and quar-
tered when the Peasants' Revolt was suppressed. So much for
English liberties for commoners.

Few decades later, the followers of Jan Hus and his religious preaching in Bohemia also found that they upset both the worldly and the ecclesiastical powers, and were bloodily repressed in the ensuing Hussite Wars (1419–1434). Jan Hus, too, was executed, but his teaching lived on. The second half of the fifteenth century still saw rulers like George Podiebrad, King of Bohemia, being condemned as heretics because of religious views derived from Hus' teachings.

Neither Hus nor, initially, Luther had intended to weaken the Catholic Church or even to break away from it and open their own separate confession. The ideas of both, however, along with those of John Calvin, Huldrych Zwingli and the other sixteenth-century reformers had just that effect. By challenging the pope and thus the central authority of the Roman Catholic Church, not only on the level of personal misconduct and Vatican policies (the sale of indulgences to raise money for the gigantic new Church of St Peter's in Rome), but also on the level of doctrine, they questioned the direct link between the pope and God; in doing so, they questioned all authority that came from the pope, including that of the emperors he had crowned. Emperor Charles V and his successors understood this very well: after attempting (notably at the Diet of Worms) to absorb the energies of the Reformation within the Catholic Church, they lined up in defence of the Vatican, spearheading the Catholic Counter-Reformation. A temporary truce was established with the religious peace of Augsburg of 1555, postulating that it was up to the heads of all states and principalities to dictate the confession of their subjects—*cuius regio, illius religio*. But the damage was done. As we have seen, the quest for sovereignty and independence from pope and Empire had arisen in France, Spain, and England well before the Reformation, but it now spread to princes within the Holy Roman Empire who at the very least wanted to keep the pope from meddling in their religious affairs, and reduce the power of the Catholic Church within their states. The confessional disputes made conflict about the future distribution of power and competences, within Western Christendom and Europe as a whole, but particularly within the Holy Roman Empire, structurally inevitable. The ensuing wars, including the Peasant Revolts in the German-speaking lands in 1524–1525, the internal French Religious Wars, the 80-years' struggle of the Protestant Dutch to free themselves from Catholic Spanish overlordship, and finally the devastating Thirty Years' War, and in parallel, the Wars of the Three Kingdoms on the British Isles, all contained elements both of civil war and inter-state war. This originated in the resistance of Protestant rulers in the Holy Roman Empire, especially in Bohemia, against attempts by Emperor Ferdinand II to renege on the 1555 Diet of Augsburg agreement on religious tolerance, and to roll back Protestantism. In 1618, the Bohemian Protestant nobles chose a Protestant elector of the Holy Roman Empire, Frederick V of the Palatinate for their king instead of the Habsburg emperor, who claimed the crown by heredity and whose military intervention marked the outbreak of the Thirty Years' War. Frederick ruled Bohemia for less than a year, gaining him the nickname of the 'Winter King'. He had hoped in vain that his father-in-law, King James VI of Scotland and I of England, would come to the aid of his and the Protestant cause. James, by not interfering, put off the eruption of the religious wars on the British Isles, but his heir's pro-Catholic leanings and pro-absolutist political experiments catalysed their outbreak in 1642.

It was in campaigning unsuccessfully for English intervention on the Protestant side in the Thirty Years' War that the ardently Protestant John Donne, poet, diplomat and soldier, wrote the famous lines:

> No man is an Iland, intire of itselfe; every man is a peece of the
> Continent, a part of the maine; if a Clod bee washed away by the

Sea, Europe is the lesse, as well as if a Promontorie were, as well as if a Manor of thy friends or of thine owne were; any mans death diminishes me, because I am involved in Mankinde; And therefore never send to know for whom the bell tolls; It tolls for thee.[3]

Even a century later, this current of thinking that Britain should be more, not less, actively involved in European inter-state affairs was still going strong in Britain, as we shall see. Meanwhile, however the notion of any unity even just of Western Christianity was shattered forever.

Imperium and Global Competition

The effects of Martin Luther's 95-point accusation of the Roman Catholic Church, nailed onto the door of the palace church in Wittenberg in the middle of the Holy Roman Empire in 1517, were not yet fully felt when in 1519, the Habsburg scion King Charles or Carlos I of Spain was elected 'Roman King' (the title of the Holy Roman Emperor-elect before his coronation). In 1519, Charles, as fifth emperor of that name, united a larger empire than even that of the Mongols. It was described as an empire in which the sun did not set, as it included colonies around the globe. While he claimed the succession to the old West Roman Empire, albeit half a century after the fall of Constantinople, he also explicitly claimed the succession to the East Roman Empire, as a symbol of which he adopted the dou-ble-headed eagle as the imperial emblem.

In this he was not alone: the Caesars or 'Tsars' of all the Russias' from Ivan III 'the Great' onwards also claimed this suc-cession, although this would not matter greatly before the eigh-teenth century, when Russia became a major player in the European state system. So did the sultans in Kostantiniyye. A temporary armistice between the Holy Roman Emperor and the Ottoman Sultan, concluded in 1606 and renewed ten years later (as the Koran forbade any longer armistices with the infidel) described both men as '*imperatores*'.[4] Indeed, some relativity was contained even in the very word with which Pope Clement VII crowned Charles V Emperor in Bologna in 1530: he referred to the imperial crown as '*la prima corona dell Imperio del Mondo*', the first crown of the world empire,[5] which arguably downgraded the emperor to a first among several 'emperors'. Nevertheless, this concentration of power in a single pair of hands worried the other rulers of Europe. Maps like that on the cover of this book, dating from 1588, depicting Europe in the form of a queen or empress with Spain as her head, circulated from 1537. The symbolism was not lost on contemporaries: Charles, King of Spain, ruled Europe.

Then, Charles did something unprecedented: in 1554–1556, he retired to a monastery where he died a couple of years later. And he resumed the early Germanic custom of dividing up his lands. In this case, the heirs were his brother Ferdinand who received the Austrian Habsburg possessions and was elected Emperor Ferdinand I after him, and his son Philip, to whom he bequeathed Spain and a range of other smaller states from the Netherlands to parts of Italy, plus Spain's overseas empire. Even then, Philip II of Spain, while not emperor, had a global realm.

English critics could rightly claim that Spain was seeking *imperium*, but it was not necessarily *imperium universalis*. As noted above, confusingly, the widely-used Latin word for sovereignty was *imperium*. As we have seen, this was claimed by France, England herself, but also Spain, where already in 1104–1114, King Alfonso I of Aragon, married to Urraca the heiress of Leon and Castile, was called 'emperor of Spain, king and magnificent emperor of all of Spain, emperor by the Grace of God'.[6] After him, King Alfonso VII of Leon and Castile in the twelfth century called himself *imperator* of all of Spain so as to affirm his superiority to and overlordship of Portugal, recently promoted from county to kingdom. In Philip II's time, as he ruled over a large collection of different principalities, but not the Holy Roman Empire, his court philosophers could easily place him on a level above that of an ordinary king, but could not ascribe to him universal monarchy. Instead, they could proclaim him '*Emperador del Nuevo Mundo y de Europa*'—emperor of the new world and of Europe (the latter, by implication, meaning his possessions that were outside the Holy Roman Empire: Spain, Southern Italy, Sicily...).[7]

The discovery of new worlds whetted appetites on all sides: the monarchs of countries other than Spain also adopted symbolism implying claims to the globe. The Portuguese, whose royal prince Henry the Seafarer (grandson of Edward III of England) had pioneered naval discoveries in the Atlantic, adopted an armillary sphere symbolizing the globe as their emblem, seen still today on the national coat of arms. King Manuel I of Portugal (1469–1521) brazenly had the motto '*spera mundi*' (sometimes rendered '*espera mumdi*') inscribed on one, which could be seen as a misspelling of *sphera mundi*—the global sphere, or else 'the hope of the world'. Elsewhere we find an illustration of him enthroned, holding the armillary sphere, with the caption '*deo in celo tibi autem in mundo*', as to God in heaven, to you also on earth.[8] With the motto of the French King Henri II (reigned 1547–1559) you had to look twice to see that it stopped a little short of claiming world rule: '*Donec totem impleat orbem*' simply meant, until the whole world is filled, not ruled (*imperat*), by implication by France.

Queen Elizabeth of England came late to this game, but the iconography is just as clear: on her famous Armada portrait, her elegant hand is posed delicately on—a globe. Against such competition, Philip II could only proclaim that for him, the world was not enough, as it said on a medal that was issued, with his head on one side, and the inscription '*non sufficit orbis*' around a globe on the other, with a horse jumping off the globe, into space. His grandson, Philip IV, had himself painted by Rubens on horseback, balancing the globe on his shoulder with the help of angels. None of them could seriously hope to be 'world rulers', but they did rule areas all around the globe, geographically a quantum leap from the pretensions of certain monarchs of Antiquity to be 'world rulers'. Such was their global competition.

The Holy Roman Empire vs Bodin's Sovereign State

Luther's Reformation was well underway and the Ottoman Empire was steadily expanding into Europe when instead of standing shoulder to shoulder against these two major threats to their world and their world views the French King Francis I brought balance-of-power politics between his own and the Habsburg dynasty to a new intensity. During the imperial elections of 1519, both he and Henry VIII of England threw their hats into the ring, along with another prince from within the Empire; only electoral interference in the form of large bribes made to several electors by the Fugger banking family delivered the choice of the Spanish Habsburg king as Charles V. Francis' disappointment was followed by a deep humiliation as he and Charles fought over the domination of Italy, Francis was not only defeated by Charles' imperial forces at the battle of Pavia in 1525, but taken prisoner and forced to make huge concessions to Charles in the Treaty of Madrid of the following year: the renunciation of all claims on Italy, Flanders, and the surrender of Burgundy to the Habsburgs. (Later Francis reneged on his treaty commitments, arguing that it had been made under duress; this would become an important precedent in international law.) Francis's humiliation turned into deep, lasting resentment of the Habsburgs. In 1526 the Ottoman Empire had defeated and killed the King of Hungary at the Battle of Mohacs, and occupied his kingdom; in 1529 the Turks stood before Vienna. Nevertheless, Francis I preferred to conclude a treaty of alliance with Kostantiniyye, rather than come to the defence of his Habsburg rival. A subject of the French king, Guillaume de Rochechouart blamed both sides equally—the French king and emperor Charles V (whom he referred to as the king of Spain). Despite two meetings between Charles and Francis in 1538 and 1539 designed to establish peaceful relations, their antagonism lived on. This is how Rochechouart commented on their relationship in the latter year:

> The kings of France and Spain [i.e. emperor Charles V] know from their own experience and that of their predecessors that they cannot ruin each other, nor establish a general [=universal] monarchy in Europe, as it is partitioned under the domination of several princes and republics who have an interest that no such large monarch could come into being who might swallow them up, and because they will always balance [throw in their weight on the side of] the weaker of the two to equal the stronger ...

> The best would be to unite to ruin the general enemy of all Christendom [that is, the Turk]. The will of their majesties, if they were the same, would make all the rest of Europe work, being able to lay down the law to all the others if they were united, and they could declare those [other leaders in Europe] who would not help as enemies.[9]

Instead, they pig-headedly put their own dynastic interests first.

The Reformation and the confessional wars of the sixteenth and early seventeenth century much reduced the standing and influence of the Holy Roman Empire. It is almost a miracle that it survived the Thirty Years' War, and that its outcome was a confirmation of the system of internal checks and balances elaborated under Emperor Maximilian I in 1495–1496. While Maximilian's attempts to create a fully centralised administration and an imperial army had in large part been thwarted by the princes and the cities of the Empire, the Empire had established a Court of Justice to deal with any issues arising among its constituent parts; the Aulic Council (*Reichshofrat*) acting as a check on the emperor as much as an executive organ; a parliament or Imperial Diet consisting of three Councils: the Council of the powerful Electors (the archbishops of Cologne, Mainz and Trier, each of whom was simultaneously ruler over extensive lands; and as secular electors, the Duke of Saxony, the Count Palatine of the Rhine, the Margrave of Brandenburg; and the King of Bohemia); the Council of other Princes or heads of sub-states that formed part of the Empire, and the Council of the representatives of the Empire's free cities, that is, cities that were not ruled by a prince or bishop. The Empire practised what today is called 'subsidiarity': issues were decided at the lowest level of government at which they could be settled. This can also be called layered sovereignty: there was no entirely centralised government in a structure in which the imperial Diet met in different places, such as Augsburg and Frankfurt on the Main, and later mainly Ratisbon; where the imperial court was peripatetic for a long time before settling more permanently, first in Prague, then in Vienna; where its Court of Justice for the adjudication of quarrels among its constituent entities was located successively in Frankfurt on the Main, Worms, Augsburg, Nuremberg, Esslingen on the Neckar, Speyer, and finally in Wetzlar. Even though from the fifteenth century, the Holy Roman Empire was often given the epithet 'of the German nation', its population was never exclusively German-speaking. After the Empire was finally shorn of its Italian states, Flemish and Slav populations remained within it until 1806, and by then the Habsburgs had long ruled over territories outside the Empire where Hungarian, Romanian, Polish, Ukrainian, Croat, and Italian was spoken. And a particularly curious arrangement even gave two of the

Holy Roman Empire's great neighbours a formal check on its foreign polices: enshrined in the Peace Treaties of Westphalia of 1648 which restored this multi-layered shared-sovereignty constitution of the Holy Roman Empire after the Thirty Years' War was the right of France and Sweden to be guarantors with the right to intervene in the Empire if the Treaty commitments were not upheld.[10]

Consultation was the hallmark of this structure. Consultation had to take place on all levels, beginning with the consultation by the electors of other princes before they cast their vote in the election of the new emperor. While it is true that from the reign of Maximilian I, most emperors belonged to the Habsburg family, there were several occasions when the outcome of the election was not a foregone conclusion: we have already alluded to the candidacy of Francis I and Henry VIII for the emperorship in 1519. Later, when the power of France in Europe reached a new peak and that of the Holy Roman Empire had been reduced by the Thirty Years' War, Louis XIV of France, let it be known during the imperial election of 1658 that he was a candidate for the office—although again, the French candidate was passed over in favour of the Habsburg. The third time was when the Prince-Elector of Bavaria, and not a Habsburg, was actually elected as Charles VII in 1742, in the absence of a male Habsburg heir. His reign was no great success, strengthening the support for the succession of Maria Theresia; to circumvent the annoying fact of her gender, her husband Francis Duke of Lorraine was elected Emperor Francis I. But it took a war to confirm this outcome. (Maria Theresia's adversaries would obstinately continue to refer to her only as 'Queen of Hungary'.)

In any case, the Holy Roman Empire was a structure accommodating the needs of many different entities through elaborate consultation mechanisms amounting to internal checks and balances. And had it not been for the confessional wars triggered by the Reformation, the Empire would have been remembered above all as a zone of peace. As Machiavelli commented in his *Discourses on the First Ten Books of Titus Livius* (written before the consequences of the Reformation were fully felt), the Holy Roman Empire:

> is divided among the Swiss, republics called free states, princes and the emperor. And the reason why amidst such diverse forms of constitution wars do not arise, or, if they do arise, do not last long, is the Imperial title. For, though the emperor has no power to enforce his will, yet he has such standing among them that he acts as arbitrator, and by imposing his authority, mediates between them and at once puts an end to any dissension.[11]

Not only was the Empire thus a large area of peace; members of the Empire were banned from fighting against one another or against the Empire itself. On a rare occasion when this rule was broken outside the religious wars, punishment followed. When Frederick II of Prussia went to war against Saxony in the Seven Years' War, the Imperial Diet declared war against him. Only defensive war—against the never-ending Turkish onslaught— was immediately possible for the Empire as a whole, and even then, the different parts of the Empire would send as many soldiers as they saw fit and would only grudgingly contribute their 'Turk's penny', the taxes demanded by the central imperial administration, to pay for its standing army.

Meanwhile, the kings outside the Empire proudly claimed and exercised their sovereign right to go to war. The king of France was in the pole position, as the eventual defeat of the English in the Hundred Years' War led to the integration of the parts of France formerly held by the English kings into the royal domain. This gave the French king a permanent income from these lands (their liberated populations had no choice in this) for which he needed no parliament's approval: the road to absolutism was thus clear, the rule without parliamentary checks and balances.

While in England, Spain and the Holy Roman Empire, monarchs were limited in their legislation and their ability to tax by their parliaments, diets or *cortes*, already the French philosopher Philippe de Beaumanoir (c.1250–1296) in his late-thirteenth century *Coutumes de Beauvaisis* defined sovereignty as the being above the law: 'the king is *souverains* [sic] above all others and by his rights has the general protection of the whole realm, because he can make all statutes for the common benefit and what he decrees must be followed.'[12] This ideal type of a sovereign polity was captured by the French political theorist Jean Bodin when in 1576 he published his *Six Books on the Republic* (or commonwealth). In it, in this context of a ruler who did not depend on parliament for his freedom of action, but also in the context of a complete independence from any higher power, Bodin defined 'sovereignty' as follows, elevating it to an indivisible principle:

> SOVEREIGNTY is that absolute and perpetual power vested in a commonwealth...The true sovereign remains always seized of his power. Just as a feudal lord who grants lands to another retains his eminent domain over them, so the ruler who delegates authority to judge and command, whether it be for a short period, or for as long as it is his pleasure, remains seized of those rights of jurisdiction actually exercised by another in the form of a revocable grant, or precarious tenancy. (Book I.8)

And he continued, 'there are none on earth, after God, greater than sovereign princes, whom God establishes as His lieutenants to command the rest of mankind...'(Book I.10) Bodin thus put into words what French and English monarchs had aspired to since the twelfth century, but what only the French, given their special independence from any parliament for their revenue, could put into practice:

> The first attribute of the sovereign prince ... is the power to make law binding on all his subjects in general and on each in particular.

But to avoid any ambiguity one must add that he does so without the consent of any superior, equal, or inferior being necessary. (Book I.10)

Bodin thus postulated de facto tyrannical powers for the sovereign monarch, who was free to break any inherited contracts and even to change his mind regarding promises made by himself (Book VIII). Bodin feebly added that it would be unwise to do so, or that one should do so only in exceptional circumstances, and that the monarch should refrain from tampering with the constitutional law. But the sovereign's freedom to do what he wished was what the casual reader would take away from this tract. Moreover, breaking with almost two millennia of just war tradition, Bodin thought it quite acceptable that such a sovereign would wish to expand his power:

Offensive weapons must also be provided if one would extend one's frontiers and subjugate the enemy, for the appetites of men being for the most part insatiable, they desire to secure great abundance not only of what is necessary and useful, but of what is pleasant merely, and redundant. (Book I.1)

Crucially, wherever this view of the absolutist sovereign state was accepted, war was also accepted as a tool that the sovereign state could deploy as it pleased. Insistence on sovereignty meant (and still means) insistence on the freedom to go to war, to beggar one's neighbour or invade him, by simply stating that it is in one's own state's interest. Adding the adjective 'national' has not changed anything about this: *raison d'état*, reasons of state, and today 'national interest' can be the excuse for any behaviour and is the chaotic force that turns inter-polity relations into anarchy, insecurity and war. Bodin's and his followers' idea of sovereignty was essentially the freedom of the sovereign to do as he or she pleased, freedom from external and internal checks. And all monarchs aspired at least to freedom from external checks.

Liberties vs Universality

Freedom or liberty was inscribed on banners on all sides. The Imperial cities were forever defending their special privileges or *Libertäten*, the Protestant princes fought the Thirty Years' War in defence of religious freedom and in 1648 won this concession (already made once in 1555 but challenged in the Counter-Reformation moves of the Habsburgs), confirmed by the Treaties of Westphalia; only, after 1648, the princes of the Holy Roman Empire no longer had the right to impose their religion on their subjects. The (Catholic or Protestant) monarchs outside the Empire wanted freedom of action, unchecked by the pope or emperor, and ideally also unchecked by any internal powers represented in parliaments. Freedom—their sovereign freedom of action in foreign affairs—was also how the French monarchs explained their successive treaties with the Ottoman Empire. After the alliance of 1536, France also joined the Ottomans in waging naval war against the Habsburgs in 1550, and deliberately went to war with the Holy Roman Empire to attract imperial forces to the West, to facilitate the Ottoman assault on Vienna in 1683. Catholic France took the side of the Protestants against the Catholic League of the Habsburg emperors in the Thirty Years' War, and her wars with Catholic Spain over disputed territories would only end with the War of the Spanish succession 1701–1714. This unrestrained competition, devoid of religious or ideological affinities, was one main strand of European inter-polity relations from 1519 until the French Revolution, even during the Confessional Wars.

As we saw in the precocious revolutionary teaching of the fourteenth-century agitator John Ball, Protestantism also could go hand in hand with calls for democracy, the rule of the people. Reasons to rebel were always present in the context of the huge and persistent social inequalities of Europe which time and again pushed peasant communities on the brink of famine to revolts against unbearable taxation and/or land hunger. From the French Jacquerie of the mid-fourteenth century and Wat Tyler's Peasants' Revolt to the German Peasants' and then the Tudor Rebellions of the sixteenth century, the pattern was robust and recurrent. Self-confident burghers and townsfolk in cities from London to Würzburg and Florence with privileges and a proud heritage of self-government rose against overlords or even kings a great many times from the late fourteenth to the early sixteenth centuries. Most of these uprisings tended to be focused on individual grievances; few rebels or leaders saw and attacked the basic inequality of European society with quite such clarity as John Ball. The rebellious Netherlands since their Union of Utrecht upheld above all their *vrijheid* in all its forms—religious freedom above all, freedom from Spain's tutelage, and sovereignty of the individual provinces making up the Union.[13]

Notwithstanding the English commoners' readiness to stand up for causes of religion that manifested itself in the Tudor Rebellions, in England it was only in the seventeenth century that such ideas were once again fully mobilised. This led to the Civil War, a forerunner of the French Revolution that equally resulted in the execution of a king, and the appointment of Oliver Cromwell as Lord Protector by the not particularly democratic proclamation of his close companions. (Edmund Burke who in 1790 protested that he loved a 'manly, moral, regulated liberty' as much as anybody, thought that his country did not need an elected ruler, having already had its own revolution with the Bill of Rights of 1689. For Burke it was freedom from persecution and terror, and national independence from great-power oppression, rather than freedom to vote for a government or a leader, that were important.)[14]

Both Cromwell's and the French Revolution of 1789, despite fighting for republicanism, resulted in the creation of autocratic regimes, here in the person of Cromwell, there first in the person of Maximilien Robespierre and then Napoleon. Both set up republics (a.k.a. a commonwealth). 'God's Englishman' Oliver Cromwell and his supporters were distinctive, it is true, in marrying a revolutionary political ideas and puritan Protestantism. But in both cases, their political (and in the case of the Commonwealth, religious) ideals led these republics into direct confrontation with neighbouring monarchies (and with Catholics anywhere, in the case of the Commonwealth). If any evidence were needed, these two experiments in republican governments, that is, governments supposedly in the interest of the nation and not that of dynasties, showed that in the midst of polities with different constituent ideologies, republics with a strong missionary zeal promoted war, not peace. For underlying their demand for (religious or democratic) liberty was the conviction that these liberties should be applied universally, that their world view was the only valid one. (This latter part of their convictions was, of course, heartily reciprocated by their adversaries.) Conflict was ideologically preordained, as with the clash between Communist autocracies and Western democracies in the twentieth century, but without being contained by the fear of nuclear war.

Just as the Wars of the Three Kingdoms fused religious and constitutional-political disputes, the Thirty Years' War brought together in Central Europe three sets of approaches: the religious fervour rooted in Reformation and Counter-Reformation (which drove Emperor Ferdinand II on the Catholic side, but also the Swedes on the Protestant), narrow dynastic or state interests (France) and proto-nationalism (which we find particularly in the Holy Roman Empire). In other words, 'realists', and 'idealists' of two kinds—religious and nationalists—clashed. Some contemporaries were aware of these conflicting world views and concomitant approaches to inter-polity relations. In the 1640s, during the negotiations leading up to the Westphalian

Treaties, Henri-Auguste de Loménie, Count of Brienne, the French Secretary of State for Foreign Affairs, complained about France's allies, the Swedes:

> On the [aims] we concur with the Swedes but not on the means. Weakening the excessive power of the House of Austria, establishing the liberty of the princes of the Empire; that has, indeed, been the aim of our union [i.e. alliance] and of the [Thirty Years'] War. But to reach it by strengthening the Protestants, by weakening the Catholics, that is what we do not concur with. On the contrary, our aim must be to love [both] Catholics and Protestants ... always defending and strengthening our own without allowing ourselves ... to weaken it by an ill-founded fear that being Catholic means being dependent on the Spaniards.[15]

The French diplomat Abel Servien agreed with Brienne that what was annoying about the Swedes as allies was that 'the Protestant religion much more dominates their minds than *raison d'état*.' By contrast, wrote other French diplomats, the German princes 'are much more affected by their love of their fatherland, and cannot approve of foreigners dismembering the Empire, no matter what gain we hold out to them...' Indeed, they would constantly talk about their 'beloved fatherland of the German nation'.[16]

Balance-of-power games were central—Cardinal Mazarin, who was himself adept at this game, complained that the emissaries of the pope and of Venice were constantly speaking about 'the equilibrium in Christendom, [*la raison de l'équilibre dans la chrétienté*], which is one of the chief maxims of these gentlemen' who 'take the side of our enemies and wish to favour them as being the weaker party.' In 1638, the French Henri Duke of Rohan, in a treatise on the interests of the princes and the states of Christendom wrote that there were:

> two powers in Christendom that are like two [magnetic] poles, that is the Houses of France and of Spain, which align all the other states

in war and peace. [The House] of Spain having suddenly found itself more powerful cannot hide the design it had to make itself mistress and to let rise in the West the sun of a new monarchy. That of France has precipitated itself to become the counter-weight. The other princes have aligned themselves with one or the other, according to their interest.[17]

Indeed, to aim for the creation of an equilibrium within Christendom seemed to be good guidance for individual rulers. Johan Adler Salvius, adviser to the Crown of Sweden, instructed young Queen Christina that:

The first principle of statecraft is that the security of the whole consists in the equilibrium of the single realms. When one of them begins to become too powerful and a threat to the others, they throw themselves by means of leagues and alliances into a scale against it, so as to create a counterweight and to preserve the balance.[18]

Thus dynastic competition began to be disguised as the nobler aim of creating a balance of powers. In this context Englishmen resurrected the notion of England as the decisive 'the tongue of the balance', throwing in their weight with that party of such a dynastic balance-of-power game that was in England's greatest interest. As Slingsby Bethel, an MP with one foot in both the Commonwealth and the Restoration camps, wrote in 1671:

it is in the interest of the king and kingdom of England to make use of the advantages their strength and situations gives them, in weighing the imperial [= sovereign] powers of Christendom, keeping the balance, by adding to, or diminishing from any of them, as best suits with justice and their own interests.[19]

An anonymous author who published *Discourses upon the Modern Affairs of Europe* wrote nine years later that 'The great thing which has disturbed the Peace of Europe ... has been the huge designe of the Universal Monarchy; a designe which ... has possessed the Genius of the Spanish and French Monarchies.' He concluded that 'what is needed is (for England to be) a 'separate Kingdom or State in Europe sufficient to balance the weighty body of the French Monarchy'.[20]

Englishmen claimed that the defence of this balance was essential for the defence of English liberties, or even the liberties of all of Europe.[21] So the balance and the defence of liberty, in the fight against supposed aspirations to 'universal monarchy', in the English mind at least, were welded together as one big guiding principle of foreign policy.[22]

As Andreas Osiander has shown in his seminal studies of European state systems, the balance of powers would be elevated to a recognised condition for a lasting peace with the treaties of Utrecht.[23] These multiple peace treaties, however, simultaneously elevated to a guiding idea of international law the idea that the desired end-state of war should be in the interest of the greater good of Europe, which had to be put above the interests—even the very legitimate interests—of any individual power (see below). This idea of the prevalence of the wellbeing of the whole, over the narrow interests of one state, was perhaps first formulated by Francisco de Vitoria, who in his *Law of War* of 1539 wrote that the just war had to have as its purpose the 'good of the whole world', *bonum totius orbis*. For Vitoria, the 'whole world' did indeed mean the whole world, as much of his writing was concerned with the treatment of Spain's new conquests on other continents. Subsequent writers who we shall encounter in the next chapter were concerned only with the wellbeing of Europe, but this change of priority is crucial and in keeping with Vitoria's (and ultimately St Augustine's) argument that even if justified, the evil consequences of a war must not outweigh the benefit derived from pursuing justice.[24]

Both approaches put dynastic and state interests in relation to a universal balance of interests, but in two radically different ways: the first served to promote the ambitions of dynasties in dealing with their rivals, the second to subordinate them to the interests of others.

The Turkish Threat

While dynastic rivalry and confessional wars tore Europe apart, the Turks' assaults on the external borders of Christendom continued. Such aggression from the outside was nothing new; the Roman Empire had been battered in this way. Incursions and invasions had never ceased since the fourth century. Pagan invasions had more often than not ended with the invaders—from Goths and Franks to Saxons, Normans and Magyars—being converted to Christianity, although there had been the exception of the Mongols who turned back after the death of their Great Khan. The Arab expansion had peaked in the eighth century. Only, the Turks had never stopped assaulting Christendom since they first appeared on the scene in the tenth century. Converted to Islam, they subjected even other Muslim rulers. It was they, we recall, who with their brutal behaviour in the Middle East finally pushed Western Christianity to undertake the Crusades to save the Christians of the East from Turkish tyranny. Despite the amazing triumph of the First Crusade—illustrating the great strategic advantage of surprise—these Christian wars aimed at liberating what had until the Arab Muslim conquest been Christian territories had no lasting success. But given the consistent expansionism of the Turks, the idea of the crusade along with the pressing need for self-defence would remain a key theme of European foreign policy for centuries to come.

To echo Rochechouart, the most logical action to take would have been for the powers of the West, especially the Holy Roman Empire, to ally themselves with what was left of the East Roman Empire to stave off the Turks. Self-centredness, but above all greed, stood in the way, as the sack of Constantinople in 1204 and the establishment of a Western or 'Latin' kingdom in its place illustrated. Even after the restoration of the Byzantine Empire and its precarious subsistence, encircled on all sides by Ottoman conquests which had already spread to the Balkans and thus to Europe by the mid-fourteenth century, this did not change. When Constantinople fell in 1453, it was too late: the Christian state system had irreversibly lost Asia Minor.

After 1453, the Ottomans were not content with their 'Golden Apple', Kostantiniyye, as the Second Rome was henceforth called. New booty beckoned in Europe. By the end of the fifteenth century, they held not only most of the Balkans but also the northern littoral of the Black Sea, and were eying the riches beyond the Carpathian Mountains and the Eastern Alps. By 1529 they besieged Vienna, the gateway to the Holy Roman Empire. Winter came early that year and for logistical reasons, the Turks withdrew, but in the following decades, they subjected all of modern Bulgaria, Romania, Hungary, Macedonia, Kosovo, Serbia and Bosnia, while conquering the entire southern littoral of the Mediterranean up to Algeria, both coasts of the Red Sea and the southern littoral of the Gulf. It was only a matter of time before they would again assault Vienna.

How was the Holy Roman Empire and Christendom to deal with this challenge? Christendom was singularly lacking in solidarity not only when it came to defending the last remnants of the East Roman Empire, but also when it came to the defence of the Holy Roman Empire itself, now a front-line state. Franco-Turkish alliances made both Ottoman sieges of Vienna possible, and periodic defences mounted by the Holy Roman Emperor against Ottoman attacks elicited only weak responses from the princes whose realms lay at a greater distance from the confrontation. In 1683, when the Ottomans besieged Vienna for a second time, it was Poland that came to the defence of the Holy Roman Empire, while Spain, the Netherlands and other Christian states stayed well out of the fray and France mischievously supported the Turks.

Given how divided Christendom was, the Habsburg general and diplomat Lazarus von Schwendi (1522–1583) advocated accommodation with the Turks:

> Reason and nature teach us that we should humble ourselves somewhat before those who are stronger [than us], and we see this even among the irrational animals. Powerful and strong kingdoms and regimes have always eventually vanquished and subjected the weaker, just as we now see with the Turks and others. Therefore peace is much better, in such cases, if it can be obtained in a bearable way, and to humble oneself and cede, rather than running headlong towards one's own perdition.

> The Christian countries and princes who could not withstand the Turk have done better if they agreed in time to pay him tribute and render him other services, while preserving their own régime and a little freedom, than those who, albeit weaker, opted for unwarranted resistance and were exterminated or came under the Turk's yoke.[25]

From 1529 until 1547, there were permanent skirmishes and raids along the border of (unoccupied) Hungary and Turkish-controlled territories. In 1547, less than two decades after the first Ottoman siege of Vienna, Emperor Charles V concluded a truce with the Turks by *de facto* accepting a form of vassalage to the sultan, and agreed to the payment, by the Holy Roman Empire, of annual tributes to Kostantiniyye in return for a non-aggression promise. Hostilities resumed in 1556 and carried on until a new truce was concluded in 1562, in which Emperor Ferdinand I renounced his claims to Transylvania, and resumed tribute payments. When Maximilian II followed Ferdinand to the imperial throne, he refused to pay the tribute and a new war broke out. Further battles and truces followed, but no stable peace, until the end of the seventeenth century.

The structural problem with any lasting accommodation with the Ottoman Empire was posed by Islam which ruled out a permanent peace with the *Dar al-Harb*, the 'realm of war', the

Muslim label for all lands beyond the world of established Islam. Peace treaties were in fact truces, and thus only temporary. Only under the impact of the Austrian roll-back assault at the very end of the seventeenth and the early eighteenth centuries, did Sultan Mahmud I break with this Muslim norm. In 1747, for the first time in the history of the Ottoman Empire, a peace treaty (that of Belgrade, of 1739) was extended for an indefinite length of time. Only after this could the Ottoman Empire gradually become a part of a European state system, when it began to behave as a partner respecting terms of war and peace according to prevalent European norms.[26] Paradoxically, the Ottoman Empire gained full recognition as one of the European great powers only in the late nineteenth century, barely half a century before its demise at the end of the First World War.

Raison d'état, *Dynastic Competition and Balance-of-Power Wars*

We might have expected the end of the long period of confessional wars to usher in more peaceful times for Europe. Instead, with the medieval Church's restraints on war and the emperor's moral influence beyond the confines of the Empire fatally weakened or even gone, the prevailing pattern of European inter-polity relations was one of continuing intense competition between the great powers. If anything, this could now assume wider geographic dimensions as the whole globe had become the theatre for such competition with colonial expansion. Let us take a step back to explain the background to this.

We have seen that the kings of France claimed leadership in Europe and competed for it with the Holy Roman Empire. Direct wars between the two polities had occurred sporadically, as with the Battle of Bouvines of 1214, in which the French king prevailed against a coalition of the emperor and the king of England. The competition had drawn in the papacy. But it really took off and became very personal under the later Valois and then the

Bourbon monarchs, who saw the Habsburgs—in their Spanish and Austrian branches—as rival claimants to leadership in Europe. The French monarchs stopped at very little to deal a blow to the Habsburgs, claiming always that they were doing this 'in the interest of Europe'. The Bourbon kings of the seventeenth century continued the previous Valois antagonism to the Habsburgs who with their Spanish and Austrian branches had dominated Europe in the sixteenth century. By ensuring that the two branches of the Habsburgs would not join up again to recreate the global empire of Charles V, Cardinal Richelieu, the chief minister of King Louis XIII, claimed to be fighting for 'the liberty of Christendom', as he put it in 1624. And yet, only five years later, Richelieu articulated as the overall aim of his grand strategy 'to make the [French] king the most powerful monarch of the world and the most esteemed prince.'[27]

While the Habsburg-led Holy Roman Empire, staunch defender of Catholicism and a bastion against further Turkish expansion, still held a position of pre-eminence in Europe after the confessional wars, if nothing else due to its sheer size which exceeded that of all the other states, it could no longer make any claim to universal primacy. Other great powers could step up their competition with it: even during the Thirty Years' War, Gustavus II Adolphus of Sweden, the 'Lion from Midnight', and at one point leader of the Protestant coalition, was seen as a potential future European hegemon. France had followed her own *raison d'état* and sided with the Protestant forces, not least to check Sweden's ascent. Soon thereafter, Louis XIV, loyal to the ideals of Cardinal Richelieu, was accused of aspiring to universal monarchy. In a satire published in 1657, a 'vendor of spectacles' explained the world to his myopic client:

> In my view ... the French desire to assume the regime over the entire world and thus to get all humans to submit to them, as they claim orally and in writing that the monarchy of Charlemagne belongs to

them. They profess without shame that the origins of their wars lie in their frustrated attempts and unsatisfied hopes, the presumptuousness of their aspiration to regain the regime of Charlemagne, i.e. the emperorship. They are not ashamed of these ambitions, nor do they refuse to shoulder the hostility [of others] resulting from their claim to universal monarchy—of which they had hitherto accused the Spanish, with much clamour.[28]

And the instrument of Louis XIV's ambitions was the Treaty of Münster of 1648. As we have seen, as one of the twin Westphalian Treaties of 1648, it had made France the guarantor of its observance by the member entities of the Holy Roman Empire, just as the Treaty of Osnabrück conferred the task of guaranteeing the *status quo* within the *Reich* to Sweden. As Brendan Simms put it, 'the Westphalian Treaties were nothing less than a charter for intervention.' Far from acknowledging any equal sovereignty of the states of Europe over their domestic affairs, as is often claimed in works of IR Theory, the Treaties placed the whole peace settlement of the Holy Roman Empire 'under international guarantee', thus providing a lever for interference in the internal affairs of the Empire throughout the late seventeenth and eighteenths centuries.'[29] Louis XIV was the first to use his treaty right as leverage to extend his rule to the Imperial cities of Alsace.[30] As the Thirty Years' War ended, France was still at war with Habsburg Spain. Louis embarked upon a series of further wars, usually but not only involving the Habsburgs, mainly over Spanish possessions on the frontiers of France, but also to wrest the Palatinate from the Holy Roman Empire. But Louis also managed to secure temporary alliances with his adversaries' adversaries, among them Charles II of England and Scotland, and/or the Dutch Estates General. The effect of these wars was an anarchy as described by Hobbes, hardly a 'state system' at all: as one of Louis' chief ministers, Vauban, commented, when wars were drawn out, 'bizarre con-

junctures arise and other changes of the interests of neighbouring states (naturally enemies of each other's prosperity) which
result in your friends becoming your enemies who cease to help
you, or don't help you in good faith, or change sides overtly.'[31]
Vauban thus famously persuaded his king to invest in the defensive fortifications for which the former is so renowned. But even
Frenchmen—especially Protestants, whom the king chased away
in 1685 by ending their toleration that had been enshrined in
the 1698 Edict of Nantes—accused the king of being set on a
path of enslaving Europe, calling upon England to break
Europe's chains.[32] This is how Hobbes described inter-polity
relations shortly after the end of the Thirty Years' War, being
under the impression that things had ever been thus:

> [I]n all times, Kings, and Persons of Soveraigne authority, because
> of their Independency, are in continuall jealousies, and in the state
> and posture of Gladiators; having their weapons pointing and their
> eyes fixed on one another; that is, their Forts Garrisons and Guns
> upon the Frontiers of their Kingdomes; and continuall Spyes upon
> their neighbours; which is a posture of War.[33]

Cities and kingdoms, he argued, stood in perpetual fear of one
another, yet were wont 'to robbe and spoyle one another', just as
men had done in the state of nature, seeking to 'enlarge their
Dominions, upon all pretences of danger, and fear of Invasion'.
They 'endeavour as much as they can, to subdue, or weaken their
neighbours, by open force, and secret arts...'.[34] (It is not acciden-
tal that Hobbes described a world reminiscent of that of the fifth
century BC Greece of Thucydides—he was himself a translator
of the *Peloponnesian War* into English.)

Louis XIV was quite aware of the reactions he caused among
other European dynasties with his ambitious policies, yet he
continued regardless. He wrote to his ambassador in London
in 1699:

I know how much Europe would be alarmed at seeing my own power rise above that of the House of Austria, so that this type of equality on which [Europe] makes its repose depend would no longer obtain. But at the same time the Emperor's power is so much increased now, both on account of the submission of the princes of the Empire and of the advantageous peace [=the Peace of Karlowitz in 1699] that he has just concluded with the [Sublime] Porte [= the Ottoman Empire's foreign ministry] that it is in the general interest that, if it becomes even greater, my own power should still be such as to counterbalance it.[35]

Meanwhile Archbishop François Fénelon, tutor to the French princes, wrote that:

The natural ambitions of sovereigns, the flattery of their counsellors and the defences of entire nations cannot allow us to believe that a nation that *can* subject the others will abstain from doing so for centuries. ... One thus has to count on reality, which is that each nation will try to prevail over the others around it. Each nation is thus obliged to be ceaselessly on the lookout for its own security to prevent the excessive aggrandisement of each of its neighbours.

To prevent a neighbour from being too powerful is not to do wrong; it is to hedge against one's own servitude and to that of one's other neighbours; in a word it is to work for liberty, tranquillity and the public good, as the aggrandisement of one nation beyond certain limits changes the general system...

Indeed such a development would 'overturn the equilibrium and would result in the inevitable ruin of all the other members of the same body. All that changes ... this general system of Europe is too dangerous and brings along infinite evils.'[36]

Ironically, it was to counterbalance Fénelon's employer, Louis XIV, that William III urged Charles XII of Sweden 'to adopt such policies as may rescue and preserve the liberty of all of Europe from the enormous power of the French, aimed at establishing supreme dominion.'[37]

William himself of course owed his British crowns to the Glorious Revolution: he and his wife, Stuart princess Mary, had invaded Britain to depose Mary's father, King James VII of Scotland and II of England, when the latter formally became a Catholic and produced a Catholic son who superseded his older sister as heir to the throne. The Glorious Revolution was undertaken, as one of William's supporters put it, 'for the service of God, the defence of the laws of England and the liberty of that state *and the interest of the whole of Europe*' (my emphasis).[38]

From then until well into the nineteenth century, England and then the United Kingdom would indeed follow a strategy of intervention in European wars against expansionist rulers in the name of safeguarding a balance of powers advantageous to the British Isles. It was of course France, not any Habsburg emperor, who was to be counter-balanced by the 1689 League of Augsburg that brought together William's multiple realms and the Holy Roman Empire. Where the Tudor monarchs had seen Habsburg Spain as main antagonist, after the restoration of religious tolerance in the Holy Roman Empire with the Westphalian Treaties of 1648, its Austrian Habsburg rulers now became allies of the Stuarts to defend Europe's 'liberties' against Louis XIV's France.[39]

Louis' faithful minster Colbert wrote of the subsequent War of Spanish Succession (1701–1714) that 'there was not the least room to expect that the neighbouring princes, who were so greatly alarmed at the power of France would tamely suffer [Louis XIV] to extend his authority so as to have the supreme direction, in the name of his grandson, of the dominions subject to the crown of Spain in the old and new world.'[40] The commander of the United Kingdom's armies in this war, the Duke of Marlborough, boasted that his victories had 'rescued the [Holy Roman] Empire from desolation, asserted and confirmed the liberties of Europe', and Britain was celebrated at beacon of liberty that fought to 'set all Europe free'.[41]

Yet Louis persisted with his land-grabbing wars, and by the time he died in 1715, spelling the end of the *Grand Siècle* of French domination of Europe, he had prized away territories to France's north that had remained in Habsburg possession after the independence of the Netherlands was confirmed in 1648, and had successfully appropriated Spain for the House of Bourbon. French government officials justified this grand strategy by claiming that they had only aimed to check Habsburg ambitions to universal monarchy. As Louis XV's foreign ministry put it in instructions to its newly appointed ambassador to Vienna in 1757:

> The political objective of the [French] crown has always been to play in Europe the superior role appropriate to its age [*ancienneté*],[42] its dignity and its grandeur; to reduce [*abaisser*] any power that attempts to elevate itself above that of [the French crown], be it by usurping its possessions, be it by claiming an unjustified pre-eminence, be it by stealing its influence and credit in general affairs.[43]

A more sober appreciation was that of Irénée Castel, the Abbé de Saint-Pierre, writing in 1712, as the peace was being negotiated after the Spanish War of Succession:

1) The present constitution of Europe could only produce almost continual wars, as it could never provide sufficient security for the [full] application of the treaties.
2) The equilibrium of powers between the House of France and the House of Austria cannot produce sufficient security against foreign wars or against civil wars and consequently could not furnish sufficient security for the protection [*conservation*] of the state, nor for the protection of commerce.[44]

But already in 1725, France and Britain would re-align in a rekindled fear of a Habsburg bid for universal monarchy.[45] A decade later, Russia, in one of her wars against the Ottoman Empire, once again made it her war aim to seize Constantinople. Her military leaders dreamt of seeing Tsarina Anna crowned in the Church of Saint Sophia, resurrecting the East Roman Empire, consummating a claim that had existed since the days of Ivan III.[46] Thus the perpetuum mobile of balances and counter-balances, the swings and roundabouts would not come to an end until well into the twentieth century.

Even intermittent dynastic marriages between the Bourbons and Habsburg designed to create peace (especially that of Louis XIV to the Spanish Habsburg princess Maria Theresa, and that of Louis XVI to Empress Maria Theresa's youngest daughter, Marie Antoinette, were cause for further wars rather than peace. Louis XIV used his wife's inheritance claims as reason for two wars of succession which won the Bourbon Dynasty more lands to the North and then the Spanish succession. Then as Louis XVI and Marie Antoinette were embattled by the French Revolutionaries, their situation if anything was exacerbated by the intervention of the Habsburg Emperor Leopold II, brother of Marie Antoinette: it contributed directly to her execution following that of her husband.

Relations between France's and England's rulers had been equally competitive until 1558 when English Queen Mary I had lost Calais (until the capture of Gibraltar in 1704 the last English possession on the Continent). Periodic dynastic marriages between the ruling dynasties of France and England, again intended to bring peace and friendship, were no more rewarding in this regard than those between the Bourbon and Habsburg dynasties. It was from those marriages that the Plantagenet and Lancastrian kings had derived their claims to the French throne (which had precipitated the Hundred Years' War). And it was the attempts of Charles I of England and Scotland to rule without parliament, emulating the absolutism of his father-in-law and brother-in-law, kings Henri IV and Louis XIII of France, that ultimately cost him his head in 1649.

Dynastic rivalries included non-martial aspects, such as the European princes' jealousy of Louis XIV's palace of Versailles.

Many copied it—the Habsburgs with Schönbrunn outside Vienna, the Hohenzollerns with the New Palace in Potsdam, the Dukes of Bavaria with Nymphenburg near Munich, Peter the Great with Peterhof outside his new capital city of St Petersburg. While these colossal building projects were of course realised at the expense of their subjects, the cost of the wars, in blood and treasure, was naturally much greater.

These dynastic rivalries and the lack of religious or other ethnical restraints in the balance-of-power politics and wars of the Early Modern period already led contemporaries to realise that this was not a healthy state of affairs in inter-polity relations. Even Charles Davenant, who advocated the 'balance-of-power' as best approach to European (and de facto, world) politics, admitted that implied 'long, bloody and expensive' wars.[47] This realisation led to the quest to replace this anarchic pattern of great-power competition with a new rule-based system that would give peace a chance. It is worth underscoring that several projects for putting these relations on a different and more peaceful footing came from France.

But dynastic competition continued. Nor were the Valois, Bourbons, Habsburgs and the successive English dynasties alone in their competitive attitude towards their fellow-monarchs. The 'interest of the state' was now the excuse that could be made for all actions. As Frederick II of Prussia put it in 1762, 'War is good if it is made to support the interests (*considerations*) of a state, to maintain its safety or to contain the projects of an[other] ambitious prince consisting of conquests harmful to your interests.' And, 'The first preoccupation of a prince must be to protect what he has (*de se soutenir*), the second his aggrandisement.'[48] Any state's interest was thus the interest of its ruling dynasty, and that was invariably territorial expansion, second only as priority to self-defence. Given the balance-of-power mechanism that by now was well established, any such expansionism automatically triggered push-back on the part of the other powers of this European system. The result of this was, of course, more wars.

6

THE QUEST FOR A PEACE SYSTEM
OR A EUROPEAN UNION, 1305–1796

Tired of the state of Europe with its endless number of wars that were fought mainly for selfish dynastic interests, a number of observers proposed schemes which amounted to syntheses of the two great dialectically opposed themes of inter-polity relations we have encountered. The first of these themes was the Empire, the components of which were firmly tied together in one area of peace with all the consultative and deliberative mechanisms that kept them, and the emperor, in check. It was, as we have seen, a super-State with an internal conflict-solution mechanism that was unable to unleash wars, and could only act defensively. The second theme, its antithesis, was that of the fiercely independent, sovereign states with their competing dynasties and their balance-of-power politics which time and again led to wars to increase the possessions of individual players. The syntheses proposed would try to bring together elements of both.

Pierre Dubois and King George Podiebrad

The earliest schemes designed to create long-term peace, following the logic of the *Pax Dei* movement, linked it to external defence or campaigns. The first of these was written by Pierre Dubois, a counsellor of French King Philip IV (the Handsome) who shared the French monarch's aversion to the domination in Europe by the pope and by the emperor. Dubois was at once against the domination by any one power, and against unrestrained competition among many sovereign powers in Europe, who could not but live in discord, given their clashing interests. In 1305–1307, Dubois addressed a treatise to the French king entitled *On the Recovery of the Holy Land*. He boldly claimed that 'nobody serious can really imagine today, at the end of time (*in hoc fine seculorum*), that the entire world can still be governed by only one temporal monarch whom all would obey as their temporal lord.' After all, the kings were '*superiorem in terris non recognoscentes*', they did not accept that there was anybody superior to them on earth.[1]

But leaving Europe subject to the politics and rivalries of so many equals who did not recognise any higher secular authority turned her into a theatre of war, sedition and infinite disagreement.[2] Dubois understood what for centuries, thinkers and practitioners would try to ignore: namely, that multiple entities existing alongside each other without any enforceable rules create an anarchic society with endless wars. How to resolve this dilemma?

The monarchs themselves, Dubois argued, had to choose voluntarily to form an association. To preserve peace, Christendom as a whole should 'form one single republic that was so close-knit that nobody could ever prize it apart.' How to proceed? The pope—whom he recognised as moral and spiritual head of Christendom—should convene a *concilium generale*—a General Council, an established form of ecclesiastical decision-making, but this time including 'all princes and higher Catholic dignitaries', especially 'the kings and other [heads of state] that do not recognise a superior on earth'. This Council would have the power to decide on war and peace. If a member of this Republic were victim of an injustice, it would seek justice by referring to the Council. If the dispute could not be settled in this way, war was still a possible option, but the Council could designate arbiters in an attempt to resolve the dispute. If one party remained dissatisfied, it could refer the matter to the pope. If a vassal went to war against his lord, the Council would punish him through confiscation of his goods.[3] We have no evidence that King Philip ever followed Dubois' suggestions to approach the King of England with this project to build an alliance of supporters for it; for all we know, the project was shelvded.

The second proposal had a more concrete impact on the politics of its times. It was put forward in 1462–1464 by George Podiebrad, King of Bohemia, one of the electors of the Holy Roman Empire. It was ostensibly a belated reaction to the fall of Constantinople less than a decade earlier and a general complaint about the sorry effects of wars on Europe, but probably mainly due to a falling out with Emperor Frederick III (the first Habsburg to be crowned emperor). In a draft charter, King George of Bohemia proposed the creation of a Perpetual Union (*unionem perpetuis temporibus duratam*) of Christian princes, which he called variously *pax* (peace), *unio et fraternitas* (union and brotherhood) and *unio, amicitial et fraternitas* (union, friendship and brotherhood), or *congregation* (congregation), or *foedus* (federation, alliance).[4]

The draft charter began with a commitment of mutual non-aggression, followed by a mutual defence commitment and a renunciation of any conspiracies against each other. Third came a promise to punish any subjects who might deviate from this commitment by undertaking a private raid or war. Fourthly, if a third party attacked a member of the Union without having suffered previous injury or provocation, the others should try to mediate, and failing success, should support the attacked party's self-defence financially. A court of justice should be set up to mediate in any disputes between members.

King George identified as the most pressing need the mounting of a defensive operation against the Turks who since their capture of Constantinople had moved even further into Christian European territory. The signatories of this charter should 'pledge and swear ... that we shall defend and protect the Christian religion and all the oppressed faithful ... until [the Turk] is driven out of Christian territory or until it is jointly resolved to conclude peace, which may only be done if the security of neighbouring Christians is deemed ensured.'

They should set up an Assembly which would, by majority decision:

> determine when it is suitable to attack the enemy or what land and naval forces should be used to conduct the war or under which generals this should be done, what machines and instruments of war should be used, and at what place all the land forces should assemble that will march against the Turks. Also, in what manner it would be possible to obtain at decent prices victuals and billets in towns villages and other suitable places. Also, in what manner a common coin should be provided so that the troops would not find themselves in difficulties on the march...

The Assembly should be set up during Lent in 1464 in Bâle where it should meet for five consecutive years, followed by a city in France and then a city in Italy, for five years each.

> The Assembly shall have its own and special Council whose president shall be N[5] as its father and head and we, the other Christian kings and princes, shall be its members. The said college [i.e. the Council] shall also have ... jurisdiction with ... authority over all of us and our subjects as well as those who voluntarily submit thereto ... Finally, it shall have its own coat-of-arms, seal and common treasury as well as public archives, a syndicate, a fisc, clerks and all the other rights allowed and appertaining to a proper corporation.

The Assembly would have a secretariat, be financed collectively, and vote by majority. There would only be very few votes in total: the King of France and his nobles would jointly have one vote, similarly the Italian polities collectively, ditto the *reges et principes Germanie*, the kings and princes of Germany; insultingly, there was no mention here of the emperor. Should the Iberian kingdoms join, they too should have one vote for them jointly. The Charter was to be binding to the heirs and successors of the original signatories, but the Assembly could add new provisions provided they were in the same spirit of defending Christendom and peace. New members could be admitted.[6.]

The scheme was drawn up with the help of Antonio Marini of Grenoble, by background an engineer. King Casimir IV Jagellon of Poland and King Matthias Corvinus of Hungary—the latter the son-in-law of King George—were enthusiastic about this scheme, as was Venice. In 1464 Marini, representing Poland and Hungary, and Albrecht Kostka of Postupice, representing King George of Bohemia, presented the draft covenant at the Court of French King Louis XI in Bourges. Pope Pius II opposed the project. He had already been at loggerheads with King George over the revocation of the act of tolerance of the Hussites; now he declared King George, a supporter of the Hussite teachings, and thus a heretic. This put an end to the immediate political life of the project—the King of France avoided answering Marini and Kostka—but not the idea of such a federation.[7]

Crucé, Sully, and Penn

A multilateral alliance for peace that for the first time was not explained in terms of solidarity against the Turks was suggested was by Erasmus of Rotterdam, in the early sixteenth century, although his *Querela Pacis*, a treatise purporting to be a complaint made by the personification of Peace, contained no concrete suggestions as to how eternal peace was to be arrived at. On 2 October 1518 Charles I of Spain, the future emperor Charles

V, and his rivals for the imperial crown Henry VIII of England and Francis I of France, did indeed conclude an indefinite peace treaty or non-aggression pact which did not end any specific war. Charles's grandfather, Emperor Maximilian I, and the pope both acceded to the treaty. The treaty had no political consequences at the time given the rapidly growing rivalry of the three principal signatories, but especially between Francis and Charles.[8]

Nevertheless, the idea lingered, and a century later, the chief minister of the late King Henri IV of France, the Duke of Sully (1560–1641), devised a 'Grand Design' or peace proposal (published posthumously) that he attributed to the late king, presumably for greater effect, claiming also that it had been the subject of negotiations with other monarchs and that it had won the support of Queen Elizabeth of England, for example (yet no trace of it could be found in the English State Papers).[9] Like King George Podiebrad before him, Sully proposed the creation of a confederation in which the Holy Roman Empire would merely be one among several equal states, 'a political system through which one could divide up and lead all of Europe like a family.' Always attributing this scheme to King Henri IV, Sully explained that the king's only aim with this had been:

> to spare himself as much as to [his fellow-monarchs], the immense sums which so many millions of soldiers cost them, so many fortified places and so many other military expenses; to deliver them forever from the fear of bloody catastrophes which is so common in Europe; to procure for them enduring rest; and finally to unite them all through an undissolvable bond, so that all these princes could have lived henceforth as brothers...

Once this was achieved, the Christian princes would no longer have to tolerate that a 'foreigner' (that is, the Sultan) shared Europe with them. Yet they could then attempt to spread this (civilised) form of inter-state relations beyond Europe, to Asia and especially North Africa, creating new states there that might be integrated into *la république chrétienne* (that is, this Christian Commonwealth), to be shared out among some of the lesser princes of Europe.[10] Sully's underlying theory of international relations which implicitly saw Christian Europe as the natural leader of the world was that such newly created states in Asia and Europe should be colonies of smaller European states, the weight of which would thus be increased in relation to the larger states of Europe. As a counsellor to the French king, he accepted the principle that the states of the Christian Commonwealth of Europe should be equal, which of course served France by promoting it to the level of the Holy Roman Empire, while conceding that stability would be increased by making some of the other states more powerful (and thus also upgrading their influence) through the acquisition of these colonies. If France wanted equality with the Empire, thus the implicit logic, it had to tolerate the equality of others with France.

It is uncertain when precisely Sully developed this scheme. He may have known a similar proposal that was put forward by French mathematician Emeric de Crucé (c.1590–1648), as it was published with Royal privilege.[11] In 1623, when the great war that engulfed Central Europe had been underway for only five of its thirty years, Crucé proposed a permanent assembly of ambassadors of the princes of Europe to settle any disputes among them. He projected the model of the Swiss Confederation upon Europe on a larger scale. Crucé was even more outspoken in addressing the question of how one could make the component parts of this European confederation one of equals: by cutting down all the states of the world to more or less the same surface—we see here the emergence of the notion that a state should ideally have a compact, contiguous territory, forerunner of the idea of a 'territorial state'. Of all the theorists considered here, only Crucé was open to the inclusion of the Ottoman, Persian, Chinese and Ethiopian empires, and even the 'Tartars' in his peaceful confederation of states, as differences of religion must not prevent perpetual peace. In this association, again, the Holy Roman Empire would merely be one state among equals.[12]

Another series of wars involving his own country, England, moved the Quaker William Penn in 1690 to develop a similar scheme. Although he was the founder of the American state of Pennsylvania, his world view was still a strictly European one and he clearly did not foresee the development of America into an independent entity. Directly inspired by Sully's Grand Design (which he attributed to Henry IV) and by the inner workings of the Dutch Republic (the Estates-General), Penn thus proposed to set up a European 'Sovereign or Imperial Diet, Parliament', an assembly invested with sovereign powers to take decisions to which the individual state-member had to bow, indeed to form 'Estates' or a 'State of Europe' which elsewhere he called 'European League or Confederacy'. He proposed that:

> the empire of Germany to send twelve [emissaries]; France ten; Spain ten; Italy which comes to France, eight; England six; Portugal three; [Sweden] four; Denmark three; Poland four; Venice three; the Seven [Dutch] Provinces four; the Thirteen [Swiss] Cantons, and little neighbouring sovereignties two; dukedoms of Holstein and Courland one: and if the Turks and Muscovites are taken in, as seems but fit and just, they will make ten apiece more. The whole makes ninety.

Not least to ensure against corruption (which usually only affects a small swing vote), Penn in a striking anticipation of Qualified Majority Voting in the EU's Council of Ministers pre-scribed that 'nothing in this imperial parliament should pass, but by three-quarters of the whole, at least seven above the balance'. He went into some detail concerning the layout of the assembly hall in which delegates were to meet, and opined that the language of deliberations should be Latin or French, a nod to the diplomatic practice of his times (French would remain the main language of diplomacy until the First World War).

A PEACE SYSTEM OR EUROPEAN UNION?

Penn ran through many objections, such as that the Holy Roman Emperor would not agree to cede his powers to such an assembly, to which he replied that the other states must jointly persuade him to do so, given that jointly, they were stronger than him. He thought that the member states would disband their armies:

> after such an empire is on foot.... However, the question may be asked, by order of the sovereign states, why [another state] either raises or keeps up a formidable body of troops, and be obliged forthwith to reform or reduce them; lest anyone, by keeping up a great body of troops, should surprise a neighbour. But a small force in every other sovereignty, as it is capable or accustomed to maintain, will certainly prevent that danger and vanquish any such fear.

He answered a further objection:

> that sovereign princes and states will hereby become not sovereign: a thing they will never endure. But this also... is a mistake, for they remain as sovereign at home as ever they were. Neither their power over their people, nor the usual revenue they pay them, is diminished: it may be the war establishment may be reduced, which will indeed of course follow, or be better employed to the advantage of the public. So that, the sovereignties are as they were, for none of them have now any sovereignty over one another: and if this be called a lessening of their power, it must be only because the great fish can no longer eat up the little ones, and that each sovereignty is equally defended from injuries, and disabled from committing them...

Penn argued that the realisation of his project would save the states much money, ease travel and commerce, 'a happiness never understood since the Roman Empire has been broken into so many sovereignties'. It would make it much easier for the Christian princes to join forces against the Turks—seven years earlier, the Turks had only just about been turned away from Vienna a second time. 'Wars', wrote Penn, 'are the duels of princes', and what he was proposing was to put in the place of the selfish pursuits of the interests of the princes a European government. For government 'prevents men being judges and executioners for themselves, over-rules private passions as to injuries or revenge, and subjects the great as well as the small to the rule of justice, that power might not vanquish or oppress right, nor one neighbour act in independency and sovereignty upon another'. Just as a state needed a government, he argued, building on Hobbes's defence of the state as bastion to fend off anarchy, Europe needed a government to contain the selfishness of her princes. To summarise, Penn argued that scheme offered 'the benefit[s] of an universal monarchy, without the inconveniences that attend it', such as the central taxation by the Holy Roman Empire.[13]

Nijmegen 1678 to Utrecht 1713: Balance of Power and Common Good over Dynastic Interest

The background to Penn's writing, as we have seen, was another series of wars, mostly involving France. Yet each peace treaty concluded at their end was designed by the diplomats to be a lasting one. Since the 1648 Treaties of Westphalia which had brought peace only to the Holy Roman Empire, peace treaties generally purported to be of infinite duration.[14] There had been occasional treaties of perpetual peace aiming at universality, such as that concluded in London in 1518, but usually peace treaties only concerned parties that had previously been at war with one another; the treaties generally did not purport to apply to Christendom as a whole.[15] The peace congresses following the Westphalian Treaties, as far as France was the main signatory, began by confirming the Westphalian settlement of the Holy Roman Empire, then to constitute a wider peace, recognising that much of Europe had been churned up by war. In the Peace of Nijmegen of 1678 we thus find a new aim: the peace that had been brought to the Empire in 1648 should now be spread more widely in Europe. However, the treaties were drafted by French diplomats and thus favoured France, to the point where philosophers and artists at the court of Louis XIV could praise France for 'havings given' peace to Europe.[16] This was the background to William Penn's design for a reform of inter-state relations.

At least one indirect effect of Penn's and the earlier works of Sully and Crucé may have been that, from the 1690s, a new justification of war and peace would be introduced: 'the security and tranquillity of Europe'. By the time of the Utrecht negotiations, a stable balance of powers or even an equilibrium, the repose of Europe, and the tranquillity of Europe were established as aims, while references to traditional rights occurred much less frequently. Among the eleven bilateral treaties signed at Utrecht in 1713, the Treaty between France and Portugal included the phrase that it sought to 'contribute to the repose of Europe', as did the Treaty of Friendship between France and the Estates-General, which had at its aim 'the re-establishment of the tranquillity of Europe.'[17] The use of the term 'Europe' was not unprecedented, but it now increasingly replaced the term 'Christianitas/Christendom' which one would have seen in previous times.[18]

At least the diplomats now agreed formally that the chief aim of peace treaties was no longer to confirm traditional rights of individual parties, but the promotion of the common interest of Europe over that of individual dynasties. They put it differently: beyond achieving Europe's repose, her tranquillity, a recurrent terminology throughout the Utrecht negotiations, they spoke of the 'public interest', *le bien de l'Europe* (the welfare of Europe), *le salut de l'Europe* (the salvation or wellbeing of Europe), *la tranquillité générale*. The 'equilibrium of Europe' was also invoked, as a legitimate overall aim. In the Treaty between Sicily and Savoy (one of the Utrecht treaties) it actually said: it is 'the duty of every Christian prince to desire the repose and tranquillity of the world.' An argument put forward in the peace negotiations by Britain (and later echoed by France) was that 'something must be done for the general sake of peace, and the interest of one individual [monarch] must yield to the general interest of Europe.' And with this in mind, old rivalries could still aim to ensure that no one power would 'swallow up everything'—but this now applied to the Habsburgs and the Bourbons alike. At Utrecht, Louis XIV was persuaded to 'consent willingly and in good faith that all just and reasonable measures be taken to prevent the crowns of France and Spain from ever being united in the person of a single prince; His Majesty being convinced that such an excessive power would be contrary to the good and repose of Europe.'[19]

One characteristic of the Utrecht Peace Treaties has been underscored by historians: the formal proclamation of the principle of the balance-of-power as a fundamental condition for peace.[20] What was previously merely selfish competition among Europe's monarchs was thus elevated to a principle creating order and stability, comparable to the equilibrium of the planets in the heavens above. Utrecht was also a milestone in the history of European state systems, whereby the interest of Europe as a whole was now elevated above the pursuit of revenge cloaked as 'justice' and the affirmation of traditional rights by each individual signatory.[21] Henceforth there would be appeals even in the British Parliament to keep in mind the higher interest of Europe rather than to focus exclusively on self-interest.[22] Among the Utrecht treaties, it was the British-Spanish treaty which articulated the aim of a general perpetual peace in the Christian world (*Christiani orbis*) which would be vouchsafed by a 'just equilibrium of powers'.[23] This was not by accident, as it was probably Charles Davenant, who first used the term 'balance of power'.[24]

A PEACE SYSTEM OR EUROPEAN UNION?

If the balance of powers meant peace, to state that this balance was upset or endangered henceforth was a call to arms, particularly but not only in Britain. In 1734 one British politician expressed his unhappiness that the British were, 'for the sake of preserving the balance of power', inclined 'at our own charges, to defend every power in Europe, and to prevent their being invaded or conquered by any of their neighbours', while another, a decade later, criticised the 'ridiculous custom' of engaging 'in the quarrels of almost every state in Europe that has, by its impudence or ambition, brought itself into any distress', and that 'under the pretence of preserving a balance of power in Europe.'[25]

It is comprehensible in this context, as ships brought in ever more riches from around the world to the Western shores of Europe and religious quarrels had almost disappeared from Europe, that Britons began to fancy the idea of a splendid isolation of Britain from matters continental. Around 1738, Henry St John, First Viscount Bolingbroke and a Tory politician, refuted John Donne's line by pointing out that Great Britain was an island after all:

> The situation of Great Britain, the character of her people, and the nature of her government, fit her for trade and commerce ... The sea is our barrier, ships are our fortresses, and the mariners, that trade and commerce alone can furnish, are the garrisons to defend them.

Great Britain, he argued, should avoid any entanglement in continental wars and should instead give her 'continual attention to improve her natural, that is her maritime strength.' The myth of the British separateness from Europe was born, and with it the illusion that some Britons could refrain from European wars by either turning her back on them, or by financing others to fight for her interests. Even Whigs saw some attraction in this if they realised that the 'balance of power' had become a rallying cry that once evoked almost automatically triggered British involvement in continental wars, with all the taxes and cost in lives of British soldiers that entailed.[26]

In response, however, some British politicians including John Carteret, second Earl Granville, and John Perceval still argued in the face of growing isolationism that 'our own independence' is closely linked to the 'liberties of the continent', and that it was not enough for Britain 'to attend our commerce and our pleasures'. Perceval explicitly dismissed the new isolationist:

> doctrine ... that it is of no importance to this nation what may happen on the continent; that this country is an island intrenched within its own natural boundaries, that it may stand secure and unconcerned in all the storms of the rest of the world.[27]

The other widely celebrated characteristic of the eighteenth-century European System is that at and since Utrecht, all states parties to the negotiations were for the first time in modern history formally treated as equals, regardless of their size.[28] Utrecht is supposed to have ushered in the era of equality of states in which we supposedly find ourselves even today. Even then this was an illusion, a matter of courtesy, perhaps, but one not seriously reflecting reality—no more, at any rate, than the claim of the UN Charter that all members are equal, when only five are permanent members of the Security Council, and have veto rights (see below).

The Abbé de Saint-Pierre and Jeremy Bentham

Writing during the Utrecht peace negotiations, the Abbé de Saint-Pierre (1658–1743) devised a plan about how to create perpetual peace, which was already being discussed among those present at the negotiations. As an eye-witness reported, already in 1712 at Utrecht, everybody was talking about the Abbé's project, and two factions emerged, the 'irénistes' and the 'anti-irénistes',[29] labels which played on Saint-Pierre's Christian name,

Irénée, which by happy coincidence meant 'the peaceful one'. As a diplomat, the clergyman had taken part in the negotiations, and written the first version of his *Project to render Peace perpetual in Europe*. In knowledge of Sully's Grand Design, Saint-Pierre proposed a Treaty to establish a perpetual European Union (sic!) or Society of Europe. It should have a Permanent Congress or Senate, at which all questions at issue between the contracting parties were to be settled and terminated by way of arbitration or judicial pronouncement. The Permanent Congress of plenipotentiary state representatives should be able to decide, initially by a simple majority, later with a three-quarter majority, on any issues which the states members wanted to settle through the European Union. To this Congress, Europe's 18 main 'sovereigns' should send plenipotentiary representatives—that is, ambassadors with the full right to make decision on the part of their states. The 'sovereigns' he listed (in this order) as: 1. France, 2. Spain, 3. England, 4. Holland, 5. Portugal, 6. Switzerland and its associates, 7. Florence and its associates, 8. Genoa and its associates, 9. The Vatican State with its still extensive territories, 10. Venice with its possessions throughout the Eastern Mediterranean, 11. Savoy, 12. Lorraine, 13. Denmark, 14. Courland with Danzig, 15. The Emperor and the Empire (!), 16. Poland, 17. Sweden, 18. Muscovy. Arguing that no member was to be sovereign of more than one state, Saint-Pierre proposed that the electors of the Holy Roman Empire were to be added to the signatories-members of the Treaty, thereby de facto dismembering the Empire and reducing it to its components (with the emperor reduced to the Austrian hereditary lands). By counting the archbishops as one entity, he thus produced a list of 24 members, each with one voice.[30]

The member states should continue to have the legislation and the internal political system they had before, each with their own way of choosing their government, by heredity or election. They would promise not to meddle in each other's internal affairs and would support each other against anybody taking advantage of the rule of a child monarch or other times of internal instability. Meanwhile the present frontiers of each state should be frozen. The European Union could then conclude a peace-treaty with the 'Mohameddan sovereigns'.

Saint-Pierre explicitly used the model of the internal institutional structure of the Holy Roman Empire as a model for this 'European Union'.[31] It should have a rotating presidency, and its member states should make payments to it to cover common expenses. Before joining, they should renounce any attempt to revive past disputes, while future disputes should be settled by arbitration of the Congress and not by force. A member who would break its treaty obligations, that is, if it refused to abide by the decisions of the European Union, if it prepared for war, if it concluded a treaty against another member of Union or against the Union's overall purpose, would be put under the ban of the Union and proscribed as a public enemy. The Confederates could oppose it, by joint use of force if necessary, until it laid down its arms and complied with the Union's demands as formulated by its Permanent Congress, made amends, paid all the accrued costs, and atoned for having gone to war against a fellow-member of the Union.[32]

Here then was the first full-blown proposal for the creation of a European Union, simultaneously projecting the structure of the Holy Roman Empire (minus the emperor) onto the whole of Europe while breaking down the Empire itself into its component polities. As we have seen, Saint-Pierre envisaged that this new super-state would be coterminous with Europe, able to conclude treaties with powers outside Europe to establish peace and defend its territory.

During his lifetime and after, Saint-Pierre's proposals were much discussed but usually dismissed as unrealistic, including by

Jean-Jacques Rousseau despite his admiration for them. Rousseau thought that '[t]he whole life of kings, or of those on whom they shuffle off their duties, is devoted solely to two objects: to extend their rule beyond their frontiers and to make it more absolute within them. Any other purpose they may have is either subservient to one of these aims, or merely a pretext for attaining them.' Consequently, he saw no way that they could be persuaded to form a European Union and to desist from following their selfish dynastic aims.[33] Saint-Pierre's ideas would only be resurrected in the twentieth century, and it is with a nod in his direction that the European Communities fused into one single organisation in 1993 was named the European Union.

Then, in the very year of the outbreak of the French Revolution, it was an English philosopher, Jeremy Bentham, who advanced another proposal that would also have an important influence on the world. Bentham put forward the following propositions: that it was not in Britain's or France's interest to have foreign dependencies (colonies), or alliances (offensive or defensive) or trade treaties excluding third nations with any other power, or to possess a navy other than 'to defend its commerce against pirates'. Bentham postulated:

> That the increase of growing wealth in every nation in a given period is necessarily limited by the quantity of capital it possesses at that period.

> That Great Britain, with or without Ireland, and without any other dependencies can have no reasonable ground to apprehend injury from any one nation upon earth.[34]

As far as France was concerned, on her own he thought she had 'at present nothing to fear from any other nation than Great Britain: nor, if standing clear from her foreign dependencies, should she have anything to fear from Great Britain.' If now Britain and France could be made to agree on these points, 'the principal difficulties would be removed by the establishment of a plan of general and permanent pacification for all Europe.' Once this had been achieved, he recommended the conclusion of 'general and perpetual' arms control treaties to number the soldiers any state were allowed to have, the constitution of 'a common court of judicature for the decision of differences between the several nations, although such court were not to be armed with any coercive powers.' And finally he demanded 'That secrecy in the operations of the foreign department [ministry] ought not to be endured in England; being altogether useless and equally repugnant to the interests of liberty and to those of peace.' This last clause would later become echoed in US President Woodrow Wilson's call in 1918 for 'open treaties, openly arrived at'.[35]

Like all the previous authors cited, Bentham wanted to give this 'European Fraternity' a:

> Congress or Diet ... by each power sending two deputies to the place of meeting; one of these to be the principal, the other to act as an occasional substitute. The proceedings of such Congress or Diet should be all public. Its power would consist,
>
> 1. In reporting its opinion;
> 2. In causing that opinion to be circulated in the dominions of each state.
> 3. After a certain time, in putting a refractory state under the ban of Europe.[36]

> There might, perhaps, be no harm in regulating, as a last resource, the [military] contingent to be furnished by the several states for enforcing the decrees of the court. But the necessity for the employment of this resource would, in all human probability, be superseded for ever by having recourse to the much more simple and less burthensome expedient, of introducing ... a clause guaranteeing the liberty of the press in each state...[37]

So crucially, while Sully, Crucé and Saint-Pierre thought some coercive power was needed by these 'security communities' (to employ an expression coined in the twentieth century by Karl Deutsch) to keep their own members in line and to organise them for collective self-defence, Bentham optimistically thought such a 'European Fraternity' could manage without an enforcement mechanism, and that public opinion in the states collectively would be a sufficient constraint upon governments to put the collective well-being over any selfish agendas.

Guibert, the French Revolution, and Kant

By the time Bentham completed this plan, shortly after America's declaration of independence, Europe had reached boiling point, and the French Revolution erupted, with sympathisers throughout Europe. Here we must take a step back and consider the views of one French thinker of the Enlightenment, who unlike Sully, Crucé, Saint-Pierre and to a large extent also Bentham saw a link between the internal constitution of a state and its foreign affairs. This was Count Guibert (1743–1790). He was a French nobleman and officer who as a young cadet had witnessed France's humiliating defeat, in the Seven Years' War, at the Battle of Rossbach against a new power that had made her appearance on the European stage: Prussia. Until that war, for a century or more, Louis XIV's France had dominated Europe through warfare. Rossbach came as a shock, and thenceforth France had a new German-speaking adversary in Prussia. For in the Seven Years' War, the Holy Roman Empire had for once been aligned with France against Britain and Prussia.

Just after the war, young Guibert wrote a manuscript that circulated for twenty years before being published anonymously in London so as to escape censorship. In it, he pondered the poor performance of France's once so great military in the Seven Years' War, especially against Frederick II of Prussia's forces. In an emotionally-laden preface, he drew a link between a system of government that would lead a state in the interest of its people (that is, a republic, in the terminology of the times), rather than in the interest of its dynasty (that is, a monarchy), and a generally pacific posture in foreign relations—unless it were attacked. He began his explanations by dividing politics 'into two parts, domestic and foreign policies.' Only a state in which domestic policies were designed entirely to build up the prosperity and the moral fiber of the population as a whole could a strong army be formed from its citizens, he argued, an army able to defend the country and underpin an influential foreign policy. Indeed, he thought that the citizen-soldiers of such a state would be invincible. It would be respected externally, and yet open and free in its relations with other states with which it would trade freely and which it would not fear.

Like Bentham forty years after him, young Guibert saw the secrecy of inter-state negotiations and treaties as the source of great evil:

> It is the folly of all our governments to practise in their negotiations so much obliquity and little faith. It is that which foments disorder in a state, which reciprocally endeavours to corrupt the members of administration. It is that which makes the nations watchful of one another, vying amongst themselves, bargaining for and purchasing peace, mutually rising out of troubles and distress. It is that which creates base and dangerous rivals of every kind; that perpetual encroachment of the trade of one nation on the trade of another; those laws of prohibition, those privileges which exclude the foreigner; those treaties which favour one country to the disadvantage of the other; those chimerical calculations of the balance of exports and imports; vile and complicated methods which never did, even by those who employed them with the greaten skill at the end of an age, add the least to the increase of government. In a word, it is the folly of our governments that make us jealous of the prosperity of other nations, desirous either to weaken or corrupt them.[38]

At the same time, Guibert thought that a country governed for the benefit of the society as a whole was more likely to turn all its neighbours into admiring trading partners and even friends, and that prosperity through trade, economic and technological progress would benefit all sides, so that there was no need for competition and conflict. To this man of the Enlightenment, inter-state relations could be conducted with mutual benefit, as a win-win game, as long as states were governed in the interest of the whole polity, and not just of the ruling dynasty. If anybody, Guibert should thus be seen as the originator of what should be called the 'Republican Peace' Theory of International Relations (and what is instead called Democratic Peace Theory), namely the theory that states governed in the interest of their populations, not of a ruling dynasty, are unlikely to go to war with one another.[39]

Half a century later, Guibert's idea of the link between the domestic constitution of a state and its foreign policy was taken up by Immanuel Kant in Königsberg. He has become renowned for postulating that republics, in co-operation with one another, could arrive at a situation of perpetual peace: 'The civil constitution of every state is to be republican'.

But what did Kant mean by 'republic'? Believing that the French Revolution with its *terreur* was a monstrous aberration, Kant distinguished between a 'republican constitution' which he thought necessary to create a system of peace, and a 'democratic constitution' which he associated with the French Revolution and disliked strongly. 'The forms that a state', he thought, 'can be classified either (1) according to who has sovereign power in the state; or (2) according to how the sovereign power is used, by whoever has it, to administer the affairs of the state.' The first he called 'a classification of forms of sovereignty', of which he thought there were three:

autocracy, in which only one person, the monarch, has sovereign power; aristocracy, in which an associated group, the nobility, has sovereign power; democracy, in which all those who constitute society, the people, have sovereign power.[40]

The second he called:

a classification of forms of government, i.e. in terms of how states use their power (this being based on the constitution, which is the act of the general will through which the many persons become one nation).

He could only conceive of two forms of government: republican or despotic:

Republicanism is the political principle of the separation of the executive from the legislative power; despotism is the principle of the state's making the laws and administering them. In a despotic system, the public will is administered by the ruler (or rulers) as his (or their) own private will. Of the three forms of the state, democracy ... is necessarily despotism; because it establishes an executive power in which 'all' settle things for each individual, and may settle some things against an individual who does not agree with the policy in question. Decisions are made by an 'all' that does not include everyone. In this, the general will contradicts itself and [the concept of] freedom.

He added:

Every form of government that is not representative [of the general will] is really a shapeless monster, because a legislator (who chooses what laws there will be) cannot possibly also be an executive (who implements those choices) ... Autocracy and aristocracy are always defective ..., but it is at least possible for them to govern in a way that conforms to the spirit of a representative system ...[41]

By contrast, he thought:

the democratic mode of government makes [a representative system] impossible, because everyone wants to be in charge. So we can say: the smaller the number of those who govern..., the greater is their representation and the closer their constitution comes to the possibility of republicanism; so that there's room for hope that it will through gradual reform finally to rise to the level of outright republicanism. For these reasons it is harder for an aristocracy than for a monarchy to achieve the one perfectly legitimate constitution, and it is impossible for a democracy to do so except through violent revolution.[42]

This definition of a republic is somewhat surprising for the twenty-first century reader, but we still capture it in the statement that the President of the USA or of France sees himself as 'President of all the Americans' or 'President of all the French', and is enjoined to act in their common interest, and not just that of those who brought him to power. This passage is worth quoting at length, as it illustrates that Kant (much like Guibert before him) saw polities governed in the interest of the polity as a whole as peaceful, but had no interest in plebiscites or even regular elections. With an idea of what would be in the interest of the people similar to that of Jean-Jacques Rousseau's concept of 'the general will', Kant thought the former could be achieved without the latter.

Kant then in the form of six articles laid out his theory of how to achieve peaceful inter-state relations, several of which recall the postulates of Saint-Pierre and Bentham:

1. 'No peace treaty is valid if it was made with mental reservations that could lead to a future war.'
2. 'No independent states, large or small, are to come under the dominion of another state by inheritance, exchange, purchase, or gift.'
3. 'Standing armies are eventually to be abolished.'
4. 'National debts are not to be incurred as an aid to the conduct of foreign policy.'
5. 'No state is to interfere by force with the constitution or government of another state.'

6. 'No state during a war is to permit acts of hostility that would make mutual confidence impossible after the war is over—e.g. the use of assassins and poisoners, breach of capitulation, incitement to treason in the opposing state.'[43]

None of these projects had any immediate impact, other than to raise sniggers among sceptics—few people if any thought they could be put into practice. It was an easy game for self-acclaimed Realists to dismiss the Abbé Saint-Pierre and Kant in particular as dreamers. But perhaps it was just as unrealistic in the eighteenth century to expect there to be a huge revival of the idea of Empire, that unitary pole in the great dialectic of inter-polity relations. Yet that was what came next.

Napoleon's Succession to the (Holy Roman) Empire

For the great sibling rivalry between France and the Holy Roman Empire still lingered, notwithstanding the 'turnabout of alliances' (*renversement d'alliances*) which the Seven Years War and the Bourbon-Habsburg marriage of Louis XVI and Marie Antoinette had represented. The French Revolution had swept this realignment away and put in its place a new enmity between the revolutionary forces of France and the reactionary forces of Europe, led by Marie Antoinette's brother, the Emperor Leopold II, and his descendants. This enmity would persist until the Revolutionary armies, transformed into Napoleon's *Grande Armée*, defeated the forces of the Holy Roman and the Russian Empires at the Battle of Austerlitz in December 1805. Napoleon could dictate the terms of the peace, and his terms were finally to wipe out France's long-standing sibling competitor, the Holy Roman Empire: he decreed its dissolution after a millennium of its existence. He could not quite bring himself to destroy what was left, but instead sought a new *renversement d'alliances* to bolster his own legitimacy: allowing the Habsburgs to turn themselves into the ruling dynasty of a merely *Austrian* empire, he married another Habsburg princess, Marie Louise, to put the capstone on a new dynasty in which his brothers and sisters would become the new monarchs of the countries he had vanquished. He had already crowned himself, two years earlier, as—emperor. (He made quite sure that he did not fall into the same trap as the medieval emperors—he did not let the pope crown him but merely bless him, and crowned himself.)

Napoleon's coronation robes were modelled on those of Charlemagne whose succession he claimed, and the crown he commissioned for his coronation recalled that of the Charlemagne, even though he modestly restricted his title to that of *Empereur des Français*, Emperor of the French. There was no sign, however, that he intended to be emperor only of the French, or intended to stay within the boundaries of Charlemagne's Empire: his military exploits indicated that he was after universal monarchy, at least in Europe, as his army occupied the whole continent from Spain to Moscow. He had himself painted by Ingres wearing a gilt laurel wreath recalling that of the emperors of ancient Rome, whose eagle he of course adopted as his own symbol, but also holding the medieval French monarchs' hand of justice. When Marie Louise gave birth to a son, he was made King of Rome, recalling the title of the Holy Roman Emperor-elect before his coronation by the pope. With this descendant of the Habsburgs and the Bonapartes, the succession seemed guaranteed. Thus France was finally not just the cadet descendant of the Carolingian monarchy, but could take her place as Charlemagne's imperial heir, downgrading the older sibling. This was another possible synthesis, of course, to the millennial dialectic between France and the Holy Roman Empire.

It was not to last, as we know. The great defender of the French Revolution, of civil rights (with the Code Napoléon, exported in some form to most of the countries his army occupied) and religious emancipation, had turned into a narrow defender of his own dynastic interests. The forces of progress in the rest of Europe who had admired and supported him against their own reactionary dynasties began to have doubts about him, and support for him began to ebb away. Peace and order seemed more attractive than the Napoleonic law codes and incessant war. Coalition after coalition put itself in his way, but no peace treaty lasted: Napoleon saw peace as a time to regroup and prepare the next expansionist move. After his campaign in Russia in the winter of 1812–1813, when he lost virtually his entire *Grande Armée*, it was only a matter of time until his final defeat.

While Austria had been turned into a subservient ally, Prussia and Britain were more than ever determined to put an end to Napoleon's ceaseless expansion. While Napoleon never actually realised his plans to invade the British Isles, his 'Continental system' consisted of a gigantic blockade that aimed at destroying British commerce and denying England vital food supplies. For Britain in particular, Napoleon represented the great 'other' that personified everything Britain was against. As Brendan Simms has aptly summed it up, the contest between Britain and Napoleon was cast as a struggle between balance of power vs universal monarchy, parliamentary rule vs autocracy, Anglo-Saxon vs Latin, evolutionary change vs revolution, national particularism vs 'hegemonic European integration', empiricism vs rational deduction, sea vs land, Leviathan vs Behemoth.[44] Jointly with Prussia, Britain was thus determined to crush this Franco-Imperial synthesis. Napoleon's defeat opened the way to a further experiment in ordering the European state system.

Gentz's Critique of the Confederative Proposals

Napoleon had already seized power in France when Friedrich von Gentz, adviser to Prussian King Frederick William III, wrote a treatise deliberately echoing Kant's[45] (Kant had been Gentz's teacher at the University of Königsberg). Gentz argued that the inter-state system that had dominated Europe's history of the previous 150 years had been that of the balance-of-power, one in which states tried to counterbalance large and aggressive powers with systems of alliances, and had worked reasonably well, he thought, until the French Revolution. Gentz conceded that this system had in fact often led to war, fuelled by the vainglory and selfishness of individual monarchs. Yet he argued that if the balance-of-power system could spare mankind three or four wars in every century, it might be worth keeping, despite its manifest flaws.

Gentz did not belittle the project of escaping the 'anarchy' of inter-polity relations. Treaties alone were insufficient, as long as there was no-one to enforce their observation.[46] Just as keen to eliminate war as the authors discussed above, Gentz argued that previous projects for a perpetual peace so far have proposed one of the following four solutions, all of which had their own flaws:

First, the creation of a universal monarchy or super-state, in which Rome was, of course, the obvious point of reference. This option would work only if all states were merged into one, which Gentz thought was materially impossible, not least because of natural frontiers, but also because of the great divergence of civilisations and customs within Europe, which could not be ruled in a homogeneous fashion: what would be seen as appropriate by one nation would be seen as tyranny in another. Such a state would soon face conspiracies and insurgencies, and then it would break apart, giving way once again to the chaos which it had been designed to turn into order. Had not Rome taken seven centuries to create such a super-state? Her decline and fall in the West returned the world to the chaos it had known previously. Also, a united Europe would still only constitute a part of humanity. Given the great variation in human societies, a world government would be even less workable than a European super-state. Moreover, Gentz was aware that the idea of a universal monarchy had repeatedly in the past met with great resistance in Europe.[47]

The second model of inter-polity relations he saw was that of all states closing in on themselves, becoming autarkic, as Aristotle but also, much more recently, Johann Gottlieb Fichte, had suggested.[48] This would only work with a totally controlled domestic economy that has no need for imports, and that to Gentz would be a step back in human evolution and is contrary to human sociability.[49]

Thirdly, there was the model of a federation of states ('*ein freier Bund*'), as proposed by Sully, the Abbé de Saint-Pierre, Kant and others. Here he saw two options: a completely voluntary confederation in which for any dispute a judge or arbiter would be appointed by the mutual consent of the parties; or a federation locked into legal forms and with the formal creation of a common Court of Justice which would have the power to enforce its sentences. A confederation, however (as that proposed by Bentham) would be built on sand if it were built entirely on the free will of the individual states to belong to it. 'The preferences of men and of states are more fickle than nature, and their morality is a reed, swaying in the wind.' If there were a legal obligation and framework, it would require compulsion, which in turn would necessitate a supreme authority within that federation.

A free[ly concluded] treaty among states will only be respected as long as all who concluded it do not have simultaneously the ability and the will to break it, in other words, only as long as there would also be peace without this treaty, which is supposed to create peace. As soon as one state or a coalition of states have an interest in and enough strength to resist the common interest [of the majority], the whole system will collapse.[50]

A fourth model would be that of a formal legal constitution with a legislative, a judicative and executive, a supreme authority embodying the collective will. To work, it would have to include the entire world and that would be impossible. Gentz could not imagine that all states would be willing to submit to such a world authority. In short, Gentz feared that none of the projects that were supposed to lead to eternal peace would work.

Gentz did think that it would be a great step towards peace if Europe consisted of fewer entities, and if small states were absorbed into bigger states—this would mean fewer causes of war. Small states—city states, for example—had only flourished in the past because the baronial wars of the feudal era had turned the larger states into spheres of chaos, and merchants and other elites fled them to find a safer environment in the Hanse states, the Italian cities, the canals of Venice and Holland. But things had changed since the Middle Ages, he argued, and larger states had since spread the benefits of civilisation and domestic peace over larger spaces.[51]

Ultimately, Gentz thought that only a thorough re-education of mankind in the spirit of the Enlightenment would banish war, and he claimed to have recognised big steps in that direction in the eighteenth century prior to the advent of the French Revolution which turned this world of progress into one of chaos. Had not governments learned to create prosperity, not through foreign conquest, but through new economic approaches within? Had not the world, on the eve of the Revolution, been a much more civilised one than it had been before? The only hope Gentz could envisage was a slow progress towards a change of mentality, and a return to enlightened co-operation by men. With this approach, he prepared the Congress System which assumed such enlightened co-operation at least among Europe's great powers.[52]

Indeed, he would act as Metternich's right hand and main draftsman for the Vienna Treaty and subsequent congresses, until 1922, and can be seen not only in theory but also in practice to have been one of the main architects of this first Pentarchy, the oligarchy of great powers that in the Congress System tried to bring peace to Europe in the nineteenth century.[53]

7

FROM GREAT-POWER OLIGARCHY TO NATIONALIST COMPETITION, 1813–1918

The Congress System: Concert of Great Powers

Already in 1813, after Napoleon's first defeat at Leipzig, a peace congress was assembled at Vienna to decide how to bring order to the European world that Napoleon had turned upside down. The Congress was still in session when Napoleon made his 100-Day comeback, only to be defeated one final time at Waterloo in 1815. The great powers of Europe were all at the conference table: Britain and Austria, and the newcomers Prussia and Russia. Russia had by now acquired a huge empire, even if (much as with the Roman Empire) her self-perception was that this imperial expansion occurred only in defence against the Mongols and many other invaders from the Teutonic Knights and the Poles to Napoleon. Russia had contributed greatly to the defeat of Napoleon and could thus rightly expect to be part of this new European system. Very importantly, France was soon admitted to the 'Pentarchy of Great Powers' in 1818 (a term first used during the Congress of Aix-la-Chapelle that year, when the occupation of France by the victorious powers was ended). For with Napoleon's fall, the Bourbon monarchy had been restored, and the fiction was constructed that it was not so much France that had been defeated, but Napoleon. While France lost all Napoleon's conquests—a loss justified in terms of the common good of Europe—the Bourbon King Louis XVIII was accepted as full sovereign, innocent of all of France's deeds under the Revolution and the French Empire.[1]

The Congress system or the 'Concert' of great powers established with the Vienna Congress of 1813–1815 was one step further from Utrecht 1713 towards the creation of a permanent meeting of representatives of the great powers of Europe, in war and peace, aiming eventually to settle problems before they had turned into war. The term 'concert' can be found in European diplomatic documents since the Treaties of Utrecht 1713/14. The terms *'concert européen'*, *'concert diplomatique'* and *'système européen'* are used several times in the treaties of 1814/1815 that were negotiated in the Vienna Congress.[2] Here, definite and self-conscious efforts were made to create a new state system that would help ensure peace in Europe subsequently. As it stated in Article 1 of the First Peace of Paris: 'The high contracting parties shall make every effort to preserve, not only among themselves, but also, as far as depends on them, among all the states of Europe, the good harmony and understanding that is necessary for its repose.'[3] At the instigation of Tsar Alexander I the four victorious powers in 1815 concluded a 'Holy Alliance' for peace. While the term disappeared with his death in 1825, the notion remained on all sides that the oligarchy of great powers was supposed to work in the greater interest of Europe, not just to promote the interests of each great power separately. What the great powers shared was also a fear of revolution in their own countries, even though France and Britain would support revolutionary national movements' bids to form independent states by seceding from empires, pitting France and Britain repeatedly against the interests of Austria, Prussia, Russia, and Turkey to preserve their European empires.

The 'repose' or 'rest' or 'tranquillity' of Europe was still the aim, as at Utrecht, and it was seen as conditional upon a balance of powers, even though this did not have to be an absolute equilibrium. The state system created to ensure this changed, however: the task was entrusted to the Pentarchy, an oligarchy of the five European great powers, to ensure that the balance of powers was kept.[4] The final declaration of the Congress of Aix-la-Chapelle noted that 'a political system' had come into being, 'destined to ensure [the peace settlement's] stability. The intimate union established between the monarchs associated with this system, by their principles no less than by the interests of the people, affords Europe the most sacred warrant of her future tranquillity.'[5] The functioning of this state system assumed, of course, that all five would put the wellbeing of Europe above that of their respective empires.

For a while it worked fairly well. Through a series of greater congresses or smaller conferences, the Great Powers tried to settle among themselves and over the heads of the smaller polities or peoples concerning major issues arising in Europe that might threaten peace and lead to civil or inter-state war (or both). This method of concertation among the Pentarchy foreshadowed the Council of the League of Nations, and the United Nations Security Council. A century after the peace treaties of Utrecht had famously tried to introduce sovereign equality of the states of Europe, this notion was *de facto* abandoned with the Congress System with its hierarchy of states, putting the members of the Pentarchy above the rest. Among the Pentarchy, however, there was no longer a dominant power, not even a *primus inter pares*. The Great Powers were equal: Britain and France with their respective growing overseas empires, the Austrian Habsburgs with their personal union with the crowns of several polities from Bohemia to Hungary and Croatia, partly areas that had been prized away from the Turks; the Dukes of Brandenburg who in the eighteenth century had inherited the barren Baltic kingdom of Prussia, well outside what had once been the Roman world and who now occupied Silesia and parts of Poland and the Russian Empire with its vast but infertile Eastern expanses. And these five powers, with the occasional addition of the Ottoman Empire later in the nineteenth century, assumed the right to decide over war and peace, over state boundaries and the creation or demise of polities, throughout Europe or even the world.

Gentz wrote in preparation for the 1818 Congress of Aix-la-Chapelle:

> All the European powers have since 1813 been united, not by an alliance properly so called, but by a system of cohesion founded on generally recognised principles, and on treaties in which every state, great or small, has found its proper place. ... this state of things is what ... characterized a federative or well-balanced system.[6]

And perhaps Gentz was right in arguing that under the Concert System, Europe enjoyed an unprecedented degree of stability until the mid-nineteenth century, before it was eroded by wars between members of the Pentarchy. On the eve of the first of these, the Crimean War of 1853–1856, a letter to the editor of the London newspaper *The Examiner* claimed that:

> Europe is now restored to such a state of tranquillity as she has never enjoyed before. ... What a perfect state of peace and happiness does our world enjoy! Every prince in harmony with his neighbour: universal concord and decorous silence throughout rival nations; Religion reseated on her throne, and sanctioning in a voice from above the chastisement of the refractory. ... Not a vestige of what the factious call liberty is to be seen [!], either in the fields of industry or in the sandy and less fertile tracts of literature.[7]

But even in 1818, Gentz could not exclude that through some circumstances this system would be destroyed and all states would 'enter into new political combinations, and adopt new measures for their safety; consequently new alliances, disloca- tions, reconciliations, intrigues, incalculable complications,... would bring us to another general war... that is to say ... to the definitive overthrow of all social order in Europe.'[8]

Indeed, there were fundamental ideational disagreements among the Pentarchy. Britain and France—in those periods when France was a Republic and felt generous about the freedom and self-determination of other peoples—from time to time sup- ported nations like the Greeks, the Poles or the Italians that wanted to break away from the Ottoman, Russian, Prussian or Austrian overlordship. Naturally, this support for self-determi- nation was not shared in Kostantiniyye, Moscow, Berlin or Vienna. Even as the Congress system was formed, and in fact throughout the nineteenth century, conflicting world views existed side by side. At Vienna, the religiously-inspired idealism of Tsar Alexander I was very much out of tune with the very secular thinking of British leaders who had long left the religious fervour of the Reformation and of Oliver Cromwell and the English Civil War behind. If anything, the new prevailing ideol- ogy of the British ruling elite was one of 'pragmatism' and an emphasis on economic gains, an ideology claiming to be free from ideology (with the occasional admixture of British defence of 'freedom') that would dominate British politics till this day.[9] Likewise, Prince Metternich, negotiating for Austria, dismissed the Tsar's ideas as 'philanthropic aspiration clothed in religious garb.' Metternich described the Holy Alliance as 'the overflow of the pietistic feeling' of the Tsar.[10] In France, too, the governing elite no longer felt it opportune to evoke religious motives. Thus Talleyrand advised King Louis XVIII in 1815: 'Formerly the secular power could derive support from the authority of reli- gion; it can no longer do this, because religious indifference has penetrated all classes and become universal. The sovereign power, therefore, can only rely upon public opinion for support, and to obtain that it must seek to be at one with that opinion.'[11]

Yet religious fervour was strong and on the rise among the common people throughout the nineteenth century. At an International Peace Congress organised, not by states, but by peace activists in 1849, Victor Hugo, to great applause, evoked 'religious and holy thoughts' which, with 'the Gospel as our Law' and 'the Law of God' would transform Europe into a sphere of peace with a great sovereign senate taking the place of a parliament.[12] Even in Britain, old Christian dissenters like the Baptists and new Christian confessions such as the Methodist Church recruited new members in unprecedented numbers. And when the Congress System broke down once more with France and Prussia going to war with one another in 1870–71, France's defeat precipitated French religious fervour of the gloomiest sort, with national contrition for France's sins that had supposedly led to this defeat physically represented by the Church of Sacré Coeur in Paris (a crushing architectural penance imposed on the French capital), and countless new statues of Jesus and Mary with bleeding hearts.

Such sentiments also brought forth some humanitarian progress however. In 1863, Henri Dunant founded the International Committee of the Red Cross. In 1868, Tsar Alexander II convened an international military conference at St Petersburg:

> in order to examine the expediency of forbidding the use of certain projectiles in time of war between civilized nations, and that Commission having by common agreement fixed the technical limits at which the necessities of war ought to yield to the requirements of humanity.

The countries represented in the commission agreed to ban certain weapons, considering:

> That the progress of civilization should have the effect of alleviating as much as possible the calamities of war;

That the only legitimate object which states should endeavour to accomplish during war is to weaken the military forces of the enemy;

That for this purpose it is sufficient to disable the greatest possible number of men;

That this object would be exceeded by the employment of arms which uselessly aggravate the sufferings of disabled men, or render their death inevitable;

That the employment of such arms would, therefore, be contrary to the laws of humanity...[13]

This in principle outlawed anything that would torture soldiers unnecessarily, and re-introduced the medieval restraint on war imposed by the Church and then by successive self-denying ordinances issued to soldiers that it was not legitimate in war to target civilians.[14]

But balance-of-power considerations as well as selfish interests of the great powers undermined the Congress System. It broke down with the Crimean War (1853–1856), when Russia clashed with the Ottoman Empire which in turn was succoured by Britain and France. A new Congress, held in Paris, ended the Crimean War, and in this Paris Peace of 1856, the Ottoman Empire was admitted to the great-power Pentarchy as its *de facto* sixth member. The Paris Congress was seen by all sides as having created a fairly equitable peace settlement, with the great powers showing moderation in pursuit of their narrow national interests. They seemed to recognise, once more, that a ruthless pursuit of 'realist' interests and power cost them more dearly in terms of blood and treasure than the agreement on wider shared interests, the tranquillity of Europe.

But then came the Second War of Italian Independence of 1859 in which France joined the Italians in their fight for the integration of Austrian-held territories in North-Eastern Italy to form an Italian nation-state, something that had never existed previously. Then came Prussia's rise under the political leadership of its chancellor, Prince Otto von Bismarck, who moved his pawns on the international chequer board. His first move was to prize Schleswig Holstein away from Denmark with the help of Austria. His second was to knock Austria out of the competition to lead the German states in the Austro-Prussian War of 1866. Third, he provoked France into starting the Franco-Prussian War of 1870–71, at the end of which he had his Hohenzollern master, King William of Prussia, proclaimed Emperor William I of a new German empire or *Reich,* actually a federation under Prussian dominance.[15] Nor were the Russian and the Ottoman empires lastingly reconciled after the Crimean War, where the former stepped in to support independence movements among European Christian populations under Turkish rule; the Russo-Turkish War of 1877–78 ensued.

Abandoning its interventionist stance which had led it to support the Greeks against the Ottoman Empire earlier in the century, Britain for the best part of 1856–1914 kept out of these wars between the Great Powers, assuming a new posture of non-intervention or 'splendid isolation' (not unlike that of American isolationism) and tending to its immensely large overseas empire. Curiously, this comparatively short period in the long history of the British Isles marked the British collective memory most strongly. It forged a mythical self-perception as one of Britain as detached from the affairs of Europe. Her monarch was no longer in personal union a prince of the Holy Roman Empire (as her ancestors, the Hanoverian kings, had been), owning no territories on the European Continent other than Gibraltar. The detachment from the European Continent fitted balance-of-power thinking well. This was summed up by Lord Palmerston's pronouncement in the House of Commons on 1 March 1848, as revolutions were breaking out all over the Continent and Britain refused to take sides: 'We have no eternal allies, and we have no perpetual enemies. Our interests are eternal and perpetual, and those interests it is our duty to follow.' As the Union Jack was flying from Australia to Canada and from the Falklands to her trading posts in China, Britain could turn her back on other European struggles for more freedom, for more democracy.

This did not mean, however, that the British government was indifferent to European inter-state power-politics. In 1867, a British diplomat complained about this in a letter to his Foreign Secretary, the Earl of Derby:

> During a long course of years Great Britain exercised a weighty influence in the affairs of Europe and it was always employed, and for the most part successfully, for the maintenance of peace. It cannot but be a matter of regret that from the system of absolute non-intervention which she has for [more recently] pursued, that influence is not so available as it formerly was to reconcile the differences or curb the ambitions of the other Powers of Europe, and to uphold the faith of Treaties.[16]

Robert Gascoyne-Cecil, Marquess of Salisbury, who in various roles as Secretary for India, as Foreign Secretary or Prime Minister played an important part in Britain's foreign policy in the second half of the nineteenth century, rejected any policy of 'splendid isolation' as dangerous. He said in a speech delivered in Wales in 1888, 'We are part of the community of Europe and we must do our duty as such.'[17] Even after the loss of the crown's Hanoverian possessions, British interests were affected by turbulence on the Continent. There, under the impact of growing national rivalry, the Congress System was steadily deteriorating. This was obvious also to academic observers. An article on the 'Balance of Power' in the ninth edition of the *Encyclopaedia Britannica* of 1875 (vol. III) noted that the long-standing principle of British policy to intervene on the Continent to check expansionist powers had regrettably been replaced by non-intervention. In the context of revolutions, wars, and the rise of Germany, it argued:

The general result is that, at the present time, the military power of the German empire far surpasses that of any other state, and could only be resisted by a general combination of all the rest. The balance of power ... has been totally destroyed; no alliances can be said to exist between any of the great powers, but each of them follows a distinct course of policy, free from any engagements to the rest, except on some isolated points; the minor states can appeal to no certain engagement or fixed general principle for protection, except perhaps as far as the neutrality of Switzerland and Belgium are concerned; and for the last two centuries there has not been a time at which all confidence in public engagements and common principles of international law has been so grievously shaken. Where the reign of law ends, the reign of force begins, and we trace the inevitable consequence of this dissolution of legal international ties in the enormous augmentation of military establishments, which is the curse and the disgrace of the present age. Every state appears to feel that its security depends on arming the whole virile population, and maintaining in what is called a state of peace all the burdens of complete armament...[18]

Meanwhile the other European great powers merrily resumed the rivalry that had plunged them into wars in the previous centuries. The Berlin Congress which in 1878 one last time mobilised the Concert to make peace between Russia and Turkey by containing the aspirations to national independence in the Balkans, saw balance-of-power politics in their most cynical form. Austria sought both to consolidate her grip on her possessions and to extend them, but it was swimming against the growing tide of nationalism. An Austrian eyewitness, Leopold von Gerlach, in 1854 described Austrian politics since the 1848 revolutions as based on fear: fear of insurgencies in Italy and Hungary, fear of Louis-Napoleon Bonaparte, the new President of France who was threatening to turn expansionist like his late uncle Napoleon I, fear of Russia, fear of Prussia—and that against the background of a miserable financial situation. Austria, for once with the support of Hungary, continued with its objective of chasing the Turks from Europe, and thus in the Crimean War, they took the side of Russia.[19] But then, by securing the annexation of Bosnia-Hercegovina by the Austrian Empire at the Berlin Congress of 1878, Austria would directly clash with Russia which wanted Bosnia-Hercegovina to be subsumed by her client state Serbia.

Bismarck, now the German *Reich*-Chancellor, tried to appear as the honest broker at the Berlin Congress that he hosted (and that was of course attended also by British representatives), the last of the nineteenth-century series. Bismarck claimed that Germany had no interests at all in the Balkans and Straits (commonly referred to as *'les affaires d'Orient'* or 'the Eastern Question'), but Berlin had in reality helped bring about the Eastern Crisis and had benefitted from it. In 1877, during the Russo-Turkish War, Bismarck told his son Herbert that the interest of Germany was 'not that of any acquisition of land, but of a general political situation in which all powers other than France need us and should be put off forming a coalition against us where at all possible.' In fact, he admitted, 'It is more important that we appear to be trying to secure the peace than to be securing it in reality'. Bismarck famously quipped that to him, the Balkans were not worth the bones of a single Pomeranian soldier,[20] but he was happy to see others wasting lives and treasure on the settlement of this volatile area. Bismarck admitted that his own aim at the Congress was 'to keep the Eastern sore running and thus to prevent unity among the other great powers, and to secure our own peace.' Welcoming British-Russian tensions, before the Congress he simultaneously (and of course secretly) encouraged the Russians to try to conquer Konstantiniyye, and promised Britain his support for the maintenance of the *status quo* regarding the Turkish Straits.[21] Tsar Alexander II was not far off target when he retrospectively called the outcome of the Congress 'a European coalition against Russia, under the command of Bismarck.'[22]

Meanwhile Britain had an indirect, but very strong and selfish interest in the continued presence of the Ottoman Empire in the European state system. Already in 1833, Lord Palmerston had told the House of Commons, 'The integrity and independence of the Ottoman Empire are necessary to the maintenance of the tranquillity, the liberty and the balance of power in the rest of Europe.' When Britain was still backing the Ottoman Empire in 1877, Queen Victoria opined that 'It is not a question of upholding Turkey; it is a question of Russian or British supremacy in the world.' Shortly before the Berlin Congress, the British Ambassador to Kostantiniyye Austen Henry Layard warned that the downfall of the Ottoman Empire would sow 'the seed for the downfall of the British Empire.' British Prime Minister Benjamin Disraeli came back from the Berlin Congress claiming to have brought 'peace with honour' (and Cyprus), upon which a contemporary critic quipped, yes 'the peace which passeth all understanding and the honour that is common among thieves'.[23]

For indeed, the smaller powers were by no means satisfied with the outcome of the Congress. Peace and stability in this multi-ethnic area of Europe remained elusive in an era of growing ethnic nationalism. Even before 1914, it broke down again in the Balkans where the wars of 1912–1913 became increasingly genocidal with massacres committed by all sides.

The Congress system had been supposed to replace the balance-of-power politics and wars of competition of the previous centuries. But the older competitive pattern came through and by 1878 was fully in force again, if anything, more so than ever. For dynastic rivalries had transformed themselves into fierce nationalist competition fuelled by Social Darwinism.

Bluntschli vs Moltke

In the very year of the Congress of Berlin, the Swiss-born jurist Johann Kaspar Bluntschli (1808–1881), who was by then teaching at the University of Heidelberg, put forward a proposal for the organisation of a Union of European states (a *Europäischer Staatenverein*). Bluntschli was building on previous works on international law, and like many before him argued that Europe was predestined by nature to civilise the world by bringing European law to the rest of mankind. Using rather unfortunate but at the time widespread terminology including references to the Aryan race, he discussed ways of improving European co-operation by ultimately creating a super-State. At the same time, he thought that this was not a realisable aim for the near future given the diversity of culture and custom within Europe. Like many of his contemporaries—including Karl Marx's collaborator and patron Friedrich Engels—he categorised peoples according to their capacity to form and sustain states, and based on this criterion, he dismissed the aspirations of the South-East European peoples to independent statehood.[24]

In a similar vein, he argued that Kant's dream of 'world citizenship' was—as yet—unrealizable. He was thus stuck with the assumption that in the near and medium term, projects of closer co-operation must be limited to Europe, and with the question of how this was best to be achieved without the 'Balkanisation' of such a project. Like the other authors discussed above, Bluntschli found himself caught on the horns of the dilemma as to how to protect the sovereignty of Europe's states—which he saw as historic and largely immutable entities—on the one hand, and how to ensure their co-operation on the other. His answers were inspired by two inappropriate models: those of the Helvetian Confederation from which he himself stemmed, and the United States of America. Inappropriate, because both were founded from below, as it were, with a strong perception of a joint purpose to stand up against dominating external forces. For Switzerland, these external foes were successively Burgundy, the Habsburgs, and Napoleon; for America, it was the United

Kingdom. Bluntschli thus proposed a voluntary association of European states which should grow together by adopting common laws, common legislation. He distanced himself from the projects of the Age of Enlightenment discussed above which had aimed to establish a Congress of sovereigns; Bluntschli wanted no sharing of powers and no common government.[25]

Nevertheless he hoped to see eighteen European states, with a preponderance of six great powers (Germany, France, the United Kingdom, Austria-Hungary, Russia and Italy) within the two organs he wanted to set up: a Federal Council (*Bundesrat*), consisting of representatives of the member states' governments (two each for the great powers, one for each of the smaller states) and a House of Representatives (*Repräsentantenhaus)*. The latter would be elected; the great powers would return eight to ten elected members each, the smaller powers four or five members. He envisaged that they might meet in conveniently situated continental cities such as Brussels, The Hague, or Geneva. Bluntschli's Union was supposed to have no competence in matters military or financial. All co-operation would be entirely voluntary, and be built on the common commitment to shared legal approaches and on the prevalence of international law.[26]

In the following years, Bluntschli tried to elicit the support of Europe's major leaders for his project of creating 'eternal peace' or even just to limit the effects of war, only to find that Prussian Field Marshal Helmuth von Moltke the elder, who in his youth had been peace-minded, dismissed Bluntschli's project. In a letter to Bluntschli of 11 December 1880, von Moltke wrote:

> First, I find the humanitarian striving to lessen the sufferings that come with war utterly worthy. [However,] Eternal peace is a dream—and not even a beautiful one. War is part of God's world-order. Within it unfold the noblest virtues of men, courage and renunciation, loyalty to duty and readiness for sacrifice—at the hazard of one's life. Without war the world would sink into a swamp of

materialism. Further, I wholly agree with the principle stated ... that the gradual progress in morality must also be reflected in the waging of war. But I go further and believe that [waging war] in and of itself—not a codification of the law of war—may attain this goal.

Every law requires an authority to oversee and administer its execution, and this very force is lacking for the observation of international agreements. What third state would take up arms because one or both of two warring powers had violated the law of war? There is no earthly judge.[27]

Echoing Gentz, Moltke thought the only hope in progress lay in better 'religious and moral education, the sense of honour and respect for law, of individual leaders who make the law and act according to it, so far as this is generally possible to do in the abnormal conditions of war.' He thought that war had already become more humane in his own day, compared with the 'savagery of the Thirty Years' War':

In our day, an important step toward the attainment of the desired goal has been the introduction of universal military service, which has enlisted the educated classes in the army. Certainly, the raw and violence-prone elements are still there, but they no longer, as formerly, constitute the bulk [of soldiers].

To contain their savagery, governments in Moltke's view had to enforce strict discipline, pay the soldiers regularly and provision them properly:

The best deed in war is the speedy ending of the war, and every means to that end, so long as it is not reprehensible, must remain open. In no way can I declare myself in agreement with the Declaration of St. Petersburg [of 1868] that the sole justifiable measure in war is 'the weakening of the enemy's military power.' No, [targeting] all the sources of support for the hostile government must be considered, its finances, railroads, foodstuffs, even its prestige.

He had no problems agreeing with the Institute for International Law's call for better treatment of 'the wounded, the sick, doctors,' and 'prisoners', however.[28] In short, the idea of containing the suffering caused by war through the new institution of the Red Cross was something even a cynic like Moltke in his old age could approve of. But this extreme 'realist' had no faith in the civilising power of law, not even if it was, as in the Declaration of St Petersburg, proclaimed and signed by Europe's great powers.

Colonial Empires for all and the Growth of Nationalism

With Napoleon I out of the way, no country entertained the pretension of ruling a singular universal empire any longer, even if the fear of another great power's pretensions to a universal monarchy was still very much alive, and with it, balance-of-power thinking. There were empires all round: not only were there the older colonial empires of Portugal, Spain, England/Britain and France, but also the Netherlands and even little Belgium, a state that was created only in 1830, had overseas' colonies. Austria's empire lay right at her borders. Russia was one gigantic empire. Still set on 'defensive' expansion, Russia wanted parts of the Ottoman Empire, which led it to repeated wars with Kostantiniyye.

Nor had the French quite finished with their dream of a French Empire in Europe, as their election of Napoleon's nephew, Louis-Napoléon as President of the Second Republic in 1848, and his subsequent elevation in 1852 to the title of Emperor as Napoleon III illustrated. And of course, with this, the old rivalry of the heirs of Charlemagne on both sides of the Rhine was revived. Although it was now Prussia that took the place of Austria as France's favourite adversary, their competition was every bit as strong as the Valois-Habsburg and then the Bourbon-Habsburg enmity of yore. As we have seen, it led inexorably to a dramatic clash between France and Prussia, the Franco-Prussian War of 1870/71, the first time since the

Napoleonic Wars that conscripted armies clashed in Europe in cataclysmic battles with mass casualties. This war ended the second French experiment with a French empire in Europe, but out of the corpse-littered battlefields arose a new German empire.

So this time it was Prussia, not Austria, that was in the lead. Prussia, too, had been set on expansion, ever since the eighteenth century. Prussia expanded westwards: first she collected friends and allies (through the Rhine Federation) among the Central European left-overs of the defunct Holy Roman Empire. Then her able chancellor, Otto von Bismarck, turned his skills to rebuilding a narrowly North-West German part of this Empire. Bismarck sought to apportion the lead part to the Prussian Hohenzollern dynasty by strictly keeping the Austrians out of this process, ignoring the Austrian Habsburgs' infinitely older claim to the imperial title. The claim that this meant building a 'nation-state' was therefore risible in that the Austrians were every bit as German as the Bavarians, Swabians, Hessians, Saxons or Hanoverians whom Bismarck succeeded in persuading to follow the Prussian lead. If anything, Austrian diplomat Prince Klemens von Metternich commented, the Prussians' Germanness was somewhat in doubt given their ethnic Baltic ancestry, and the strong element of Slav populations in Prussia.[29] As we have seen, he achieved his aim with the proclamation of a new empire in the centre of Europe in 1871, an entity that claimed the succession to the Holy Roman Empire which had since the fifteenth century often been referred to as 'of the German nation'. The new German empire was therefore constructed to be the (second) German Empire or *Reich*. Indeed, the imposition of a Hohenzollern emperor required some compromises: the Hohenzollerns never quite made it to be emperors of Germany (which would have implied their rule over all of it) but German emperors, to underscore that among the German princes within the *Reich*, they were merely the first among equals. Within this

Second Empire or *Reich* with its federal structures, Bavaria, Württemberg and Saxony elevated to the rank of kingdoms, and the various other great duchies, duchies and other principalities and the free (former Hanse) cities continued to be semi-sovereign entities until 1918. Nevertheless, the French (smarting from their defeat by the German coalition in 1870–71 and convinced that the new German *Reich* continued to pose an existential threat to France) and the British felt that the creation of this new German Empire had thoroughly upset the hallowed balance of power.[30]

The abolition of the French Empire in Europe and its replacement by the Third French Republic did not put an end to France's overseas' empire. A French experiment with a client state in Mexico went sour, and by the mid-nineteenth century Spain had also lost all her South American colonies to local independence movements following the model of Washington's bid for independence from London. But Africa and Asia were still open to colonial expansion, and several European states—including the latecomer, Germany—scrambled for colonies there. It was this in particular which finally persuaded the British to put a temporary end to their posture of non-alignment and to throw in their lot with Republican France, at least for the following dozen years. In 1904, Britain signed up to the Entente Cordiale with France, and barely three years later the British Foreign Secretary, Sir Eyre Crowe, wrote a now famous memorandum laying out Britain's grand strategy. Britain as a strong naval power with a huge empire would draw upon itself the envy of the world if it did not seek 'to harmonize with the general desires and ideals common to all mankind, and more particularly' aspire to be a state 'that it is closely identified with the primary and vital interests of a majority, or as many as possible, of the other nations.' Itself in need of protecting its national independence, he argued, Britain should therefore support any other nation the independence of which was threatened. Britain was also and remained the champion of free trade, and sought to check the rise of any other power with 'ambitions to extend its frontiers or spread its influence' by counterbalancing it with an alliance. It 'has become almost an historical truism', he wrote, 'to identify England's secular policy with the maintenance of this balance by throwing her weight now in this scale and now in that, but ever on the side opposed to the political dictatorship of the strongest single state or group at a given time.' In short, Britain played the balancer in world politics, or at least in European politics. And now the time had come to counter-balance the Prussia German Empire's expansionism, both in Europe and, with the German Empire's previously unprecedented quest for overseas' colonies, in the wider world.[31] The alignment of powers that would fight each other in the First World War was nearly complete. It was complemented by one further power, Russia, brought in by France to counterbalance the might of the central powers: the Austro-Hungarian Empire, and its former rival, the new Prussian-led German *Reich*, plus Italy, which had formerly also been an enemy to Austria-Hungary from which it prized away its northern Italian territories in establishing itself as an almost complete ethnic nation-state.[32] The three had formed their 'Triple Alliance' in 1882 which would survive until Italy's defection in 1915.

Meanwhile these two German-speaking empires sought to build some sort of integrated economic space in Central Europe (*Mitteleuropa*), but without any political co-ordination. This aim was still there when war came in 1914. German Chancellor Bethmann Hollweg declared:

> We must create a central European economic association through common customs treaties, to include France, Belgium, Holland, Denmark, Austria-Hungary, Poland, and perhaps Italy, Sweden and Norway. This association will not have any common constitutional

supreme authority and all its members will be formally equal, *but in practice will be under German leadership* and must stabilise Germany's economic *dominance* over Mitteleuropa [my Italics].[33]

As Germany had the largest and most dynamic economy within this planned economic association, with Britain deliberately excluded, Bethmann-Hollweg expected political domination to come automatically, in the absence of political institutions enabling the other powers to check such German *de facto* dominance. This is the essence of a sphere of influence, the alternative to a formal empire. Aiming to add larger spheres of influence to their formal empire, however, was something that all the great powers of the time were guilty of.

The *Mitteleuropa* project was elaborated and slightly modified in the eponymous book that appeared in 1915 by the theorist Friedrich Naumann, a leading German 'Liberal'[34] who like most of his contemporaries, especially in the middle of this world war, bought freely into nationalist ideas. Like Bethmann-Hollweg, Naumann was keen to strengthen the links between the German *Reich* and Austria. In Naumann's view, the German *Reich* alone was not strong enough without Austria—and Austria-Hungary not strong enough without the German *Reich*—to fashion and dominate the economic structure of the Europe of the future. Naumann thus proposed a fusion of both entities into one huge empire, into one 'united people of brothers' which would dominate *Mitteleuropa* politically and economically. In a series of chapters he discussed developments and options in agriculture, industry, customs policies, and indeed constitutional issues, including an analysis of world economic trends which he argued were spelling the end of small states as viable macro-economic entities.

Naumann recognised that his project needed the support of Hungary. He hoped to be able to persuade the Hungarian elite to join his scheme from which Germans, Austrians, and Hungarians would emerge as *Mitteleuropäer*.[35] Meanwhile Austria had a somewhat different goal, involving turning Poland into a client state comparable to that of Hungary. But neither Berlin nor Vienna had factored in the rising tide of nationalism which now flooded Eastern Europe.

To simplify complex socio-political developments, the nineteenth century transformed the call for universal human rights and democracy that had gone forth from the French Revolution into nationalism and colonial imperialism. The revolutionary potential of millions of workers living in horrendous conditions of health and poverty in the industrialising countries was bought off in part with tales of their national superiority over other peoples and the glories of the (overseas) or other empires that their states administered. In a pattern of primitive identification, the lowest and often badly exploited classes of society were made to feel proud of their imperial or royal families in ways difficult to fathom for the detached twenty-first century intellectual. While the Communist Party of Marx and Engels, founded in 1848, spread and thrived, and the International Workingmen's Association drew extensive support across Europe, little revolutionary impetus resulted from this outside France which in 1848 and 1871 saw the return to democratic republics. Even in France, as we have seen, the earlier of these two republics fell back into imperial nostalgia with Louis-Napoléon Bonaparte being turned from President of the Republic to Emperor Napoleon III. Already the Spanish had fought tooth and nail against the French occupation under the first Napoléon in order to restore their Bourbon monarchy. The Greeks who had been so keen to cast off the yoke of Turkish oppression chose to become a monarchy—and imported a minor foreign prince to be their monarch. Similarly Serbs, Romanians, Bulgarians all freed themselves from Ottoman tutelage to become, not democracies, but monarchies. Ethnic folklore, the promotion of languages that had never been written (or at least not in official documents or scientific literature) became the great fashion of the day, and more energy was expended on these and other attempts to promote minority cultures than on social justice or the right to vote and control governments democratically. Instead of demanding political rights, a redistribution of wealth, and of overthrowing their elites, increasingly literate workers and peasants followed the court news and the affairs of their royal families, and rejoiced in the overseas' exploits of their state's armies, the colonies conquered and subdued, the trade with which made the rich richer. Already Robespierre had dryly observed during the French Revolution, just before resorting to the instrument of external war himself:

> In Rome when the people, exhausted by the tyranny and the pride of the patricians, demanded its rights through the voices of their tribunes, the Senate declared war; and the people forgot their rights and their grievances to run to the banners of the patricians and to prepare triumphal processions for their tyrants.[36]

Under the influence of nationalism, the rivalries between French and English branches of the Valois dynasty of France, and later the rivalry between Valois and Habsburgs, supplanted by the rivalry between Bourbons and Habsburgs, eventually replaced by the rivalry between Bourbons and Hohenzollerns, were distorted into a narrative of centuries of supposedly national rivalries between France and England and France and Germany (even though no state called Germany had existed before 1871). The French narrative of an eternal Franco-German competition was created by none other than the First President of the French Third Republic: Adolphe Thiers, himself an historian. Even in 1866, as Prussia defeated Austria and before the Franco-German War of 1870/71, he told the French parliament:

> We shall see the remaking of a new German empire, that empire of Charles V who previously resided in Vienna [actually, he was mainly in Flanders and Spain], which will now reside in Berlin, which will

be very close to our frontier ... [France] has to oppose such a creation, in the first place in the name of the independence of the
German states; ... and in the second place in the name of its own
independence; finally in the name of European equilibrium which is
in everybody's interest, in the interest of universal society...[37]

Despite the copious and excellent literature on the origins and
effects of nationalism, it is still a riddle how thousands and millions of people were persuaded, first, to see the rivalries between
their ruling families—many of them related by marriage—as
causes to fight and die for, and then to translate them into
nationalist causes, where every Englishman, Frenchman,
'German' was seen as adversary. The 'German' stereotyping is
particularly odd, as we have seen, as beyond their language,
Bavarians, Hanoverians, Saxons, Prussians, Swabians had nothing
in common that they did not share with North Italians,
Bohemians, or the Dutch in an empire that had been under
Habsburg domination for many centuries. The most impressive
confidence trick in this context was the re-interpretation of the
Bourbon-Habsburg (in their Spanish and Austrian dimensions)
and the Bourbon-Prussian rivalry as a narrative of Franco-
German rivalry.

There was another tangible element to this competition.
Trading rivalries involving merchants and industrialists were
added into the mix as Britain, France, and at the tail end of the
nineteenth century, also the latecomer Germany, nursed their
overseas empires on the back of economic competition for raw
materials and markets. This could feed directly into nineteenth-
century nationalisms on both sides, and into militarism and a
benighted enthusiasm for war.

National competitiveness, plus a zero-sum view of a world
with limited resources and finite lands left to conquer, with the
admixture of Social Darwinism which led to the expectation that
only the fittest nation would survive (and that anything but a

very aggressive posture was a sign that one was not the Alpha-nation destined to survive) was the perfect condition for a war that would engulf all of Europe and spread to the colonies. The theorists of the Enlightenment with their prescriptions for peace had many (usually less original) successors in the nineteenth century. But they were side-lined by the time Social Darwinism and militarism had come to dominate European thinking. What moved the masses was military parades, pretty uniforms, narratives of national heroism and noble self-sacrifice. Even the polities that had long been acquainted with democratic practices were not immune to this. If anything, public politics, election campaigns and parliamentary elections presented ideal fora for rabble-rousing xenophobia. People who had not felt the effects of war for generations could fall for the old trope, reflected in Moltke's declaration, quoted above, that societies thrived on war as it purified the body politic and brought out the best in men. Even nations that had been at war within the last half century clamoured for revenge or wanted to emulate the glorious exploits of their fathers and uncles.

One further, systemic factor, aggravated what could at this point almost be called inter-national relations: the abandonment by Britain of non-intervention or isolation, and by the other great powers of their pattern of constant changes in alliances. Instead, they switched to more enduring alliances, realising that alone, they would not necessarily prevail in duels with their main adversary. Nor were ad hoc coalitions very useful for preparing the sort of mass warfare which strategists predicted would result from the technological innovations of the late nineteenth century. The Congress System gave way to two increasingly stable alliances pitting Europe's great powers against each other.[38] All these factors came together to produce the First World War.

Historians have argued over whether it could have been avoided,[39] or whether the decision-makers sleep-walked into it.[40]

FROM OLIGARCHY TO NATIONALIST COMPETITION

What is certain is that there was no state system present that could have constrained members to follow alternative means of settling their disputes. The Concert or Congress System was long dead. The system in place—adversarial alliances of mutual defence if one was attacked—did not deter a terrorist from assassinating the Austro-Hungarian heir to the throne. The Austrian threat of war if Serbia did not help arrest the terrorist did not coerce Serbia to comply, as Serbia counted (rightly) on Russia's loyal support, as Russia did on France's. All sides tried to play a deterrence game, but their bluff was called. The result of this was millions of dead, and millions of maimed.

8

RECREATING A UNIVERSAL ORDER I

THE LEAGUE OF NATIONS

From 1492 until the First World War, the world beyond Europe was seen by Europeans mainly as an area to be dominated and where possible annexed to their own realms in the form of colonies. The workings of the European system affected war and peace around the globe. From 1917, European systems in turn began to be strongly influenced by great powers outside Europe.

With the First World War, for the first time, an extra-European power, the United States, became a major actor in European affairs. But America's leader, President Woodrow Wilson, was a child of the European Enlightenment. He had read his Bentham and had understood the wish for self-determination that could be traced to the French Revolution and beyond, to the Dutch Eighty-Years' War against Spain. Unfortunately, he thought that self-determination would always bring democracy and, through democratic checks and balances, good governance. He had not reckoned with the powers of ethnic, xenophobic nationalism.

On 8 January 1918, with the outcome of the First World War still undecided, he proclaimed fourteen Points which he suggested should be the foundational principles of not just the European but the world order that should emerge from this conflagration, the bloodiest in absolute numbers that the world had seen. They included specific measures such as the creation of a Polish state, the restoration of Alsace and Lorraine (annexed to the German Reich after France's defeat in the Franco-Prussian War) to France, the evacuation of Russian territory occupied by Germany after the separate Russo-German Peace Treaty of Brest-Litovsk, the restoration of Belgium to its former frontiers, frontier adjustments to the Italian-Austrian border to benefit Italy, and the independence of the client peoples of Austria-Hungary (which included Hungary) and the Ottoman Empire.

Beyond such specific measures, Wilson also postulated the following main principles which should govern future inter-state relations:

I. 'Open covenants of peace, openly arrived at' ruling out all secret diplomacy—we see Bentham's and perhaps even Guibert's ideas here, and of course the aversion to the sort of diplomacy we have described above in the context of the Berlin Congress;

II. Freedom of navigation upon the seas in peace and war (outside territorial waters);

III. Free trade;

IV. A reduction of armaments on all sides—echoing Kant's postulate, who had aimed ultimately at the abolition of standing armies;

V. A settlement of colonial claims, with 'the interests of the populations concerned' in mind (this fell short of a promise of independence).

XIV. The creation of 'a general association of nations ... for the purpose of affording mutual guarantees of political independence and territorial integrity to great and small states alike.'[1]

Finally, the many previous proposals for such an association were about to be put into practice.

There was wide-spread consensus also in France and Britain that a new system was called for. The British foreign policy-making elite recognised the need for a new international system limiting the sovereign freedom of its members, '[u]nless we want to return to the old system of the balance of power with all its attendant dangers of competition in armaments and inevitable wars', in the words of one leading British diplomat, Sir Esmé Howard, in December 1924.[2]

Moreover, Jeremy Bentham's call for decolonisation as taken up by President Wilson now echoed around the world. French Prime Minister Clemenceau pronounced that the supreme achievement of the First World War was 'the right of nations to govern themselves' (self-determination), which of course sat very badly with any balance of great power and imperial interests.[3] It was directly influenced by Wilson's point that the ethnic minorities demanding their own states should be given this right to self-determination. Beyond that, the Paris Peace Treaties of 1918–1919 marked a further change in international law. In the prosperous Parisian suburbs where the individual peace treaties with the Axis Powers and their allies were negotiated, the defeated parties were not negotiating parties.[4] Peace treaties from the Peace of Lodi of 1454 among Italian city-states until the French Revolution had provided for 'oblivion' of all war crimes, meaning no war crimes were to be prosecuted once the peace was concluded. And until the Napoleonic Wars, peace treaties generally did not provide for any reparations to be paid.[5] The Treaty of Vienna of 1815 made France pay an '*indemnité*' of 700 million francs to the Allies. 1866 Prussia forced Austria to pay compensation for the 'war expenses of Prussia'. The German-French Peace Treaty imposed on France at Frankfurt of 1871 after the Franco-Prussian War stipulated that France had to pay 5 billion francs to Germany. There had very occasionally been such instances before 1815. But the Versailles Treaty of 1919 brought in a new angle as Germany was pronounced responsible and thus deemed guilty of having started the war (Art 231, the 'War Guilt Clause'). Emperor William II was held personally responsible 'for a supreme offence against international morality and the sanctity of treaties' (Art 227).[6] Thus for the first time, the payment of reparations was explained in terms of the 'war guilt' of one (defeated) party, which would rankle massively with the Germans, perhaps more so psychologically than the financial burden. It would provide much fuel for demagogues who could point not only to the financial hardship this implied for the German population, but also to the injustice of it, fanning moral outrage.[7]

Optimistically, or perhaps hoping that it would become true if it was said often enough, Wilson claimed that 'The day of conquest and aggrandizement is gone by....'[8] Wilson himself did his best to help create a new state system, the first of its kind spanning the globe. It took the form of the League of Nations, or *Société des Nations* in French, echoing the other term used by the Abbé de Saint-Pierre. It combined the Pentarchy of great powers (in its Council) that had existed in the Concert of Europe with a permanent Assembly with representatives of up to fifty-eight member states, the latter proposed in some form by the writings of Dubois, Podiebrad, Sully, Crucé and Saint-Pierre. The initial membership was small, as it included only sovereign states. But by implication colonies would in due course be able to govern themselves and become sovereign states with the option of membership; in the meantime, they would be under the tutelage of 'advanced nations'. The League was given a permanent Secretariat in Geneva. A Permanent International Court of Justice was established, so that the settlement of issues arising between member states would not have to be dealt with only by the mediation efforts of the Council, and if that failed, the Assembly, but through the application of a growing body of agreed international law.

The members of the League undertook to protect each other against aggression although the Council would decide how. This could include financial and economic measures (to boycott an offending country or impose sanctions upon it) with the cost of these to be shared among the members, or even the use of armed force. An offending member of the League could be expelled. The Council would meet at least once a year, and the original design was that it should include, next to the old great powers Britain and France, Italy, Japan, but also the USA.

The creation of the League of Nations and the attempt through it to create a new world system or world order was emblematic of a big change in thinking about what relations between polities should be like. The League by implication pro-scribed aggression against its members but not imperial policing (that is, actions of law enforcement or the suppression of insur-gencies in colonies). The Briand-Kellogg Pact concluded in 1928 at the instigation of the eponymous French and US foreign min-isters tried to go one step further: they renounced 'war as an instrument of national policy'. Sharing the optimism of Bentham, however, Aristide Briand and Frank Kellogg and the many signatory states of the pact neglected to put into place any mechanism to enforce compliance. Despite this, the pact argu-ably articulated a new norm to which at the time even increas-ingly militaristic Japan subscribed; it is perhaps understandable although not pardonable that the Japanese did not take it very seriously and were surprised when Western powers would in 1945 hold it against them that they had acted, with their wars of aggression of 1931–1945, much like the European great powers had done for centuries had since war became a *de facto* accepted tool of any sovereign state in early modern times.[9]

The League had two fundamental structural flaws. Even more than the Congress System before it, the League had the great disadvantage that, for any breach of the Covenant to be counteracted effectively, it needed the co-operation and willingness to assume leadership (and invest money and armed forces) on the part of the great powers members of the Council. As US Secretary of State Lansing noted in 1919:

> The League of Nations ... is relied upon to preserve the ... compromise of the conflicting interests of the great powers and to prevent the germination of the seeds of war which are sown in so many articles [of the peace Treaties] and which under normal conditions would soon bear fruit. The League might as well attempt to prevent the growth of plant life in a tropical jungle. Wars will come sooner or later.

The First World War, he argued, had been:

> fought by the United States to destroy forever the conditions which produced it. These conditions have not been destroyed. They have been supplanted by other conditions equally productive of hatred, jealously and suspicion. In place of the Triple Alliance and the Entente has arisen the Quintuple Alliance [the Permanent Five of the League Council][10] which is to rule the world. The victors in this war intend to impose their combined will upon the vanquished and to subordinate all interests to their own. ... Justice is secondary. Might is primary. ... We have a treaty of peace, but it will not bring permanent peace because it is founded on the shifting sands of [the Great Powers'] self-interest.[11]

There was a second key problem: the USA, which had largely designed the Covenant eventually did not become a member of the League, as against the wishes of its President, the US Congress preferred for America to retire into isolationism again. As David Lloyd George, British Prime Minster during the Paris Peace Conferences, said in 1923: 'Undoubtedly the great weakness of the League comes from the fact that it only represents one half of the great powers of the world.'[12] America had excluded itself, and the USSR and Germany were initially not admitted, the former as a revolutionary power that only gradually resumed its place in inter-state diplomacy, the latter as defeated and not fully sovereign entity. The only permanent members of the Council who were committed to upholding its rules of non-aggression were France and Britain. Italy and Japan, and Germany (eventually accepted into the Council in 1926) soon succumbed to nationalist expansionism, and withdrew from the League to pursue their own expansionist ambitions. France and Britain alone felt unable to contain or punish them. The USSR was admitted to the Council in 1934, but in the face of expansionist ambitions of National-Socialist Germany, Stalin preferred to engage in just the sort of secret dealing which Guibert, Bentham and Wilson had hoped to ban. Meanwhile, not only the USA, but also Britain and France had taken from the First World War the lesson that one should avoid 'entangling alliances' and commitments. By contrast, the rogue powers Germany and Italy in 1936 formed an alliance or 'Axis', later adhered to by Japan. On this basis, they more or less co-ordinated their aggressive strategies. The Western democracies by contrast entered the Second World War without a comparable alliance.

A European Alternative?

In 1923, the Tokyo-born Austrian aristocrat Count Richard von Coudenhove-Kalergi launched the idea of creating a European super-state, which he proposed under the title of *Pan-Europa*. He wanted this to be created in steps, beginning with a conference of governments, followed by a system of treaties and then a customs union, to set up, eventually, the United States of Europe. This he wanted to be modelled on the constitution of the United States of America, with the US Senate replicated in form of an upper house composed of representatives of the European member states of this United States of Europe.

Coudenhove-Kalergi sought support from all ends of the European political spectrum, but there was one country he excluded from his schemes: Russia. In his view, 'History gives Europe the following alternatives: either to overcome all national hostilities and consolidate in a federal union, or sooner or later to succumb to a Russian conquest. There is no third possibility.'[13] Coudenhove-Kalergi never committed himself entirely to one label—United States of Europe Confederation, Federation, Pan-Europe—but was more intent on persuading a wide spectrum of political forces to move in the direction of overcoming particularisms within Europe. The same applied to the many components of his proposals, among which were the creation of a European steel industry, a European customs union, European citizenship and a European currency. He was willing to bow to fashions and to make concessions to bring on board those like de Gaulle who, while generally favourable to European co-operation, wanted no European super-state. More fervent Euro-integrationists would later criticise Coudenhove-Kalergi for this.[14] Be that as it may, his is the name and the work that prepared the ground for thinking about how to overcome sover-eigntism and move towards European co-operation, with ultimate emphasis on the domains of politics and security.

Aristide Briand, a leading French politician, was one of the people whom Coudenhove-Kalergi won for the support of his project to which Franco-German reconciliation was key. And that was just the path that Briand was taking with his confidence- and security-building measures undertaken jointly with his German counterpart, Gustav Stresemann (the Locarno Treaties of 1925 guaranteeing Germany's Western borders against revisionism) and with Frank Kellogg in 1928. Briand raised the possibility of creating a 'European federation' of sorts with Gustav Stresemann at a meeting in June 1929. Elsewhere, he actually used the term 'United States of Europe'.[15] Coinciding with a big international conference organised by Coudenhove-Kalergi's Pan-European Union in Berlin in 1930, Briand issued a 'Memorandum on the

Organizaton of a Regime of European Federal Union'. He asserted that this was not anti-American, nor aimed to limit the sovereignty of member-states. In his Memorandum, he proposed a permanent parliament or 'European Conference' of representatives of European governments, a secretariat and also the creation of a permanent Political Committee which, like the Committee of the League of Nations (and after it the United Nations Security Council), would really be a great-power executive committee. Finally, Briand insisted that economic co-ordination should be subjected to political decisions:

> All possibility of progress towards economic union being strictly determined by the question of security, and this question being intimately bound up with that of realizable progress toward political union, it is on the political plane that constructive effort looking at giving Europe its organic structure should first of all be made. ... The contrary order would not only be useless, it would appear to the weaker nations to be likely to expose them, without guarantees or compensation, to the risks of political domination which might result from an industrial domination of the more strongly organized states. ... the justification of the economic sacrifices to be made to the whole should be found only in the development of a political situation warranting confidence between peoples and true pacification of minds ...

To assure that such domination of the smaller by the stronger nations did not occur, he proposed 'the general development for Europe of a system of arbitration and security, and the progressive extension to the whole European community of the policy of international guarantees inaugurated at Locarno', that is, guarantees of the inviolability of frontiers on all sides, until these treaties were overtaken by a more general treaty system. Somewhat disingenuously, given that no definition of sovereignty can bear the limitations on it which Briand intended to introduce, he added that the federation he proposed should be:

sufficiently flexible to respect the independence and national sovereignty of each of the states, while assuring them all the benefit of
collective solidarity for the settlement of political questions involving
the fate of the European community or that of one of its members.[16]

But by then Briand had lost his key German partner, Gustav
Stresemann, who had died of a stroke in the previous year, and
the world financial crisis was beginning to hit Europe hard.[17]
Instead of pan-European projects of reconciliation and co-
operation, Europeans turned inwards once more towards populist
nationalism and xenophobia.

*The 1929 Financial Crisis, the Return of National Interests,
and the Drift to War*

The League of Nations had made some positive achievements in
the 1920s, but the delicate balance of convergent and divergent
interests was upset fundamentally with the great financial crisis
of 1929 triggered by the Wall Street Crash.[18] The surge of racist-
nationalist expansionism in the political agendas of extreme parties that dominated, first Italy with Mussolini's Fascism from
1922, then Japan with an expansionist engagement on the Asian
continent from 1931, and two years later Germany with the
appointment of Hitler as Chancellor, was not an isolated phenomenon. While Wilson's Fourteen Points and the Covenant of
the League of Nations were full of the ideas of the Enlightenment
and pacific intentions, the First World War had by no means
expunged nationalism, let alone racism and bellicosity from the
mentalities of Europeans. True, the French, the Belgians and the
British had had enough of war, but throughout Europe and even
America, the economic after-effects of the war which ultimately
included the financial crisis that started in 1929 led to massive
unemployment and profound misery. Here were populations that
were open to the suggestion that the world was not as it should

be, that a strong man was needed to sort all this out. The younger the democracy, the more prone politicians were to treat one another with disrespect, the more polarised politics became, the more vicious, vengeful and extreme. Paramilitary units, siding with extreme political positions, helped Mussolini to consolidate his dictatorship in Italy and engaged in street battles in Germany until Hitler's National-Socialist storm-troopers rounded up their Communist and Social Democratic adversaries in concentration camps. People with serious problems in life—unemployment, illness, lack of housing—were open to demagogues who promised them that electing them and letting them curtail democracy to make huge changes was the answer. There was sympathy with such approaches throughout Europe, albeit to varying degrees.

Instead of moving further with arms control in a new type of conference of which the Washington Naval Conference was emblematic with its arms control treaty of 1922, states in the 1930s built up their arsenals. The key indicator of this tidal shift was the world disarmament conference which started in Geneva in 1932, really still a child of the positive trends towards the renunciation of the use of force of the 1920s. Its foundering in 1934 was symptomatic of the failure of the post-war hopes for perpetual peace through the League of Nations and voluntary interstate co-operation. Instead, the world returned to the largely Social Darwinist views that had obtained before 1914. Regardless of their actual ideological roots and background, leaders began to see wars as inevitable, including another major war of the scale of the Great War. That it would be large-scale industrialised warfare, mobilising one's own society, was taken for granted by all sides. By 1934 a new arms race was in full swing.[19]

Nor had the days of conquest and aggrandizement truly passed. Mussolini embarked on a scheme to play catch-up with the European colonial powers and belatedly to acquire for Italy a colonial empire. His motto was that he wanted to turn the Mediterranean into a Roman lake again, with colonies and dependencies on its southern shores. The Japanese leadership, Mussolini in Italy, Hitler and his National-Socialist and Conservative supporters all played a game with gusto: it was the game of scaring the *status quo* powers who did not want war into making ever more concessions, into turning a blind eye to conquests and expansion and infractions of treaty obligations. In the early rounds of this game, the three rogue states could capitalise on the reluctance of the democracies to raise the stakes. They were themselves not entirely keen on major war, but their success in these early rounds—Japan's in the Far East, Mussolini's in North Africa, Germany's against her neighbours—seemed to indicate that the losses in this game were minimal, while the gains were attractive. Until September 1939, all three powers got away with murder, territorial annexations and outright conquests by war.

Crucially, the League of Nations was not strong enough to override the return to narrow self-interests of states. Nor did defensive alliances exist this time as the lesson of the First World War seemed to have been that one should shun entangling alliances.

Let us recall that Britain and France were the only states that throughout the inter-war years were members of the League's Council. Both felt extremely overstretched with independence movements in their colonies and expansionist powers in Asia and nearer home, in the Mediterranean and Central Europe. Governments in both Paris and London were acutely worried by Rome's and Berlin's expansionism, but neither was willing to stand by the Ethiopian emperor, Haile Selassie, when Italy attacked his country in 1935–1936. Then, when Franco's Fascist forces unleashed the Spanish Civil War against the Spanish Republican government, especially members of the French left-wing Popular Front government sympathised with the latter, but even they were unwilling to come directly to the aid of Madrid. Léon Blum, France's Socialist Prime Minister, found that there was not enough Socialist or even democratic solidarity in his country or Europe more widely to stand up to Fascism in Spain. Stalin as the leader of the Communist world chose to play the game in the narrow interest of his own state, enormous though the USSR was, rather than fully to back Communism worldwide. Nor could Blum and his predecessors and successors secure the most logical alliance with the democracies Britain and the US in time to put up a truly meaningful defence for Czechoslovakia and Poland. Worse still, at the Munich Conference of 1938 France and Britain helped Hitler to the strategically most defensible parts of Czechoslovakia, the mountain range along the border to Germany known as the Sudetenland. Infamously, British Prime Minister Neville Chamberlain in a radio address on 27 September 1938 pronounced it 'horrible, fantastic, incredible ... that we should be digging trenches and trying on gas-masks here because of a quarrel in a far away country between people of whom we know nothing.'[20] Nor did his French colleagues feel strong enough to stand up to Hitler alone.

In early 1939 Chamberlain, previously determined to do almost anything to ward off another world war if at all possible, at the cost of letting down other democracies, finally realised that, British (and French) security could not be separated from that of other parts of Europe and thus would not be fit for purpose (a lesson that seems to have been forgotten by 2016). Britain and France finally plucked up the courage to draw a red line and issue Poland with a guarantee against German aggression, but it was too late for them to co-ordinate a serious defence of France, not to mention Poland. No joint exercises, no joint planning, no joint logistics had been prepared. When in the summer of that year Britain and France made visibly half-hearted attempts to co-operate with the USSR to contain aggressive

Germany, Stalin preferred to conclude a secret pact with Hitler jointly to occupy Poland, each side securing one half. For the Soviet Union this had the advantage of creating a buffer zone against German aggression. In the autumn of 1939, Poland could not be saved by Britain and France from the double aggression from East and West. Then in 1940, as Germany conducted its *Blitzkrieg* against France, Britain presented her expeditionary force's ignominious withdrawal from Dunkirk across the Channel as a great logistic achievement, to raise morale at home.

Fortunately for Britain and France, the decision on what to do was made for the USSR and the USA by Hitler and the Japanese government who crazily went to war against the two emerging world superpowers. It was this hubris that would bring the Axis Powers down in the end, not the feeble resistance put up by France nor the blood, sweat and tears of the British who held off Nazi Germany alone for a while. The Second World War was decided by the sacrifice of perhaps 27 million Soviet lives, and by American industrial might.

The war gave Stalin an opportunity to increase the buffer zone around Russia, first in Poland and the Baltic states, then in the long and immensely costly counter-offensive, which advanced the Red Army to the Elbe. Bought after it had lost more human lives than any other European country—probably more than all other European losses combined—this Eastern European buffer zone Europe would make the USSR feel more secure throughout the Cold War. Other countries, too, saw that the war offered possibilities to move frontiers. Yugoslavia for one fought a long diplomatic battle to obtain Trieste, and while that did not happen, it managed to incorporate Fiume/Rijeka which had been under Habsburg rule for centuries, and mainly Croat-populated Zadar which had changed hands many times in its history. When order breaks down, the greedy will help themselves—and in an anarchic world in which states follow narrow national interests, there is no security.

9

RECREATING A UNIVERSAL ORDER II

THE UNITED NATIONS IN THE COLD WAR

After the Second World War, once again, theorists and practitioners drew lessons from the inter-war period and the Second World War, just as Wilson, Briand and Kellogg had done so from the run up to the First World War. In both cases, not all lessons were learned. After the Second World War, statesmen thus returned to some earlier solutions which had not worked previously and would once again have their problems after 1945. One was British Prime Minister Winston Churchill's attempt to conclude a 'realist' secret arrangement with Stalin behind the back of the more principled and idealistic US President Franklin D. Roosevelt, in October 1944: it harked back to the phase of Britain's non-intervention in the affairs of the other European great powers in the nineteenth century and was comparable to the agreement of Britain and the USA to keep out of each other's hemispheres. Churchill proposed to Stalin that Britain and the USSR would have different degrees or 'percentages' of influence on the states of post-war Europe and would tolerate each other's domination of the states closest to them. It was here, not at

Yalta, and not with US participation, that an attempt was made to divide Europe into spheres of influence. Britain and the USSR could not entirely realise their plan because the USA did not see the self-determination of the states liberated from German occupation as something that could be surrendered.[1] Yet worse was to come when the USA through the Marshall Plan of economic aid sought to reach into what Stalin saw as his sphere. Moscow prevailed upon its satellites to refuse any aid and tightened its control over them. Eventually, instead of creating spheres of influence open to trade but disregardful of the self-determination of smaller powers, Europe was transformed into two mutually opposed armed camps.

The British and the French, but more importantly the American political elites learnt that to keep Europe and the world at peace, powerful America that shared the democratic values of Britain and France must not return to isolationism but must play a major part. All sides continued to profess their commitment to the outlawing of war, and indeed it is expressly articulated in the Charter of the new league that was created, the United Nations. One lesson the drafters of this Charter had learnt was that this required an enforcement mechanism. But as representatives of great powers, they drafted themselves into a logical corner. The five great powers while agreeing on paper to outlaw war did not want to tie their own hands unduly, and they definitely did not want to relinquish their sovereign ability ultimately to do as they pleased. Nor did they want to be down-graded to equality with the many new states that now aspired to UN membership. The equality of all states introduced in the Treaties of Utrecht had always been a polite fiction. There was no equality in the Congress System, when great powers decided the fate of the smaller nations. A two-tier system distinguishing the great powers from the lesser powers was embedded in the League of Nations with its Council-members and its Assembly for the others. The UN retained this oligarchy of great powers when setting up its Security Council, giving the five great powers permanent seats (the USA, Britain, France, the USSR and China, with the People's Republic replacing the Taiwanese Republic of China in 1971). These permanent Five ('P5'), a new Pentarchy, secured a veto power to protect their own national interests. The drafters of the UN Charter tried to give the Security Council greater executive power and instruments, but a planned Military Committee and a projected UN Army were never created: the great powers were too distrustful of building up a true international organisation that might be used against them.

But just as the Concert among the European great powers had broken down every time one of them saw its interests threatened, the UN Security Council would in large measure be paralysed by the ideological clash between the three Western powers and the two Communist powers in the Cold War of 1946–1990. Only once, at the outbreak of the Korean War in 1950, did the Security Council take a big decision to use force collectively, when the Soviet representative had miscalculated that his absence from the Council would prevent decision-making. This paralysis of the Security Council left the post-Second World War system of Europe uncertain: the UN alone was clearly not capable of securing peace in Europe.[2] Also, given the divergence of aims that emerged so very quickly after the defeat of the Axis Powers, no peace congress could be agreed on this time. Arguably, it was only the Conference on Security and Cooperation in Europe which took place in 1973–1975 that served as the peace congress to end the Second World War, leading to the Helsinki Final Act of 1975 that set out new rules of interstate conduct, and the creation of the Organisation for Security and Cooperation in Europe (OSCE).

Western Defence Co-operation: WU, WEU and NATO

If the UN was not robust enough to secure peaceful inter-polity relations, what else could be done? It dawned on more and more

intellectuals that finally, after a thousand years of French antagonism to the *Reich*, whether this was the Holy Roman Empire
(with or without Habsburgs in the lead), the Prussian-led German
Empire (with the Hohenzollerns in the lead) or Hitler's Third
Reich, this antagonism had to be replaced by something else. The
war was not yet at an end when a congress of representatives of
Resistance movements meeting in Switzerland in July 1944 proposed to set up a European Union of Federalists, to integrate the
German people in a larger European framework without allowing
it to become once again a danger for other peoples.[3]

Two years later, Winston Churchill told an audience at the
University of Zurich that '*We* [my emphasis] must build a kind of
United States of Europe'.[4] He added words of great wisdom when
he prescribed the equivalent of the clause of Oblivion which had
characterised European peace treaties before 1919:

> There must be what [nineteenth century Liberal interventionist
> Prime Minister] Gladstone many years ago called a 'blessed act of
> oblivion'. We must all turn our backs upon the horrors of the past
> and look to the future. We cannot afford to drag forward across the
> years to come hatreds and revenges which have sprung from the
> injuries of the past. If Europe is to be saved from infinite misery, and
> indeed from final doom, there must be this act of faith in the
> European family, this act of oblivion against all crimes and follies of
> the past.

On that basis, one could build this united Europe. Like Briand
sixteen years earlier, he thought that:

> The first step in the re-creation of the European family must be a
> partnership between France and Germany. ... There can be no revival
> of Europe without a spiritually great France and a spiritually great
> Germany. The structure of the United States of Europe will be such
> as to make the material strength of a single state less important.
> Small nations will count as much as large ones and gain their honour
> by a contribution to the common cause. The ancient states and prin-

cipalities of Germany, freely joined for mutual convenience in a federal system, might take their individual places among the United States of Europe.[5]

Yet after the establishment of peace in 1945 and the creation of the UN, the very first steps towards European integration were taken not by France and Germany, but by France and Britain. In March 1947, as a symbolic expurgation of the *acte manqué*, the Franco-British alliance that had been so sorely lacking in the Inter-War Period, France and Britain concluded a Treaty in Dunkirk. This committed them to mutual defence in case of a resurgent German threat, and unlike the alliances prior to the First World War, it was not limited in time.[6]

Meanwhile, another 'Concert' of great powers, the victors of the Second World War in Europe (among which, at British insistence, France was generously counted), was supposed to govern the defeated Germany. The latter was once again amputated of her Austrian part and other Eastern territories that were given to Poland and Russia respectively, while Poland lost some of its Eastern territories to Ukraine and Byelorussia. Germany and Austria were both put under a four-power regime of the victors as occupying powers, and the challenge for the latter was to concert their policies. By the end of 1947, it was blatant that this endeavour was failing: while the Western occupation powers were trying to build up their zones economically to stave off insurgencies, a Nazi revival or the spread of Communism, the devastated USSR was removing from its zone whatever it could, and the West had to help feed the Soviet-occupied part of Germany.[7] Communism once more seemed an internal threat to European countries, especially Greece, Italy, and France herself.

Against this background, we see a significant turning point in English and British history. In an unprecedented fashion, the British government in Whitehall decided not only to intervene in a European balance of power, but to commit itself to the construction of a European co-operative inter-state system under British leadership, with full British participation. British Foreign Secretary Ernest Bevin sought to extend the Franco-British alliance to include the Benelux countries, initially through unilateral guarantees, on the model of the 1939 guarantee to Poland. It turned out that the Benelux countries were very keen to join Britain and France in their endeavours, but as equal treaty partners with equal commitments.[8] Thus in a first step towards European integration, at the end of December 1947, Bevin proposed to the French Foreign Minister Georges Bidault the creation of 'some sort of federation [*sic!*] in Western Europe', in order 'to save Western civilisation', no less.[9] In January 1948 he told the British Cabinet that in his view, Britain could 'no longer stand outside Europe.' He saw Britain linked to Europe by 'common ideals for which the Western Powers have twice in one generation shed their blood.'[10] At the same time he told the House of Commons that guiding principles of his government's policies towards Europe were first, 'that no one nation should dominate Europe.' And secondly, 'that the old-fashioned conception of the balance of power as an aim should be discarded if possible.'[11]

The British Prime Minister, Clement Attlee, shared this view and instructed Bevin to seek French support for the creation of a 'European Affairs Committee' with the task of preparing the way for 'political and economic integration of Western Europe, under four heads: (i) political; (ii) defence and security; (iii) publicity and propaganda; and (iv) economic'.[12] In March 1948 Bevin obtained his Cabinet colleagues' approval for the negotiation of 'multilateral economic, cultural and defensive pacts between the United Kingdom, France and the Benelux countries, which would be left open for accession by other European democracies.'[13] In the same month, Britain, France, and the Benelux Countries signed the Brussels Treaty providing for co-operation in cultural, social, economic, and political affairs.

The 'Western Union' thereby created was beyond anything that had been envisaged by the theorists of the eighteenth century, and with its plans for institutionalised social and economic co-operation it went further still even than the Holy Roman Empire. Moreover, it contained an unconditional, cast-iron mutual defence clause that committed all signatories in case of an attack against one of them, 'in accordance with the provisions of Article 51 of the Charter of the United Nations' which allowed for self-defence against aggression, 'to afford the Party so attacked *all the military and other aid and assistance in their power.*'[my Italics][14] Arguably, the signatories thus limited their sovereignty: they signed away the right to do nothing or little if one of them was attacked, and committed themselves to using all means they had if the defence of a treaty partner required it.

Britain and France did not stop here, however. They sought an American guarantee for this Western Union, in the form of a similar treaty with the USA and anybody else who cared to make such a commitment. This took the form of the North Atlantic or Washington Treaty of April 1949, which created the North Atlantic Treaty Organisation (NATO). As East-West relations deteriorated even further, there were more candidates to join such a larger defence pact, such as Canada and in Europe, Denmark, Norway, Portugal, and Italy, shorn of her Fascism. Other countries followed: Greece and Turkey, and in 1955 even the re-democratised West Germany. The project received American support (on condition that America's sovereignty remain untouched, which is why the NATO Article 5 is less binding than that of the Brussels Treaty).[15] The reason for this was not merely the growing perception of a Soviet threat, and of a system of bilateral Soviet military pacts with satellites that vastly increased the USSR's already considerable military manpower that had not been demobilised after the Second World War.[16] It was also a way, the American leadership realised, to forestall any re-emergence of a threat from Germany that had twice dragged America into a European war against her will. It was recognised in Washington that German aggressiveness did not exist in a vacuum, but that it had a background of nationalist and imperial rivalries in Europe that reached back a long time. The USA decided not just to commit itself to preserving peace in Europe, but also to support, from the start, European integration with its express aim of overcoming nationalist rivalry. Despite decades of American complaints in NATO that European allies were not paying enough for their defence, Washington's elites knew that it was cheaper for America to pay the lion's share for the security of Europe and to persuade the Europeans to co-operate closely, rather than to allow them to revert to their traditional competition and balance-of-power games.

West European security depended on a fundamental change of mentality on the part of Europeans: overcoming their past rivalry, their nationalism, and the ideal of the sovereign state that can do or stand aside as it pleases, depending on its narrow national interest. They had to put in its place a new set of ideals around the settlement of conflicts of interest by negotiation, around co-operation and mutual aid in the belief, once put forward by Guibert, that this would be to their mutual benefit. It meant putting into practice and institutionalising the idea formulated in the seventeenth and eighteenth centuries that the 'tranquillity' of Europe should be placed above narrow national interests.

Six days after the North Atlantic Treaty was signed, a Council of Europe was set up, at this point still with Britain in the lead: the founding charter was signed in London, by the United Kingdom and the other Western Union members, plus Italy, Ireland, Sweden, Norway, Denmark, soon to be joined by Greece and Turkey (it has since grown to forty-seven member states). Its aim was and is to watch over the safeguarding of human rights in Europe, and the upholding of law, so as to ensure states are *états de droit*, or *Rechtsstaaten*, something Bluntschli would have greatly approved of. The European Convention of Human Rights and the European Court of Human Rights are related products.

Once the American commitment to Western Europe's security had been achieved, however, British enthusiasm for further European integration flagged, while that of other European powers increased. It has even been argued that the Western Union was 'a sprat to catch a mackerel'—the vital treaty with the USA.[17] Britain had not been in the loop when the French came up with further proposals for European integration. On 19 October 1950 Ernest Bevin, who was aware that the French government aimed to set up a supra-'national'[18] (that is, of a level of government above the member states) organisation with this initiative, submitted to his Cabinet Colleagues a memorandum drawing attention to two diverging views of the future of the Council of Europe. He claimed that 'To the majority of the Governments which set it up the Council of Europe was not an instrument for the immediate political unification of Europe, but part of the general material and moral build up of which other parts are represented by ... the Brussels Treaty and the North Atlantic [Treaty] ...' He thought that the Council's Consultative Assembly had now been hijacked by 'enthusiasts for European federation'. Britain by contrast should avoid 'commitments in Europe which would affect our position as the leading member of the Commonwealth, our special relationship with the United States, and our responsibilities as the centre of the Sterling Area...'[19] Thus Britain left the path towards European economic, political and social integration that the Attlee-Bevin Government had first identified in early 1948: Attlee and Bevin had never contemplated more than inter-governmental co-operation, not taking European integration onto a supra-national level.[20]

Britain did, however, continue to play a crucial part in trans-atlantic security co-operation. Arguably, Britain 'saved' NATO when, in the 1960s, it went through the greatest crisis since its foundation. The American commitment to the defence of Europe, assumed by all sides to be a promise to defend Europe with nuclear weapons if necessary, had been somewhat in doubt ever since Soviet missiles could reach American soil and threaten a terrible retaliation against American nuclear use. In 1965, the Franco-American political scientist Stanley Hoffman conceded:

> [W]e have reached the stage when Europeans and Americans both wonder whether the threat of a United States first strike against the Soviet Union, in the case of a Soviet conventional attack in Europe and in the absence of a conventional NATO army large enough to be a deterrent force all by itself, has not ceased to be plausible.[21]

France acquired her own nuclear weapons, and other European powers might well have followed suit, leading to extensive nuclear proliferation. Britain saved the day by insisting that, as a European power, so much closer than the United States to any attack by the Warsaw Pact, with British forces and British nuclear weapons deployed in West Germany, Britain could be trusted to take action even if America hesitated. Britain would demonstrate this commitment—explained through its Western (European) Union engagement—in NATO exercises. Britain also succeeded in persuading its NATO allies to set up the Nuclear Planning Group as a consultation mechanism. Instead of playing the old part of balancer that would throw its weight in with one side or another, Britain here and indeed throughout the Cold War assumed the role of the hinge keeping the two wings of NATO on either side of the Atlantic together, or that of the lynchpin connecting the three circles that overlapped only with Britain: Europe, the 'special relationship' of Britain with the USA, and the Commonwealth.[22]

The fruits of the British initiatives of 1946 to 1948 to bring about purely European cooperation, however, are now lost. The Western Union, renamed Western European Union (WEU) in

1954, was declared defunct in 2011 as several other parts of the EU or NATO had taken over its function. The crucial mutual defence commitment that limited the sovereignty of the WEU's member states in the interest of enhancing collective security has been absorbed into the Lisbon Treaty of the European Union as Article 42.7, which reads: 'If a Member state is the victim of armed aggression on its territory, the other Member states shall have towards it an obligation of aid and assistance by all the means in their power, in accordance with Article 51 of the United Nations Charter. ...' With the UK's withdrawal from the EU, Britain is regaining her full sovereignty, and of course simultaneously losing her share in this mutual security guarantee. Equally, Britain's European partners are losing this guarantee of their security from one of Europe's only two nuclear powers which was the more consistent of the two in honouring her WEU commitments. The implications of this are worth pondering.

In areas other than defence it was a later French initiative which would begin European integration, gradually constructing the EU as we now know it, and not the British initiatives of 1946–1948.

10

EUROPEAN INTEGRATION

BETWEEN CONFEDERATION AND FEDERATION

From 1945, there were three main options for European integration. They shared the premise that the future Europe had to be different from the Europe of nationalisms, but they diverged on which path to choose. The first model was confederative; that is, inter-governmental, meaning that no organisation would stand above that of the governments of member states. This is how a leading Italian politician, Altiero Spinelli, described it retrospectively:

> For some statesmen whose fundamental political experience had been that of the sovereign nation-state, but who had become persuaded by the course of events [leading to and including the Second World War] that there was an inherent danger in a pure and simple return to national [thinking], the unification of Europe should be, fundamentally, a confederation, a league of states of which each would preserve its sovereignty. They would all in certain areas commit themselves permanently to practice the same policy, defined and adopted in their reunions bringing together the representatives of different governments. Churchill and de Gaulle are the most presti-

gious heroes of this vision, but it is widespread, ... because its realisation requires a minimum of effort of imagination and creation...[1]

The second European model was to create institutions *de facto* moving towards a European super-state. The European Coal and Steel Community was the first and most important step in this regard. It was proposed by the former businessman Jean Monnet who during the two World Wars had worked in the allied administration of essential war materials in the pursuit of victory over the Central powers. Monnet, in close co-operation with Robert Schuman, the French Foreign Minister, hoped that through this *de facto* integration of these key European industries, one day a European superstructure, that is, a supra-national super-state would emerge.

The third model is federalist model. As we know, it has its antecedents also in the ideas of Dubois, Podiebrad, Sully, Saint-Pierre and Kant, and indeed to Aristide Briand's and Coudenhove-Kalergi's initiatives of the Inter-War period. Again in Spinelli's words:

> The federalist model proposes to maintain and respect the sovereignty of the nation-states in all areas that have a [purely] national significance [='subsidiarity'], and to transfer to a European government democratically controlled by a European parliament and acting in conformity to European legislation the areas of foreign policy, defence, economy and the protection of civic rights.[2]

In many respects this model is similar to the post-1495 Holy Roman Empire, minus the person of the emperor. Supporters of this federalist approach usually either hail from countries that were once members of the Holy Roman Empire (Germany, the Benelux Countries, Italy) or have considerable historical knowledge thereof.

The first initiative that was to enjoy lasting success in European integration came in 1950 from a few leading figures. Apart from Monnet, they included Robert Schuman, the Belgian politician Paul-Henri Spaak, the Dutch banker and later politician Johan Willem Beyen and the Italian Prime Minister Alcide De Gasperi. These men shared a vision: to replace old antagonisms by a form of co-operation which would make it structurally impossible for countries to go to war with each other again. It was thus of the 'functional' sort. They started this process of European integration in 1950 by merging their countries' coal and steel industries. The aim was always mainly political, as explained in the plan largely thought up by Monnet put forward officially on 9 May 1950 by Schuman:

> The contribution which an organised and living Europe can bring to civilisation is indispensable to the maintenance of peaceful relations. Having for over 20 years been the champion of a united Europe [reference to the Briand proposal of 1930], France has always had the aim of serving peace. [Such a united] Europe was not created, and we had [the Second World] war instead.

> Europe will not be made all at once, nor on the basis of an overall construction. It will be built through concrete achievements, first creating a *de facto* solidarity.

Echoing Briand and Churchill, Schuman continued:

> The coming together of the nations of Europe requires the elimination of the centuries-old opposition of France and Germany. Any action to be taken must first of all concern France and Germany. With this aim, the French Government proposes that action be taken immediately in one limited but decisive point. It proposes that Franco-German production of coal and steel as a whole be placed under a common High Authority, within the framework of an organisation open to the participation of other countries of Europe.[3]

The US government enthusiastically supported this project, persuaded by Jean Monnet with his extraordinary business connections to invest money in the industries affected as an incentive to realise the Schuman Plan. The pacification of Europe through this overcoming of the 'centuries-old opposition of France and Germany' seemed well worth it to the USA.

It turned out that not only France and West Germany, but also the Benelux countries and Italy, all descendants of Charlemagne's Empire—were immediately eager to join the European Coal and Steel Community (ECSE) that was the outcome of the Schuman Plan. Meanwhile the United Kingdom stayed well clear of it: 'The Durham miners won't wear it', as Labour politician Herbert Morrison argued. The ECSE was given a High Authority for its administration, a Council of Ministers, and a parliament, originally merely a consultative assembly of 78 appointed parliamentarians drawn from the national parliaments of member states, without legislative powers.[4] (Over time this would grow into the European Parliament which today is the parliament of the European Union, is elected directly by the populations of the member states and has legislative powers.) In 1952, a common European Court of Justice was set up by the member states of the ECSE which is now the Court of Justice of the EU.

The next proposal, also initiated by the French government, was the creation of a European Army. It foundered on a majority in France's National Assembly that refused to let go of France's armed forces as a tool of her sovereignty. France's old dilemma when confronted with European integration was first articulated here: in order to control any future (West) German army, France was happy to have that integrated into a European Army or the integrated military structure of NATO. Given ideas of the equality of states that had now been around since Utrecht, however, this would lead to the demand that France should do the same (at least, at the time, with those of France's armed forces stationed in Europe as opposed to those stationed overseas in the still extensive French Empire). And this would mean France giving up part of her precious sovereignty in that most sensitive area, defence—which French monarchs had of course fought to monopolise since the Middle Ages. And this France would no more do with regard to her army in 1954 than later with regard to her nuclear weapons.

Integration was easier in the economic sphere, and that is where Robert Schuman, Jean Monnet, Paul-Henri Spaak and their like-minded colleagues turned their energies. One incentive was that co-operation might allow the six European countries who pursued these initial negotiations (France, the Benelux, Italy and West Germany) to pool their resources so as better to exploit atomic research for civilian energy purposes, against the background of American reluctance to share research findings in this field. A set of treaties concluded in Rome in 1957 provided great steps forward, creating the European Economic Community (EEC) and EURATOM. The EEC laid down comprehensive plans to move in a number of steps towards the creation of a tariff-free customs union with common external tariffs, and a common domestic market, with a free circulation of goods, people, capital and later also services. A European Social Fund was created to address problems of social inequality, and a European Bank for Investment to help finance the overall enterprise. The EEC was given a Council of Ministers representing the member-states, which initially had to vote unanimously to pass resolutions (with increasing membership this would later be changed). To complement the Council, an assembly composed of members of the national parliaments of member-states was constituted along the lines of the ECSC common Assembly. One Commission was initially set up to administer the EEC and EURATOM, later merged into what is now the European Commission. The organisations thus created officially came into being on 1 January 1958.

The United Kingdom deliberately excluded itself from these further steps towards European integration. Even then, there were some who felt uneasy about this. As the Europhile

Conservative Chancellor of the Exchequer Harold Macmillan put it even in February 1956, 'I do not like the prospect of a world divided into the Russian sphere, the American sphere and a united Europe of which we are not a member.'[5] He sensed that Britain's own sphere, the Commonwealth, was shrivelling away in importance under the fierce winds of change and colonial emancipation. Britain had originally been invited to the negotiations leading to the creation of the European Communities (as the EEC, EURATOM, and the Coal and Steel Community would jointly be referred to). It was particularly the tendency towards potential further supra-state integration of the project which worried the successive Conservative governments of Britain, and the conviction that economic integration that went beyond a free trade zone but also created common external customs and trading rules was not in the interest of what was left of the British Empire. London did not want to downgrade its Commonwealth partners to be afforded worse conditions of trade than its European partners. So Whitehall proposed a European Free Trade Area (EFTA) which would have allowed the United Kingdom to export to and import freely from both the European continent and the Commonwealth.

This was not to the liking of the French government as it (quite intentionally) undermined the linkage France sought to maintain between further European political integration and free trade within the European Community. In 1958, when Charles de Gaulle became President of the French Republic and introduced a new constitution, he put a stop to the idea of extending a free trade zone to all of Europe, including both members and non-members of the European Economic Community (EEC). Britain henceforth pursued EFTA project with countries outside the EEC—Austria, Denmark, Norway, Portugal, Sweden, Switzerland—and eventually signed an EFTA agreement with them in 1960 (with the later association of Finland).

EUROPEAN INTEGRATION

Soon the impression arose in London, however, that membership of the EEC and the other parts of the European Communities was the best solution for Britain's needs, as decolonisation and the waning of the Empire was fundamentally changing Britain's overseas' commitments. Belatedly, London tried to jump on the bandwagon of European integration: in 1961, when Harold Macmillan was Prime Minister, and again in 1967, Britain made bids for European Communities membership. Both bids were vetoed by de Gaulle, not least because France as a nuclear power did not want Britain as another cockerel in the European hen-house, as wits quipped at the time. The reasons given by him were each time the very bonds that Bevin had referred to—Britain's ties with Commonwealth (which still exist today, albeit weakened by the passing of generations) and her overseas' possessions (now almost entirely gone), and Britain's very special dependency on the USA which exists until this day. The 'special relationship' which even times of strained relations consists of sharing of special intelligence and British procurement of nuclear missiles from the USA is nevertheless at the mercy of successive US Presidents' benevolence towards Britain. Another factor keeping Britain apart from Europe was the Sterling Area, an assortment of countries that had pegged their currency to the British Pound Sterling which underwent repeated devaluation in the 1960s. De Gaulle's final veto of British membership in the European Communities came shortly after a further devaluation of the pound in November 1967 which led to the final decline of Sterling Area membership until it had become largely insignificant in by the early 1970s. What was thus left when Britons decided in 2016 to leave the EU of those arguments against full British membership of its predecessor-institutions in the late 1950s and early 1960s is only the 'special relationship', and the largely symbolic and ageing family links with Commonwealth countries.

Defence Integration or a Europe of the Fatherlands?

The ideas around in the 1950s included much more radical proposals for European integration than anything that was accomplished in the following decades, up to and including that of a Monnet-inspired super-state with full state powers. The Western Union, enlarged in 1954 to include also Italy and West Germany, amounted to a partial limitation of sovereignty (in the unconditional commitment to mutual defence) made by the member states in return for greater collective security. This is reminiscent of the situation in the Holy Roman Empire from 1495, where all member entities were banned from going to war against each other, but committed to defend the Empire if it was attacked.

Within Western Europe, and even among the members of the reformed WEU of 1954, there were states with a variety of different statuses. There was the Federal Republic of (West) Germany, which until this day has American, British and French forces on its soil. There were Britain and France, the former from the mid-1950s, the latter from the mid-1960s, nuclear powers. Several countries, among them Britain and France, still had colonial empires overseas, although their colonies would progressively become independent in the 1940s-1970s. Outside the WEU, a number of states were neutral, either by choice like Sweden or Switzerland, or by political necessity like Finland and Austria.

Both France and Britain had experienced extreme dependence on the United States in each of the world wars. From this they had drawn diametrically opposite conclusions: Britain, which escaped German occupation in both conflicts, concluded that she could depend on the USA to come and save her from continental aggression, and France, for the occupation of which American aid came too late both times, that she could ultimately not rely on the US for her safety.[6] Yet both governments begged the USA to underwrite the Western Union's collective defence commitment with NATO, creating something of an 'Empire' by invitation.[7] Meanwhile both wanted their own atom bomb, with varying degrees of public acknowledgement that this implied a doubt about the dependability of an American nuclear umbrella.

The United Kingdom in particular was quite desperate to retain the close working relationship with the USA which it had enjoyed in the Second World War. This was cut off initially by the McMahon Act of 1946 passed by a US Congress which seemed to want to follow its precursor of 1919 in its retreat into isolationism. British-American military co-operation needed the North Atlantic Treaty as a legal base to restart again properly. Eventually this would also include a resumption of co-operation in the nuclear field, which had also been interrupted, even though British scientists (along with several other European physicists) had been directly involved in the Manhattan Project that produced the first atom bomb.

Washington, keen to prevent nuclear proliferation, refused to give support to the nuclear research projects even of its close allies in Europe until these forced a game change by producing their own nuclear weapons. From this point onwards, successive American administrations were prepared to give some support not least in order to gain a good insight into if not control over these allied nuclear programmes. Britain was the first of the two European countries to engage in this balancing act with the USA, between either becoming fully dependent on a US President's approval of the British use of her own nuclear forces, or facing procurement bills which Britain as a second-tier power did not want to foot. Britain emerged each time with a deal with the Americans which made her wholly dependent on the latter for the procurement of sea-launched missiles with strategic range (*Polaris*, *Trident*, and a future successor missile), and partly dependent on American satellite-produced meteorological and geodesic data for a very precise strike with such a missile on a moving target, but able to carry out a strike against a known fixed target without US approval.

This fine distinction and the nature of the first British-American deal of this sort, negotiated at Nassau in the Bahamas in December 1962, was not understood by de Gaulle who was also invited to accede to this scheme. Assuming that the US wanted to obtain a veto over all British and French nuclear use (they did indeed) and that no compromise could be found (there he was wrong), he not only refused to negotiate. He also decided that Britain—at the time an applicant to join the European Communities—had sold her freedom 'for a dish of Polaris', and was nothing but an American stooge, worse still, a Trojan Horse which America was trying to insert into the European Communities. As Paul-Henri Spaak remembered correctly, British Prime Minister Harold 'Macmillan's crime was to have reached agreement with the President of the United States on Britain's nuclear weaponry. ... In General de Gaulle's eyes the cooperation with the Americans was tantamount to treason against Europe's interests and justified his refusal to allow Britain into the common market.'[8] Admittedly, Britain accepted a greater degree of dependence on the USA in the nuclear weapons and intelligence fields (not just with regard to satellite, but all other areas of intelligence) than she ever had on any European power. Either way, the only nuclear power with which France could have worked to develop nuclear weapons jointly had chosen co-operation with the US, not with France, and this pattern would repeat itself again and again in the following decades.[9]

De Gaulle's hostility to dependency on the USA is explained not only by France's experience of US help coming late in both world wars. It is also explained by the shock which both Britain and France experienced in their expedition to reclaim the Suez Canal from Egypt in 1956. The US brought this expedition to a premature end by putting financial pressure on sterling until London ceded to US demands to terminate the operation which was close to succeeding. France felt confirmed in the conclusion that she could rely only upon herself, and that meant in modern terms, becoming a nuclear power, independent of any ally.[10]

Not least for this reason, de Gaulle on his return to power as French President in 1958 also put a stop to European defence integration. He was also much more the child of the nineteenth century with the ideal of a Europe of nation-states than his contemporaries Monnet, Schuman, Pleven etc. Nevertheless, he was a tactician, occasionally trying out new schemes—usually grand sounding ones with little substance agreed in advance—only then to discard them when the reactions were not to his liking. On 31 May 1960, de Gaulle announced that the wanted to see the Europe of the Six increase their co-operation at a state level, 'awaiting that the future might bring an impressive confederation.'[11] Having secured West German Chancellor Konrad Adenauer's support for this very vague scheme that was lacking any time-line, de Gaulle announced in September 1960 that he wanted more inter-governmental, not supra-national co-operation among the member states of the European Communities. At a press conference in May 1962, he explained this preference for a largely voluntary inter-state co-operation over further integration:

> People counter this by saying: 'Why not merge the six states together into a single supranational entity? That would be very simple and practical.' But such an entity is impossible to achieve in the absence of Europe today of a federator who has the necessary power, reputation and ability. Thus one has to fall back on a sort of hybrid arrangement under which the six states agree to submit to the decisions of a qualified majority. ... although there are already six national Parliaments as well as the European Parliament and, in addition, the Consultative Assembly of the Council of Europe ...it would be necessary to elect, over and above this yet a further Parliament, described as European, which would lay down the law to the six states. ... Can we imagine France, Germany, Italy, the

Netherlands, Belgium, Luxemburg being prepared on a matter of importance to them in the national or international sphere, to do something that appeared wrong to them, merely because others had ordered them to do so? Would the peoples of France, of Germany, of Italy, of the Netherlands, of Belgium, or of Luxembourg ever dream of submitting to laws passed by foreign parliamentarians if such laws ran counter to their deepest convictions? Clearly not. It is impossible nowadays for a foreign majority to impose their will on reluctant nations.

De Gaulle thus typically furnished the narrative we have been hearing from British Brexit-supporters in recent times. In his speech, he added that he saw two possible developments: one that no policies could be made in such an integrated Europe, and the other, that an external, non-European 'federator' would come along and make the Europeans follow in his wake (he was thinking of the USA whose President, John F. Kennedy, had in January 1962 proposed a commercial association of the European Communities and his own country).[12] Crucially, with a balance-of-power reflex unmitigated by common values, de Gaulle and a strong faction of the French élite saw America as a challenge to Europe but above all to the independence of the European states (especially France), almost as great as that of Soviet-led communism. As one Gaullist intellectual, Jean-Jacques Servan-Schreiber would later put it, the fact that the US was about fifteen years ahead of Europe in terms of development meant that it was setting the targets and defining the direction of research and technological evolution, even the evolution of society, and at the same time forcing other powers to imitate it in order to catch up. This stifled the potential originality of Europe (and Japan and other cultures) that could have led to the exploration of other paths, technologies and social models.[13]

It is interesting to note in the 1962 speech quoted above how strongly imbued with nineteenth-century national thinking de

Gaulle was. One might just as easily argue that democracy would never work: why should people ever accept the rule of a party they had not voted for? And then there was a deliberate lack of imagination—why could the European Parliament not be turned into the directly elected parliament of the European Communities (as it is now, of the EU)? What de Gaulle actually wanted was to transform Europe into France's force-multiplier, with France the lead nation of a 'Europe of the fatherlands', viz. sovereign states. French rulers from Clovis to Napoleon would have approved.

Consequently, de Gaulle played a complex game with the Federal Republic of Germany in these years. Most of what he promised Konrad Adenauer's government in Bonn in this special relationship was insubstantial or hollow. Yet the grand gestures—the signing of a bilateral Elysée Treaty in 1963 proclaiming friendship and reconciliation, the joint mass in the cathedral of Reims which had served the coronation of French kings and which had been half-destroyed by the Germans especially in the First World War, the ensuing youth exchanges and town twinnings—actually worked wonders to uproot the ghost of an eternal Franco-German enmity from the collective psyche on both sides of the Rhine.

By contrast, de Gaulle himself never had any intention of seriously pursuing the creation of a European super-state, which was how the West Germans wanted to interpret the 'progress on the way to a united Europe' promised in the Preamble of the Elysée Treaty.[14] Also, hopes that previous French governments had raised in Adenauer's government that EURATOM would eventually lead to the development of a common European nuclear force (deemed more reassuring in Bonn and Rome than the nuclear protection of a faraway alliance partner, the USA) were gradually stifled as it became clear that de Gaulle was skilfully making vague promises while always putting off the decisive decision to turn promises into concrete action.[15]

Meanwhile de Gaulle's minister Fouchet presented a plan named after him to the European Communities partners in October 1961 and again, after joint revision, in early 1962. It aimed to establish a co-ordinated foreign policy among the members of the European Communities. The plan disappointed those more committed to further integration; it was rejected both times. De Gaulle subsequently blocked progress in European construction by his 'empty chair' policy of the mid-1960s, and seriously rocked the North Atlantic Alliance by proclaiming that France would withdraw from NATO's integrated military structure.

Only in the mid-1970s, under de Gaulle's second successor as French President, Valéry Giscard d'Estaing, did European integration take off again. By now the United Kingdom, Ireland and Denmark had been admitted to the European Communities. For Britain it was only on her third application, after her withdrawal from former defence commitments East of Suez, having reoriented her military almost entirely towards the defence of NATO Europe. The Copernican revolution in British thinking about power on the European Continent, begun under Clement Attlee and Ernest Bevin, was complete: Britain would no longer counterbalance a security system that dominated the Continent, but be an integral, decision-making part of it.

The European Community's decision-making structures were in need of reform; the result was the creation of the European Council, basically a permanent, institutionalised 'congress' of European heads of state and government that takes place about once every three months, to consult on major common issues and take decisions by consensus (that is, not by voting, but by talking matters through until no member still has objections to a commonly agreed text.). We see here a realisation of a variant of the proposals of Dubois, Podiebrad and all the others who over centuries had pushed for such a body to settle issues of common concern peacefully. Giscard also pushed for steps in the direction of a common currency, which would include a freezing of the exchange rates to create a fictitious currency of reference, the Écu (from European Currency Union). This would lead in 1999–2002 to the adoption by some states of a common currency, the Euro, under a European Central Bank. And in close co-operation with the West German Chancellor Helmut Schmidt, Giscard persuaded the member states of the European Communities to accept reforms of the European Parliament resulting in the direct election of its members by citizens of member states.

The Cold War was not over when in 1986 a 'Single European Act' was signed, preparing further integration in the following decade.[16] Britain was only interested in its economic side, and as usual, sceptical about all other aspects. Prime Minister Margaret Thatcher's Bruges Speech of 20 September 1988 explained why this was a departure from the inter-governmental (or confederal) model supported by Britain in her Gaullist approach:

> [W]illing and active cooperation between independent sovereign states is the best way to build a successful European Community. To try to suppress nationhood and concentrate power at the centre of a European conglomerate would be highly damaging and would jeopardise the objectives we seek to achieve. Europe will be stronger precisely because it has France as France, Spain as Spain, Britain as Britain, each with its own customs, traditions and identity. It would be folly to try to fit them into some sort of identikit European personality.[17]

Thatcher wilfully misrepresented the European Community. It did and does make considerable allowances for national peculiarities and preferences, through variable membership of its respective institutions and arrangements. From its accession, the United Kingdom was allowed to continue driving on the left, to keep its pint measures for the sale of beer and milk, its miles and yards, and many other idiosyncrasies. What irritated Thatcher along with other Gaullist believers in strong, central government was among other things the EC's financial support for needy regions within states, and the co-operation of regions across 'national' boundaries, such as the Italian Alto Adige (South Tyrol) with Austria's Tyrol, just one of many cases where such injections of aid took the sting out of separatist movements.

In the negotiations here as in the following decades, Britain, along with the Gaullist element in France, consistently blocked advance towards the second or third models of European integration, while Germany and usually Italy and often the Benelux Countries would push for them. The beneficial outcome of this British obstreperousness was probably that the Brussels institutions continued to be forced to accommodate plural configurations and needs, in the 1990s and after adapting evermore to local needs and preferences, allowing for à-la-carte membership of the Schengen area and the Euro, rather than insisting that one size fits all.

11

FROM THE RENEWED UN CONCERT
TO THE NEW COLD WAR

The Cold War, like the Peloponnesian War, many wars of modern history and the two world wars had pitted two alliances against each other. In the Cold War, it was NATO vs the Warsaw Treaty Organisation, the latter essentially a fusion of a series of earlier bilateral treaties between the USSR and its satellite states. There was one huge difference between the Cold War and these former clashes of alliances: the Cold War did not turn into a Third World War, probably mainly due to mutual nuclear deterrence.[1] Nuclear weapons brought their own dangers—the possibilities of accidents and miscalculations of the opponent's readiness to react. But luck was on the side of humanity. It was Soviet President Gorbachev's and US President Reagan's mutual recognition that they had entered into dangerous spiral or rearmament which allowed them to break out of this vicious circle with a nuclear arms control treaty in 1987. But Gorbachev's liberalising regime could not keep the floodgates open only a little—the dam burst under popular pressure for political liberalisation, freedom of movement and consumer goods. Both the Warsaw Treaty

Organisation and the USSR collapsed in 1990–1991 respectively under the popular pressure for change in the East.

The end of the Cold War was of course marked by the reunification of East and West Germany. As previously in 1919 and 1945, Austria was excluded in this new German state (which thus is again not an ethnic 'nation-state' in the sense of containing all German-speakers). As in 1945, Austrians showed no interest in being included. Either way, this new German state with 80 million inhabitants had a larger population than the two now second-largest states France and Britain with about 60 million each. This conjured up nightmares of a resurgent and dominant Germany.

Confirming the centrality of Franco-German relations in European integration, it was the—at times quite wrong-footed—interplay between French President François Mitterrand and German Chancellor Helmut Kohl which saw the solution to these fears in greater European integration. If anything, the fall of the Wall made the case for an entity above the level of the state watching over the interests of the European populations more urgent. While the ethnic patchwork of the nineteenth century has been fundamentally changed by genocide and ethnic cleansing in the first half of the twentieth century, traces of it persist still in many areas of Europe. A new mix of populations has resulted from immigration from Africa and Asia, and from labour movements within Europe. European integration had yet to put the question of who can live, work, own property and speak which language in Northern Ireland, Alsace, Lorraine, Belgium, the Tyrol, the Basque areas of France and Spain *ad acta*. Old border issues in Eastern Europe now also came onto the European agenda: Hungarian-speaking minorities in Romania or parts of the Balkans, or the fate of Muslim minorities with European roots dating back to the sixteenth century or earlier, or recently arrived in the context of labour recruitment. Meanwhile, the countries emerging from the Soviet sphere had an enormous backlog in modernisation to overcome, ranging from infrastructure to technology. A post-nationalist approach and inter-state co-operation was dearly needed to face these challenges. Yet the liberation from the well-meant internationalisation imposed by the Communist regimes of the Cold War unleashed a renaissance of nationalism in Eastern Europe.

Against this background, François Mitterrand gave a speech on 29 February 1992 on European affairs. Previous post-war settlements, he said, had been 'the victors' peace', he said, containing in them the germs of an actual or potential future war. Could one escape from this vicious circle?

> It is the chance of the present generations that finally an occasion has appeared [to create] an order of the nations in Europe where the ethnic groups, where the states (for some among them are neither ethnic groups or states) prefer the way of the contract, the way of the peaceful resolution to that of the military resolution. ... this presupposes an act of voluntary renunciation of this or that aspect of national power... That is in any case the way to follow.[2]

Mitterrand's moves in this period are much debated, but in the end both he and Helmut Kohl, steadfast in his determination to anchor a united Germany within the Western international organisations from the European Communities to NATO, proceeded to push for further European integration.[3] On the basis of the Maastricht Treaty of 1992, by 1993 there had emerged a European state system mainly among the lines of the confederative model with small elements of the super-state model (such as the ECSC), consciously adopting the name that the Abbé de Saint-Pierre had hoped to bestow on it, European Union. A number of member states formed an area without systematic frontier controls, called the Schengen Area after the place where the agreement was signed, which became operational in 1995. Since then it really has not mattered much for those living in previously borderlands within the Schengen Area whether they are shopping, studying, or working on either side of the border. Issues that for centuries were settled by wars have been resolved ingeniously and pacifically, making possible, for example, the Northern Ireland Peace Agreement of 1999. Simple solutions were found for many problems arising for multi-ethnic areas such as the supply, with EU funding, of dual-language signposting, multilingual schooling and administrations, and large aid injections into particularly impoverished areas from Cornwall to Transylvania. Preparations for the common currency continued in the 1990s until the Euro single currency came into force by those countries that chose to adopt it (Britain remaining outside, but Ireland enthusiastically embracing it).

One by one, the newly independent states of Eastern Europe, but also formerly neutral states rushed to apply for membership of the EU and NATO, with the exception of Switzerland and Norway (which nevertheless opened their borders to the free movement of EU citizens). This rush to join came despite the existence of the OSCE which included all members of NATO and of the defunct Warsaw Treaty Organisation that was dissolved in 1990. A debate among EU members took place as to whether one should widen it or deepen it, the latter implying a move towards 'an ever closer union', or the third federalist model of European integration. Some wanted both; the United Kingdom strongly favoured widening only, as chances the were that this would prevent deepening. An alternative approach was put forward in 1994 by two Conservative politicians in Germany, Karl Lamers and Wolfgang Schäuble, who suggested that some European countries might go ahead with deepening, forming a 'core Europe', with those who wished to stay out of this doing so. They also used the term a Europe of 'variable geometry', which we have today with the different lists of EU member states that have adopted the Euro, are part of the Schengen area, are both in NATO and EU, etc. Unhelpfully Lamers and Schäuble also spoke of a 'two-speed Europe', implying that those who initially stayed out of the core would ultimately be expected to join it,[4] which again the British could not swallow.

The British position more or less prevailed; the EU expanded to become larger than the Roman Empire, let alone the Holy Roman Empire, had ever been. It now includes countries that had not been part of either, and indeed countries that never accepted the aim of a federation, like Britain. The effect is undoubtedly one of overstretch, not only in physical and financial terms, but also in terms of having brought in societies where the values of the old members are not fully shared. Divergences on what the end state of European integration should be—we recall the three models sketched above—were confirmed again when Britain and Denmark, amongst others, baulked at the idea that the EU should aspire to 'ever closer union', putting the brake on an evolution to an even more integrated superstructure. At the same time, the great problems common to states around the globe, above all climate change that began to be identified and more commonly feared with the turn to the twenty-first century, clearly demand solutions well beyond any single state's capacities, with far-reaching and expensive changes to be made in the functioning of states which only firm engagements and intensive inter-state co-operation can hope to cope with.

Defence integration has stalled since the end of the Cold War, as the perception of a common threat waned. Several initiatives to overcome this impasse were made in the 1990s, and compromise solutions devised which would let European powers use NATO assets to complement their own forces for purely European operations in which the USA (and other non-European NATO member states) did not want to participate. Nevertheless, when war broke out in Yugoslavia in the early 1990s, and the USA initially held back, the European powers could not find the resolve to contain the fire in the Balkans on their own.

Progress towards greater co-operation was made—or a regress was reversed with France's return to NATO's integrated military structure in 2009, but the taboo on the integration of her nuclear weapons holds. France is still not a member of NATO's nuclear planning group (one of several compromise solutions devised mainly by Britain in the 1960s when NATO threatened to fall apart over European doubts that America would ever use nuclear weapons in defence of Europe). Since the 1980s, French governments have periodically promised but never implemented schemes to set up similar consultation with Germany on where French short-range nuclear weapons would eventually be targeted (instead, these weapons were mothballed in the early 1990s).[5]

Key obstacles to closer defence co-operation were not just the reluctance of France and Britain to give up their sovereign control of their own armed forces and above all their nuclear weapons. Obstacles also included the extreme anti-war sentiments in Germany and Italy with their strong constitutional and cultural inhibitions regarding taking military action. Germany is still weighed down and limited in her actions by the burden of her past, and the other middle-size powers—Italy, Poland, Spain—are economically too weak to pull their weight. Britain and France, the only two European powers that are members of the United Nation's Security Council's Pentarchy and as such willing to use force to uphold international norms, became increasingly impatient. They eventually returned to bilateralism, conscious of the fact that as second tier powers, neither of them can do much any longer without alliance support (not even a fairly limited intervention such as the 2013 French operation in Mali). London became aware that the USA was steadily if slowly turning away from what seemed to be a profoundly pacific Europe, towards challenges coming from the other side of the Pacific. In 1998, Britain and France issued a declaration at Saint Malo on future bilateral military co-operation—said to be always in the larger interest of European security, and in 2010 signed an Agreement at Lancaster House in London that *de facto* put the flesh of future practical co-operation measures on their bilateral Dunkirk Treaty of 1947.[6] Britain and France have thus come full circle to the bilateral alliance they created at the very beginning of the post-Second World War era, almost as though all the other measures and treaties had been in vain. And this despite the optimism about international security that had followed the end of the Cold War.

The 'New World Order' or the Hope that the Pentarchy will Finally Work

For when on 2 August 1990, Iraq's President Saddam Hussein invaded its small oil-rich neighbour Kuwait, he could not have chosen a worse time. It looked as though the world system devised in 1945 might finally work as its designers had intended. The Pentarchy, the Permanent Five great powers represented in the UN Security Council, for once cooperated properly. On 11 September 1990, US President George Bush told the American Congress that he and Soviet President Gorbachev agreed entirely 'that Iraq's aggression must not be tolerated', and that it was impossible to allow larger states to devour their smaller neighbours. In partnership, therefore, they voted against this act of aggression in the UN Security Council. Bush thought it possible that:

> [o]ut of these troubled times, our ... objective—a new world order—can emerge: a new era—freer from the threat of terror, stronger in the pursuit of justice, and more secure in the quest for peace. An era in which the nations of the world, East and West, North and South, can prosper and live in harmony. A hundred generations have searched for this elusive path to peace, while a thousand wars raged across the span of human endeavor. Today that

223

new world is struggling to be born, a world quite different from the one we've known. A world where the rule of law supplants the rule of the jungle. A world in which nations recognize the shared responsibility for freedom and justice. A world where the strong respect the rights of the weak.[7]

Indeed, the 1990s began as a period reminiscent of the early decades of the nineteenth-century Congress System. But then Russia's willingness to co-operate with the West waned as it looked on with unease while NATO underwent the same rapid expansion as the EU. Of the countries formerly controlled by Moscow, almost all sought the protection of NATO and above all America, to forestall a Russian change of mind and reoccupation of her 'near abroad'. The alternative European security organisation, the OSCE, operational from 1994, seemed unsatisfactory to all of them because dominated by Russia, a country they continued to distrust; Russian membership was crucial to this, according to much the same reasoning that Coudenhove-Kalergi put forward in the 1920s. Russia herself knocked on NATO's door, but probably more to ensure that there was no dangerous plotting going on behind it, even though (like the Holy Roman Empire, and like the UN) NATO would have great difficulties launching a war of aggression. This is not true for its member states taken individually, but since Guibert and Kant pioneered this theory, history has shown that consultative government structures with collective decision-making and alliance mechanisms tend to obstruct aggression. There are exceptions to this, but even those are not entirely disconnected from legal arguments for the justifiability of an action: the Franco-British attempt to seize control of the formerly Franco-British owned Suez Canal which Egypt had nationalised in 1956, or NATO's military campaign in support of Kosovo's bid for independence in 1999.

Indeed, the new 'Concert' among the Pentarchy, the UN Security Council's (UNSC) Permanent Five Members (or P5), eroded as Yugoslavia, a neighbour state to the prosperous and peaceful EU, started to be torn apart by secessionist movements in its federated states, countered violently by the central, Serb-dominated Army.[8] Atavistic reflexes came to the fore: Serbia with her Slav Orthodox religion and Cyrillic writing had looked East towards Constantinople, then Russia; Croatia with her Catholicism and Latin alphabet had always been part of the Western Roman Catholic world and for many years of the Austrian Empire. Both had black records of genocidal persecutions of minorities in and immediately after the Second World War when Yugoslav losses, inflicted in large part by Yugoslavs upon Yugoslavs, in numeric proportion to the whole population came second only to those of the USSR. In the 1990s, there were plenty of atrocities within living memories that all sides could draw upon to tear open old wounds and old hatreds, and soon one federal entity of Yugoslavia after the other broke away from Serbia. In the UNSC no consensus could be found as to how the P5 should react to this: Russia staunchly defended the central (Serb) Yugoslav government in Belgrade (the Serbian heartland), while after some delays the USA, Britain and perhaps more slowly, France (also traditionally friendly towards Serbia) came to recognise that the Serb government with its many para-military groupings was more guilty of massacres and the shelling of civilians than the other parties, not least because of an asymmetry in armaments available to them. Differences came to a head when in 1999, NATO decided that something had to be done to prevent large-scale massacres in Kosovo, and decided that bombing Belgrade would be legitimate albeit not legally endorsed by the P5 as Russia blocked it in the UNSC. This action by NATO is something Moscow has not forgiven until this day. Not accidentally, 1999 was the year when Vladimir Vladimirovich Putin became Prime Minister, holding that office or that of President of Russia ever since.

Despite being one of the P5, and despite the creation of a NATO-Russia Council, Moscow felt side-lined. Left alone to handle the huge economic crisis caused by its adjustment to the post-Soviet world, ignored over Kosovo and when a Western coalition intervened in Iraq in 2003 without a clear mandate of the UNSC, Russia began to harbour resentments about the way the new post-Cold War system worked. Perhaps Moscow did not make enough effort to upstage the EU and NATO through a satisfactory working of the OSCE. In any case OSCE members were not enthusiastic about this alternative organisation.

As with Germany in 1929–1933 after the Wall Street Crash, the economic crisis of the 1990s in Russia was not a fertile context for democracy to take root in a country that had never before fully practised it. The autocratic Russian state with Putin as its leader that has grown out of this unfavourable biotope seems to think more in terms of nineteenth-century empire-builders than of co-operation. Putin is comparable to Louis XIV, and the broad majority of the Russians supporting him would like to see the Russian Empire rebuilt, albeit perhaps not the Soviet Union. Claiming special powers over Russia's neighbour-hood, especially the former Soviet, now independent republics, which he dubbed Russia's 'near abroad', Putin is reviving old spheres-of-influence thinking, which we encountered in the Moscow agreement of 1944 of Churchill and Stalin. Moscow's sphere of influence was tacitly observed throughout the Cold War, when the Soviet Union's nuclear might deterred any Western intervention whenever the Red Army quashed uprisings within its Communist Bloc such as those in East Germany in 1953, Poland and Hungary in 1956, Czechoslovakia in 1968, and threatened to do so again in Poland in the early 1980s.

A true child of the Cold War, Putin hoped to restore Russia's status as a very great and respected power on the world scene by resorting to Cold War measures: a reform and build-up of the armed forces, and bullying behaviour towards former member states of the Soviet Union that did not want to restore close collaboration. In 2008, Russia staged a brief war with such a neighbour, Georgia. Around the same time, it resumed very large-scale military exercises reminiscent of those of the Cold War, while NATO had ceased to do anything of the sort in 1989. When in 2013/2014 Ukraine made moves towards EU and NATO membership, political turmoil ensued. In March 2014, Russia surprised the world by annexing Crimea, a peninsular appendage of Ukraine which had admittedly been part of a large succession of empires and other polities, before being integrated into Ukraine within the USSR for administrative reasons in 1954. Despite post-Cold War treaty obligations to protect Ukraine's frontier, the West did not react with more than sanctions—it remains the case that Russia is a nuclear power, and deterrence continues to work, at least against the West. If anything, NATO powers were self-deterred from taking stronger measure to defend the integrity of Ukraine, guaranteed by Britain, the USA, and Russia in return for Ukraine's surrender of Soviet nuclear weapons that had been based on its soil, with the Budapest Memorandum on Security Assurances of 1994. Moreover, civil war flared up in Ukraine's East, with those elements of the population favouring independence from Ukraine supported by Russian volunteers and Russian arms.

A new field of conflict opened up with the civil war in Syria, with a similar configuration as in Yugoslavia: in Syria, too, the central government of (now in the second generation of a ruling dynasty, under Bashar al Assad) is a long-standing client of Russia, and Putin clearly thinks that Russian prestige and great-power status are on the line if he cannot prevent an out-right attack on Damascus. Even when in 2013 Assad's forces used chemical weapons against populations associated with anti-government rebels, punishing strikes proposed in the UNSC were blocked by Russia.

The fourth Concert Era, as we might call the period between the old and the new Cold Wars from the point of view of the interstate system which was operational, thus came to an end in steps from 2008. This was not least because of Russian perceptions are still deeply rooted in the balance-of-power thinking that had been elevated to an ideal with the Utrecht state system. The balance seemed to have shifted greatly to Russia's disadvantage in the 1990s and early 2000s, with the extension of both EU and NATO membership. For crucially, balance-of-power thinking completely ignores the ideals and internal political dispositions of each entity: thus each has to be counter-balanced whether it is totalitarian and racist, or democratic and peaceful.

Cold War II and the Return to Sovereigntism

If anything, recent developments seem to have confirmed the need for European solidarity, even though the over-extension of the EU has led to divergent priorities and a heterogeneity of political values among its members. The financial crisis starting in America in 2008 which has hit Europe particularly hard and landed EU member states which huge debts and programmes of austerity designed to pay them off is producing effects similar to those the Wall Street Crash of 1929. The Mediterranean EU states and Ireland seem to have been affected more than the rest of Europe, and have since benefitted massively from aid from their partners. The tool box of policies used by the governments hailing from traditional parties to deal with the problems seems inadequate; new ultra-nationalist, even neo-Nazi parties, new populist leaders have sprung up, have even got into parliaments, with demagogues promising simple solutions in simple language to extremely complex problems. The decade since 2008 looked like the early 1930s all over again, with a cushioning that had not existed in the times of Mussolini, Hitler, and Franco: the

European welfare systems and free movement of people mitigates some of the worst pain, despite policies of austerity adopted by all governments. Nevertheless, the similarities are pronounced: resentment of aid given to others welling up among the poorest and those struggling most to keep their enterprises afloat, resentment of cutbacks in government spending and welfare, resentment of cheap labour especially from other EU countries undercutting salaries. As in the 1930s, xenophobia and nationalism returned. False facts, propaganda and manipulation were as much tools of the rise of Fascism and Nazism as they have been in the very recent past, and rumours existed then as now, only now they are spread even more quickly with new means of communication. Expert judgements are considered on par with the opinion of the man on the Clapham omnibus in a false understanding of popular equality embraced by the media.

Several years into the financial-economic crisis, mainly from 2015, a wave of immigration both from war-torn areas of the Middle East and from poor areas in Africa (the latter long predicted) swept into Southern Europe. Mass migration as such, as we have seen, is far from unprecedented in European history. What is unprecedented is that it did not lead to war and bloodshed, and that both states and the EU as a whole created structures and processes designed to deal with the migrants in a humane way. Perversely, countries and areas least exposed to the in-bound flow of asylum seekers and refugees—the United Kingdom, Poland, Hungary, the Czech Republic and Slovakia—saw the greatest expressions of hostility to this new immigration. Added to fiscal austerity measures and much unemployment still arising from the ongoing comprehensive restructuring of the labour market, as in the 1930s, substantial segments of the populations of EU member states form Britain to Hungary, have become vulnerable to the lure of politicians who would promise magic solutions. These included the delusionary claim that states and their population would be better off outside the EU, cutting links of mutual support and joint decision-making on common problems with their neighbours, extracting their economies from EU legislation and standards, as though the autarky which Aristotle prescribed for his ideal state was achievable in the twenty-first century. This of course is the background to Britain's 2016 referendum on whether to stay in or leave the EU, largely a measure introduced by one British Prime Minister to silence dissent in his own party.

The decision to opt out of this co-operative structure—this Holy Roman Empire in which the member states had replaced the emperor—goes in the opposite direction to all the measures that are most needed in Europe today. The financial and immigration crises are far from being the only ones. If we accept the conclusions drawn from the survey of inter-polity systems in Europe since Antiquity presented above, then several recent developments, not necessarily in this order, are further cause for concern.

One is that there are more signs than ever that the US commitment to defend Europe's security—by encouraging the Europeans to live in peace with one another, by providing the necessary leadership when the Europeans could not decide alone to pull in one direction, and by keeping potential expansionist ideological adversaries at bay—may not last, or at least not in the form it had from 1950–2017. Since 2017 the USA has had a president who has encouraged Japan to acquire its own nuclear weapons, and has threatened to pull out of NATO, putting its financial cost to the USA above the overall benefit, of suppressing security competitions in Europe, East Asia and the Middle East. As one astute observer, Adam Garfinkel, put it, the initial post-1945 rationale for US support for European defence and integration was that:

> U.S. power would substitute, and in so doing render impossible, the internecine disasters of the twentieth century's world wars that had

been so dangerous and costly to the United States. U.S. support across every postwar administration for integrative economic institutions in Europe, first the Coal and Steel Community and later the European Economic Community, were designed and supported as denationalizing accompaniments to the demilitarizing core of the strategy. ... These aspects of U.S. strategy were as important in the original design as deterring would-be hegemons in Europe and Asia—the Soviet Union and the People's Republic of China...[9]

As Europe recovered from the Second World War, it continued to be in America's interest that European nations other than its allies Britain and France would become strong military powers again, and this seems to have been a matter of relative consensus in Washington until recently, despite periodic American pleas that their NATO allies should spend more on defence and share the burden of their common defence more evenly. US President Trump however is seen to be going further than any of his predecessors with his insistence on greater European defence spending, by actually raising questions about America's future commitment to NATO, placing 'America first' in every respect. Trump's Presidency follows a longer trend of America's 'pivoting' away from Europe and the Middle East and towards its West, including a reorientation of US defence and trade towards East Asia, a trend that was well under way in the 1990s.[10]

Coming at much the same time, British disengagement from Europe has parallels in the opting out of integration negotiations 1950–1957; but this time, Britain's unquestioned defence commitment in the WU/EU Article 42.7 will be gone. There is only the vague commitment in NATO's Article 5, and much reduced physical underpinnings of that commitment, as British forces are largely being repatriated by 2020 from their previous deployment in Central Europe. At the same time, the reasons for this disengagement in 1950–1957, as given by Bevin in 1950, are much diminished or gone: Britain is no longer at the hub of a 'Sterling

Area'. While in 1950, Europe only took a quarter of Britain's trade, in 2017 44% of UK exports were going to EU countries in 2018 and 53% of her imports came from the EU.[11] In 2017, while 2.4 million Britons took their holidays in the USA and 5.4 million in Asia, Australia, New Zealand, Canada, Africa, or Latin America, 38.8 million Britons went to Europe for leisure.[12] Britain's Empire is gone, and her Commonwealth connections have aged and become more remote, while the population configuration by ethnic origin within the 'old' Commonwealth member states has changed dramatically. With these transformations, created by the natural disappearance of old kinship bonds between Australia or Canada or New Zealand and the 'mother country' Britain, and the immigration from other parts of the world to these former colonies, the *syngeneia* as the ancient Greeks would have called it, is diminishing. All three 'old Commonwealth' countries have long turned towards the USA for protection, indeed for their cultural orientation, which is also true of elites in the Commonwealth countries such as India and Pakistan. If a choice of a British university for their children is made, this is likely dictated by the lower fees in the UK, rather than by nostalgic affection for British civilisation. As Britain discovered, for example, in the FIFA member states' vote of 2010 to take the Football World Cup of 2018 to Russia, ancient Commonwealth links did not sway countries to vote for Britain: to the surprise of the British, Britain obtaining only two votes scored worst among the other candidates to host the World Cup and dropped out of the second round altogether. Meanwhile, the 'Special Relationship' with the USA still carries its intelligence sharing and nuclear dimensions for Britain's rock-bottom minimal nuclear force, but in every other way is subject to the whims of whoever is American President at the time.

Meanwhile all the reasons for which thinkers like Coudenhove-Kalergi focused only on Europe in their plans for a peace-system still apply. It seems that a functioning world system is still elusive. Even the EU and NATO have undermined their own strength and cohesion through over-extension. Countries in Europe's North, South, East and West are chiefly concerned with divergent threats and problems. Elections in recent years raise questions as to whether fundamental ideals, such as the Utrechtian prioritisation of Europe's overall wellbeing over narrow national interests, is still shared. This is an issue particularly for NATO, which resolved the centuries-old question of whether the Ottoman Empire should be treated as part of the European system or not by admitting Turkey to NATO. The turn back under Erdoğan from the secular-national(ist) ideology of Atatürk to one that is both strongly Muslim and nostalgic about the Ottoman Empire and yearns to restore the lost Turkish leadership role in the Muslim world questions the appropriateness of this membership. Here too it is worth noting Adam Garfinkel's admonition that:

> alliances are not effective by dint of capabilities alone. They are ultimately dependent on shared perceptions of threat and, in enduring alliances of democracies, ultimately on shared principles about civic life. It matters not what capabilities exist, or what mid- and lower-ranking NATO defense officials do together on a daily basis, if there is no will, no trust, and no convergence of principles on the political level.[13]

Or, one might add, in the collective mentalities of the populations.

We also see divergences about these principles arising within the EU, where old resentments of empires perceived as foreign occupation are still alive in the collective mentality of Czechs, Hungarians, and indeed Poles. Not just in the governments of these three countries, but throughout Europe, we see huge challenges to principles and values which we assumed we shared within the EU, such as the equal value of all lives, the importance of combatting unfairness within our society by supporting victims of physical, mental or social misfortunes (that is, the welfare state), the moral imperative of helping refugees from persecution and war, all of which are expensive values to have, yet essential to our identity. And then there is the value of religious tolerance coupled with rigorously secular politics. This last point is not self-evident even within the once again multi-ethnic societies of Western Europe. Substantial minorities especially in big cities belong to a religion which does not accept the separation of the religious from the political/public sphere which Christianity could establish on the basis of 'rendering to Caesar what is Caesar's, and to God what is God's'. Moreover, many of them see themselves as the diaspora of a mother country to which they still feel they belong, and to which they return periodically, if they can afford to do so, intermarrying with people from that mother community, rather than within the country the passport of which they carry. This is nothing new: it recalls patterns of marriage in old trading city networks, from the Phoenicians and Carthaginians to the Hanse and the Venetians, but it is not conducive to assimilation.

Divergences of views on principles about civic life exist with militarily strong but economically unbalanced Russia which are not just about social welfare, or the corruption of a small elite, or homosexuality. More importantly, they revive the contradiction between self-determination (the free choice made by the USSR's former client states to apply for EU and NATO membership) and a great power's national interests, still seen by Russia through a nineteenth-century great-power spheres-of-influence prism.

In short, there are ample reasons for Europeans to work together to uphold human rights they all believe in, tackle their common problems jointly, in a highly competitive world of globalised market forces. Whether a state the size of Britain can protect her social welfare system without the support of her neighbours with shared social commitments, against competition from countries that do not provide for their sick, their old, their disabled, is a question that goes beyond the remit of this book. But that the days are past where a major European player could stand by if there were a conflagration in Europe, as Britain could during its period of splendid isolation in the second half of the nineteenth century, is not an unreasonable claim to make. In 1939–1945, Britain learnt at great cost that events in Europe could not be ignored as happening in 'a far away country as a quarrel between people of whom we know nothing.' But this lesson seems forgotten. The pressure of migration on all of the European Continent from areas rent by war and suffering from poverty is unlikely to abate, and oddly Britain, although furthest away, is in the forefront of European quarrels with Russia. Nor can one imagine a large island off the European coast, confronted with the EU bloc, play 'the tongue on the scales' as England and Britain did in previous centuries. Europe in turn will sorely miss the massive contribution that British politicians, diplomats, civil servants and military officers have made in the past. It is largely to their credit that NATO stayed together and America committed to European defence. And with its highly developed diplomatic culture, Britain helped to smooth out the frequent arguments occurring between other members of NATO but also the EU, seeking compromises and proposing feasible solutions. Arguments for or against a Common Market aside, British disengagement from the EU will not be conducive to British, let alone European, security.

12

CONCLUSIONS

The patterns of relations between polities in Europe, from the Greeks and Romans up to the present, have turned around two antithetical themes. On the one hand, there was the defence of independence and sovereignty by polities engaged in competitions for primacy and competitive wars, jealous of any growth of power, as anyone's independence could not be guaranteed against a stronger polity with the ambition to extend its power. Alliances were crucial to these struggles, but were rarely enough to prevent war; indeed, they could even serve to escalate a local quarrel to a much larger war, as seen in 1914. Bids for neutrality—whether by Melos or Belgium—were shrugged off by stronger powers that would rather destroy a neutral state than live with the possibility that it would join the adversarial side. Polities embracing this approach put their narrow 'national interest' first, defended their own sovereign rights to act as they saw fit, including the right to go to war, resisting the idea of giving up the means to do so in exchange for collective renunciation of war as a means of politics and collective disarmament.

And on the other hand, there was the recurrent theme of a large overarching polity, an empire, a universal monarchy, that attempted to provide peace internally and defend only against foreign aggression.

The competitive Greek city states formed the chief model for the first, and the *Pax Romana* and the *Landfrieden* of the Holy Roman Empire for the second. On the whole, the *Imperium Romanum* thus was remarkably successful, although prone to turn into a tyranny from time to time. Its East Roman branch lasted until 1453, even if occasionally unsettled by civil wars, and shrinking over the centuries. No wonder that Medieval Western Christendom tried to recreate it in the West, and the Medieval system of polities regulated by norms of peace within the *Universitas Christianorum* or Christian Commonwealth did much to contain war. It had the structural flaw that emperor and pope had to cooperate for it to work well, and that a series of monarchs outside the Holy Roman Empire were determined not to submit to the emperor and chose to become his rival instead. Yet had it not been for the Reformation and the profound ideological conflict it brought on, the Holy Roman Empire within a Christian world would be remembered as a sphere of peace and prosperity. The emperors' powers were limited by internal checks and balances. Sovereignty was shared at several levels. If you take away the confessional wars that tore it apart and weakened it, its internal structures in many ways rightly served as a model for the many forms of confederations that were proposed over time and eventually tried out in the twentieth century. Given the longevity and success (aside from the religious wars) of the (West) Roman, the (Byzantine) East Roman and the Holy Roman Empires, one can understand why the classicist Ian Morris has argued that empires convey far more benefits than disadvantages, and are worth the toll in death which their establishment has tended to exact.[1] One can agree with him with regard to the Roman Empire (if one wasn't a slave), the Byzantine Empire (if one was orthodox), the Holy Roman Empire (but for the religious wars),

and even for the benefits brought by Napoleon with his legislation and modernisation, or Bismarck's Second German *Reich*
with its domestic social welfare programme, as Frank-Lothar
Kroll has argued.[2] The argument breaks down completely, however, when considering Mussolini's, Hitler's, or Stalin's empires.
One can thus well understand the resentment which empires—
all empires—caused among those forced into them, or those
threatened by their expansionist aspirations.

However weak the central power of the Holy Roman Empire
was in reality, princes outside it increasingly regarded it with
fiercely competitive eyes and engaged in lasting rivalry with it.
One can understand how French monarchs saw the Empire with
the same irritation with which de Gaulle regarded the USA—
only, the Empire was right next door to them and constantly
demanded precedence over other polities. The French and other
rulers who engaged in competition with the Empire claimed that
this was done in defence of their sovereignty, but their behaviour
in turn led others to suspect (sometimes rightly, as with Louis
XIV, Napoleon and to some more modest extent, de Gaulle) that
they themselves aspired to become the hegemon, the dominant
power in Europe.

A sea-change came with the confessional wars which removed
the medieval Christian restraints on dynastic rivalries. These
were now masked as the virtuous pursuit of a stable balance of
powers in Europe, but they brought the great Age of Battles
(Russell Weigley)[3] and wars so atrocious (culminating in the
Thirty Years' War) that statesmen and political theorists yearned
for a new state system. The proposals they dreamt up were for a
system no longer to be dominated by the Church or the Holy
Roman Empire, and yet designed to check any power aspiring to
universal monarchy. The new state system that was put in place
at the Utrecht peace congress of 1712–1713 was supposed to put
the general interest and peace (tranquillity) of Europe above the

dynastic interests of the individual states. But without any enforcement mechanism, it had no chance of success.

After Napoleon's ephemeral attempt to replace the Holy Roman Empire by France's (or rather his own) universal monarchy, the Congress System combined the Utrecht ideal with an enforcement system of sorts: the Pentarchy of European great powers, which by co-operating should keep the peace in Europe. This was one synthesis that was supposed to replace the thesis and antithesis of anarchic interplay of sovereign states on the one hand and empire/universal monarchy/hegemony on the other. This was not bad, as long as the five great powers agreed with each other, and as long as you were not a small state the interests of which were sacrificed to the greater good without consulting it. The need for co-operation among the Pentarchs was a its fatal weakness, and co-operation gave way several times to wars among them. The goodwill among the leaders of the Pentarchy on which the Congress System was based evaporated under the rising heat of nationalism which, combined with the old competitiveness (now transformed into rabble-rousing nationalism) ultimately plunged Europe into the First World War.

The world-wide League of Nations System that emerged from it was again built on voluntary great power co-operation. With the USA remaining aloof, however, and several great powers espousing a strategy of aggressive expansionism, this variation on the Congress System was unable to prevent the Second World War. Yet the same structural flaw was built into the next worldwide variation on the Congress System, the United Nations, constructed after this even more devastating global conflagration. Like the nineteenth-century Congress System and the League of Nations, the UN relies for its effectiveness on the will to co-operate of a Pentarchy of great powers. While at least it has aligned the USA with Britain and France, which since 1945 has been a crucial underpinning of European security and integration while their interests converge, the interests of the three Western democracies on the one hand and the USSR/Russia and China on the other have rarely coincided.

Since the League of Nations, the Briand-Kellogg Pact and the creation of the UN, all member states have signed up to the outlawing of war (implying a limitation of their sovereignty), but do not trust each other sufficiently to take the next step of disarming or disbanding their standing armies, as Kant had proposed. Neither the Roman nor the Holy Roman Empires ever gave up their armed forces; both saw the need to defend their realm of peace against external enemies. But then both empires bordered on hostile powers, needing to defend themselves against bellicose tribes which raided Roman territory and eventually brought the West Roman Empire to its knees, or the expansionist great powers Persia until the seventh century, and later the Ottoman Turks.

It should make any sovereigntist stop and think that for seven hundred years, a series of well-informed statesmen, diplomats and entrepreneurs from all over Europe—from Bohemia to Britain—kept despairing of the anarchy of sovereign state competition. While some like Bartolo da Sassoferrato of Dante saw the solution in a strengthening of the (Holy Roman) Empire, and John of Salisbury and Jean Bodin devised concepts that would make their kings more sovereign and independent, a significant number put forward proposals which would have limited the sovereign freedom of their own polities to use force as they pleased. These latter proposed to resolve the dialectic between universal empire and sovereign states through the synthesis of a council/permanent congress/parliament of representatives of the states of Europe, for them jointly and peacefully to resolve the problems of the continent. The parallels in their proposals—from that of Pierre Dubois to those of Richard Coudenhove-Kalergi and Aristide Briand—are striking. Some idealistically thought it could be put into practice without any enforcement mechanism, others wanted to be able to enforce commitments voluntarily made. But all stressed the importance of escaping a situation where either one state ruled Europe or there was an anarchic competition between sovereign states all aiming to put their own interests first, unconditionally.

Only from 1950 were measures influenced by such proposals put into practice. The resulting European Communities and their successor, the EU, have proved to be, not the best of all possible worlds, but the most successful mechanism devised so far for the maintenance of peace in Europe. It has put an end at least to the bloody dimensions of the persistent rivalry which, among Charlemagne's heirs, especially France, entertained with its great power neighbours, ranging from Germany and/or Austria to Spain and England/Britain. It complements the competences of member-states in protecting ethnic minorities or migrant workers who enrich their host countries, in assuring human rights and a high degree of standardisation of safety and quality criteria, legal norms, consumer protection, workers' rights, social welfare, and the interchangeability diplomas.

At the age of sixty, the present European co-operation structures have so far demonstrated less longevity than the Roman Empire which (counting from the annexation of the first province, Sicily, in 241 BC) survived for almost 1700 years; or Charlemagne's Empire and its Holy Roman successor, which existed in some form for 1000. Moreover, the European Communities would not have been so successful had they not been underpinned by the firm commitment to the defence of most of its members that were also in NATO, by the United States, and also by Britain that kept NATO together in times of crisis.[4] And nothing is more conducive to solidarity than a strongly and commonly perceived external threat, which in the Cold War seemed to be posed by the USSR and the client states it had marshalled in the Warsaw Pact. Nor is the EU beyond perfectibility. In its essence, however, it is above all the answer to Europe's internal security problems.

Throughout the history we have sketched, the circles that had to be squared to give Europe internal 'tranquillity' were how to create a *Pax Augusti*, without an enforcement mechanism, an Augustus, a universal monarch, who even as benevolent dictator would be resented by his rivals; how to preserve the freedom of action, the sovereign option of self-defence of the individual member states, while curtailing their ability to attack others; how an ever larger number of members could take decisions collectively without clogging up the decision-mechanism by vetoes.

The quest for absolute sovereignty that can be traced back to the twelfth century if not to Aristotle is not the answer: one power's absolute sovereignty is another's absolute insecurity and one power's sovereign right to use war as an instrument of its policy is another's sovereign right to attack it. Neither furthers stability. Sovereignty, and that is the lesson of the Holy Roman Empire, can instead be shared at several levels. Subsidiarity—the principle that decisions should be made at the lowest level possible—was widely practised even there. After these two-and-a-half millennia of experiments with state systems, is seems clear that bilateral quarrels can more easily be resolved by bringing in other parties who have a common interest in a peaceful settlement. A permanent council and parliament of representatives of the states of Europe are essential to replace 'war war' with 'jaw jaw', to echo Churchill's catchy phrase. The coincidence of great power interests is not a reliable enforcement mechanism, and that there are few reasons why smaller powers should trust the great powers not to put their own interests first; it is in their interest that not just a great power Pentarchy, but representatives of all nations should have voting rights in the decision-making forum.

It is hard to prescribe complete disarmament or even only a reduction of armaments on all sides, and mutual limitations on sovereignty, on the ability to go to war unilaterally. But structures allowing for multilateral consultation all are excellent inventions of the past that will be of great use for the future if they survive, and if the EU is not torn apart by divergent priorities and the resurgence of national selfishness. The legal *acquis* of the EU, the adoption of a European Charter of Human Rights, are remarkable achievements that would have satisfied Bluntschli. A return to balance-of-power competitions and rivalries, to sovereigntism, to nationalism and empire-building with the many wars they brought, and the return to laws and standards applying to one medium-size polity only, do not.[5]

All this suggests that the EU is the least bad state system Europe has known, despite its many flaws and shortcomings. Or to paraphrase Churchill, it is the worst form of government for this continent except for all the others that have been tried. In many areas it is in desperate need of reform. The idea of a strongly federated core Europe surrounded by more loosely confederated states, as proposed by Lamers and Schäuble, was the best recent proposal by far, and deserves to be reconsidered. Nothing suggests, however, that from a security point of view, any individual state of Europe will be better off outside this EU and its consultation mechanism, its burden-sharing and its economic support for weaker powers, which in the long term through prosperity can help stave off intra-European mass migration and radicalism. Just as the rich are never entirely safe from robbery or revolution as long as their neighbours are poor, rich countries enhance their own security by aiding less prosperous ones.

In this context, the sovereigntism espoused and defended by the British Brexiteers is no more conducive to British or European security or the long-term banning of war from the Old

Continent than was the proud pursuit of sovereigntism by the French and English kings and the British governments of previous centuries. The absence of war from Europe, the protection of the human rights of its inhabitants, and not only questions of free trade are at the heart of the European project—how would these priorities not also be the core priorities of any British government? What sense does it make to try to achieve those on a 'national' basis, given all we have said above about the illusionary concept of the 'nation-state'?

It is difficult to see what past role could serve as a model for the United Kingdom outside the EU: the counter-balancer of which power? The transatlantic hinge without being connected up with the European wing? The head of an ever less significant Commonwealth? The great colonial power and exporter of industrial goods to its colonies which it long ceased to be? The exporter of financial and insurance services, when it refuses to meet the standards of the EU? A world-policeman as a member of the UN's Pentarchy, when it has long been stripped of its empire as force multiplier and needs partners for all but its smallest security operations? How can the United Kingdom continue to justify its seat on the UN Security Council when in the recent past, Britain like France has told European partners that having two European seats on the Council is better than one EU seat?

What is not difficult to recognise is that the EU will emerge weakened militarily and in other aspects of its security by the withdrawal from it by Britain. It is after all one of only two larger European powers with an unbroken tradition of the use of force to counter aggression, genocide and other major crimes. The other, France, cannot shoulder this responsibility alone on behalf of all the EU, and we see too much historical baggage still today for anybody to be happy with Germany beginning to pull its weight, quite apart from the hard-wired anti-use-of-force reflexes stopping her. Meanwhile, the EU desperately needs new ideas to work out how to influence, without force, the politics of its own member states that are drifting back to nationalism and authoritarianism and away from post-nationalist ideals of democracy and human rights. All of Europe's old states face ideological threats from within, from parties and movements far too reminiscent of the radical parties that sprang up in the 1920s and 1930s for anybody to feel complacent about Europe's political future. Perhaps more than ever, Europe needs all hands on deck, including the experience and patience of old, stable democracies. The major events in European history suggests—whether this be the great invasions starting in late Roman times and ending with 1066, or the ideological/religious wars of early modern times or of the twentieth century, or threats emanating from expansionist powers in Europe—that the major storms of continental Europe also ravage Britain.

In short, however one defines security, whether in narrow military terms vis-à-vis external threats, or whether one includes major domestic challenges, mostly shared across the EU countries, the British exit from the EU stands to diminish the security of Europe as a whole. Core contemporary British values such as the maximum protection of the individual's rights and freedoms and policy-making through consultation and co-operation stem from and are still shared with Britain's European partners, not with Russia, not with China. Ultimately, whatever its political choices, the British Isles and their security are part of Europe's.

NOTES

1. INTRODUCTION: THE DIALECTIC OF EMPIRE, SOVEREIGNTY, AND CO-OPERATIVE SYNTHESES

1. Heinz Duchhardt: Das Reich in der Mitte des Staatensystems: Zum Verhältnis von innerer Verfassung und internationaler Funktion in den Wandlungen des 17. und 18. Jahrhunderts', in Peter Krüger (ed): *Das europäische Staatensystem im Wandel: Strukturelle Bedingungen und bewegende Kräfte seit der frühen Neuzeit* (Munich: Oldenbourg, 1996), pp. 1–9.
2. Crucial exceptions include Martin Wright: *Systems of States*, Hedley Bull ed. (Leicestr University Press 1977); Adam Watson: *The Evolution of the International Society* (Oxford University Press, 1992); Barry Buzan & Richard Little: *International Systems in World History* (Oxford: Oxford University Press, 2000); Andrew Linklater: *Violence and Civilisaiton in the Western States System* (Cambridge University Press, 2016), and above all Andreas Osiander: *States System of Europe, 1640–1990: Peacemaking and the Conditions of International Stability* (Oxford: Clarendon Press, 1994).

2. INTER-'NATIONAL' RELATIONS? PROBLEMS OF TERMINOLOGY AND BASIC ASSUMPTIONS

1. D.C. Watt: *What About the People?: Abstraction and Reality in History and the Social Sciences* (London: London School of Economics and Political Science, 1983)

2. The term 'geopolitics' was long used as a synonym for International Relations, especially in France. It is in many respects helpful, albeit not for our purposes, as this book focuses especially on the relations between entities, especially in Europe.

3. Brendan Simms: *Britain's Europe: A Thousand Years of Conflict and Cooperation* (2016, repr. Harmondsworth: Penguin, 2017), p. 39.

4. Georges Bischoff & Nicolas Bourguinat: *Dictionnaire historique de la Liberté* (Paris: Nouveau monde éditions, 2015), p. 158f.

5. Dean Hammer: *Roman Political Thought from Cicero to Augustine* (Cambridge: Cambridge University Press, 2014).

6. Simms: *Britain's Europe*, p. 53.

7. Texts in Gearóid Ó Tuathail, Simon Dalby and Paul Routledge (eds): *The Geopolitics Reader* (London: Routledge, 1998), pp. 27–32 and 33–35.

8. Carl Schmitt: *The Nomos of the Earth* (1950), trs. by G.L.Ulmen (New York: Telos Press, 2003)

9. Till, Geoffrey (ed.): *The Development of British Naval Thinking* (London: Routledge, 2006), p. 61.

10. Quoted in Simms: *Britain's Europe*, p. 141.

11. Michael Howard: *The Continental Commitment: The Dilemma of British Defence Policy in the Era of the Two World Wars* (Harmondsworth: Penguin, 1974), p. 81.

12. Ibid., p. 110

13. Alfred Thayer Mahan: *The Influence of Sea Power Upon History, 1660–1783* (Boston: Little, Brown, 1890).

14. For data on European migration, see for example Gérard Chaliand, Michel Jan, Jean-Pierre Rageau: *Atlas Historique des Migrations* (Paris: Seuil, 1994).

15. For further reading, see Michael Burleigh: *Ethics and Extermination: Reflections on Nazi Genocide* (Cambridge: Cambridge University Press, 1997); Mark Mazower: *Dark Continent: Europe's Twentieth Century* (London: Allen Lane, 1998); Alfred de Zayas: *A Terrible Revenge: the Ethnic Cleansing of the East European Germans* (Basingstoke: Palgrave Macmillan, 2006); Timothy Snyder: *Bloodlands: Europe between Hitler and Stalin* (London: Bodley Head, 2010).

16. The terminological confusion is aggravated by the fact that the USA consists of fifty states, and that a term is needed to distinguish the 'nation-state' from the component 'federal states'.

17. Gérard Chaliand & Jean-Pierre Rageau: *Atlas des Diasporas* (Paris: Odile Jacob, 1991).

18. Benedict Anderson: *Imagined Communities* (London: Verso, 1983).

19. Gérard-François Dumont: *Les populations du monde* (Paris: Armand Colin, 2001).

3. IDEAS INHERITED FROM ANTIQUITY

1. 2 Kings Ch. 15.

2. 2 Kings Ch. 16.

3. Numbers 31.

4. Ibid.

5. Alexander Gillespie: *A History of the Laws of War*, Vol. 2 *The Customs and Laws of War with Regards to Combatants and Captives* (Oxford and Portland, OR: Hart, 2011), pp. 109–114.

6. Herodotus VIII.143.

7. Plato: *Laws*, 626a. See Cian O'Driscoll: 'Rewriting the just war tradition: Just war in classical Greek political thought and practice', *International Studies Quarterly*, Vol. 59 No. 1 (2015), pp. 1–10, and idem 'Divisions Within the Ranks? The just war tradition and the use and abuse of history', *Ethics & International Affairs*, Vol. 27, No. 1 (2013), pp. 47–65.

8. Plato: *Laws* 627a-628e.

9. Hans van Wees: 'Broadening the Scope: Thinking about Peace in the Pre-Modern World', in Kurt Raaflaub (ed.): *Peace in the Ancient World: Concepts and Theories* (Chichester: John Wiley & Sons, 2016), p. 168.

10. Aristotle: *Nicomachean Ethics* X.7.

11. For Cicero's ideas, see Neff: *War and the Law of Nations*, pp. 18–30.

12. Cian O'Driscoll: *The Renegotiation of the Just War Tradition and the Right to War in the Twenty-first Century* (Basingstoke: Palgrave Macmillan, 2008).

13. Thucydides 1.23.5–6.

14. Thucydides 3.82.1–5.

15. Plato: *The Republic* Book V, 469e–471c.

16. See the translation into French by Raoul Preulles/ de Presles of 1375, first published in Abbeville: Iehan du Pre & Piecre Gerard, 1486, repr. by Olivier Bertrand (ed.): *La Cité de Dieu de Saint Augustin traduite par Raoul de Presles (1371–1375)* (Paris: Honoré Champion, 2013), Vol. 1 pp. 829, 879.

17. Thucydides 1.76.2.

18. Thucydides 5.84–116.

19. O'Driscoll: 'Rewriting the just war tradition', op. cit.

20. Hans van Wees: *Greek Warfare: Myths and Realities* (London: Duckworth, 2004), pp. 8–10.

21. Dominique Gaurier: *Histoire du droit international—De l'Antiquité à la création de l'ONU* (Rennes: Presses universitaires de Rennes, 2014), p. 59f.

22. Aristotle: *Nicomachean Ethics* X.7

23. Hans van Wees: 'Broadening the Scope: Thinking about Peace in the Pre-Modern World', in Kurt Raaflaub (ed.): *Peace in the Ancient World: Concepts and Theories* (Chichester: John Wiley & Sons, 2016), pp. 169–173.

24. Diodorus 17.24.1.

25. Diodorus 17.9.4–6.

26. Polybius 3.6.

27. Arrian, *Anabasis* 1.16.7.

28. Arrian, *Anab.* 3.18.11–12.

29. P.A.Brunt: The Aims of Alexander, *Greece and Rome* Vol. 12 (1965), p. 210.

30. John Rich: 'Warfare and the Army in Early Rome', in Paul Erdkamp (ed): *A Companion to the Roman Army* (Oxford: Blackwell Publishing, 2007), pp. 8–23.

31. O'Driscoll: 'Rewriting the Just War Tradition', op. cit.; Eric Adler: 'Late Victorian and Edwardian Views of Rome and the Nature of "Defensive Imperialism"', *International Journal of the Classical Tradition* Vol. 15, No. 2 (June, 2008), pp. 187–216.

32. In the original, it is: « tu regere imperio populous, Romane, memento. /

Hae tibi erunt artes pacisque imponere morem, / parcere subiectis et debellare superbos. » *Aeneid* (VI, 852–854).

33. Adrian Nicholas Sherwin-White: *The Roman Citizenship* (Oxford: Clarendon Press, 1939).

34. *Res Gestae.*

35. *Res Gestae.*

36. Agnès Bérenger-Badel: 'Caracalla et le Massacre des Alexandrins', in David El Kenz (ed.): *Le massacre, objet d'histoire* (Paris: Gallimard Folio, 2005), p. 132.

37. Quoted in Arthur Herman: *The Idea of Decline in Western History* (New York, the Free Press, 1997), p. 18.

4. THE MIDDLE AGES: THE CHRISTIAN UNIVERSE

1. Klaus Oschema: *Bilder von Europa im Mittelalter* (Ostfildern: Thorbecke, 2013).

2. Philippe Contamine: *La Guerre au Moyen Age* (2nd edn Paris: PUF, 1986), pp. 478–485; and see the contributions to Frank Tallett & D.J.B. Trimm (eds): *European Warfare, 1350–1750* (Cambridge: Cambridge University Press, 2010).

3. Gregory of Tours: *Historia Francorum*, II.38.

4. *Annales laureshamenses*, in Georg Heinrich Pertz (ed.): *Annales et chronica aevi Carolini* in *Monumenta Germaniae Historica*, Series *Scriptores* Vol. 1 (Hanover: Hahn, 1826), p. 38.

5. '*Rex qui super unam gentem vel multas. Imperator qui super totum mundum aut qui precellit in eo.*', quoted in Georg Baesecke: De gradus Romanorum in: *Kritische Beiträge zur Geschichte des Mittelalters.* Festschrift für Robert Holtzmann, *Historische Studien* 238 (Berlin 1933), pp. 1–7.

6. Widukind of Corvey: *Historia Saxonum*, I. 34.

7. This was before benighted medieval churchmen imposed the view that the earth was flat: it was well known in Antiquity with its Ptolemaic understanding of Physics that the world was a globe.

8. The *Gospel Book of Otto III* is now in the Bavarian State Library in Munich.

9. Honoré Bovet: *L'Arbre des Batailles* (c.), ed. by Reihnhilt Richter-Bergmeier (Geneva: Droz, 2017), IV.83, pp. 413–426.

10. Ibid., IV.2, pp. 209–211.

11. Jonathan Riley-Smith: *The Crusades: A History* (London: Bloomsbury Academic, 2014).

12. M.H.Keen: *The Laws of War in the Late Middle Ages* (London: Routledge, 1965), p. 104.

13. Ibid.

14. Bruno Arcidiacono: *Cinq types de paix: Une histoire des plans de pacit-ication perpétuelle (XVIIᵉ–XXᵉ siècles)* (Paris: PUF, 2011)

15. Herbert Grundmann & Hermann Heimpel (eds): Alexander von Roes: *Memoriale de prerogative Romani imperii'* (c.1281) in *Monumenta Germaniae Historica, Schriften des Späten Mittelalters* Vol. I piece 1 (Stuttgart: Anton Hiersemann, 1958), pp. 91–148.

16. First published as G. Bruschius (ed): *Engelberti Abbatis Admontensis, qui sub Rudolpho Habspurgio floruit, de Ortu et fine Romani Imperii Liber* (Bâle: Johann Oporinus, 1553).

17. Lupoldus de Bebenburg: *Tractatus de iuribus regni et imperii Romanorum* (Strasbourg: Rietschius, 1603).

18. *Dialogus de potestate Papae et Imperatoris*, for a translation, see http://www.nlnrac.org/classical/late-medieval-transformations/documents/dialogue, accessed on 8 VIII 2018.

19. Bartolo da Sassoferrato: *In secundum Digesti novi partem commentaria*, see Harald Kleinschmidt: *Geschichte des Völkerrechts in Krieg und Frieden* (s.l. Narr Franke Attempto Verlag, 2013), p. 99.

20. Giovanni da Legnano: *Tractatus de Bello, de Represaliis et de Duello*, ed. by Thomas Erskine Holland, trs. by James Leslie Brierly (Oxford: Oxford University Press for the Carnegie Institute, 1917), ch. xiii, p. 93.

21. Aurelia Henry (ed.): *The De Monarchia of Dante Alighieri* (Boston & New York: Houghton Mifflin, 1904), also at http://oll.libertyfund.org/titles/alighieri-de-monarchia accessed on 8 VIII 2018.

22. Bruno Arcidiacono: *Cinq types de paix: Une histoire des plans de pacit-ication perpétuelle (XVIIᵉ–XXᵉ siècles)* (Paris: PUF, 2011), pp. 209–211.

23. Rolf Grosse: 'Der Friede in Frankreich bis zur Mitte des 12. Jahrhunderts',

in Franz-Reiner Erkens & Hartmut Wolff (ed.): *Von Sacerdotum und Regnum: Geistliche und weltliche Gewalt im frühen und hohen Mittelalter* (Köln: Böhlau Verlag, 2002), pp. 77–110; Thomas Gergen: *Pratique juridique de la paix et trêve de Dieu à partir du concile de Charroux (989–1250)* (Frankfurt am Main: Lang, 2004).

24. Ghislain Brunel and Élisabeth Lalou (eds & trs): *Sources d'histoire médiévale: IXe-milieu du XIVe siècle* (Paris: Larousse, 1992), p. 142f.

25. „*[rex] in regno suo vel eundem vocat regem et imperatorem*' was used by Etienne de Tournai (1128–1203), quoted in Harald Kleinschmidt: *Geschichte des Völkerrechts in Krieg und Frieden* (s.l. Narr Franke Attempto Verlag, 2013), p. 101.

26. John of Salisbury: *Policraticus* V.2, ed. by Clemens C.I. Webb (Oxford: Clarendon Press, 1909), p. 539.

27. Quoted in J.R. Hale: *War and Society in Renaissance Europe, 1450–1620* (Baltimore, MD: The Johns Hopkins University Press, 1985), pp. 22.

28. Ibid., p. 25.

29. Philippe de Commynes: Discours sur ce que les guerres et divisions sont permises de Dieu pour le chastiement et des prince et du peuple mauvais (1497–1498)': in Denis Savvage (ed.): *Mémoires de Messire Philippe de Commines* (s.l.: Iaques Chouët, 1603), ch. 18. pp. 463–65.

30. Bruno Arcidiacono: *Cinq types de paix: Une histoire des plans de pacit-ication perpétuelle (XVIIe–XXe siècles)* (Paris: PUF, 2011), pp. 92–94.

31. Dupuis: *Le Principe de l'Equilibre*, p. 17.

32. Moorhead Wright: *Theory and Practice of the Balance of Power, 1486–1914* (London: Dent, 1975), pp. xi-xvii.

33. Francisco de Vitoria: *De Indis* ('On the American Indians') in Anthony Pagden & Jeremy Lawrence (eds): *Francisco de Vitoria—Political Writings* (Cambridge: Cambridge University Press, 1991), p. 282.

34. Stephen Neff: *War and the Law of Nations* (Cambridge University Press, 2005), p. 99.

35. Many monarchs arguably had to consult their parliaments, *de facto* in order to raise money for their campaigns, or even *de jure* and by prec-edent, as Charles Davenant argued for the English case, see Charles Davenant: *Essays upon I. The Ballance of Power. II. The right of making*

war, Peace, and Alliances. III. Universal monarchy (London: Charles Knapton, 1701), Part II.

36. Quoted in Stephen Neff: *War and the Law of Nations* (Cambridge University Press, 2005), p. 7.

37. Ibid., p. 157.

38. Jean-Marie Moeglin & Stéphane Péquignot: *Diplomatie et « relations internationales » au Moyen Age* (Paris: PUF, 2017), pp. 708–17.

39. Fernando Luis Corral: 'Alfonso VIII of Castile's Judicial Process at the Court of Henry II of England: an effective and valid arbitration?', *Nottingham Medieval Studies*, Vol. L (2006), pp. 22–42.

40. Jean-Marie Moeglin & Stéphane Péquignot: *Diplomatie et « relations internationales » au Moyen Age* (Paris: PUF, 2017), pp. 705–707.

41. Jean-Pierre Bois: *La Paix: Histoire politique et militaire* (Paris: Perrin, 2012), p. 30.

42. *Le Livre de Fais d'Armes et Chevalerie*, I.iv, trs. by Sumner Willard, ed. by Charity Cannon Willard: *The Book of Deeds of Arms and of Chivalry* (University Park, PA: Pennsylvania State University Press, 1999), I.iv, p. 17f.

43. Bois: *La Paix*, pp. 36–44.

44. Bois: *La Paix*, p. 292.

45. Translation in excerpts of both in Edward Peters: *The First Crusade: The Chronicle of Fulcher of Chartres and other Source Materials* (2nd edn, Philadelphia, PA: University of Pennsylvania Press, 1971), *passim*.

46. Rudolph I in the thirteenth century had been elected King of Rome but never been crowned emperor.

47. Quoted in Brendan Simms: *Britain's Europe: A Thousand Years of Conflict and Cooperation* (2016, repr. Harmondsworth: Penguin, 2017), p. 29.

48. Quoted in Beatrice Heuser: *Strategy before Clausewitz* (Abingdon: Routledge, 2017), p. 72.

49. Quoted in loc. cit..

50. Charter to Sir Walter Raleigh of 1584, in Francis Newton Thorpe (ed.): *The Federal and State Constitutions Colonial Charters, and Other Organic Laws of the states, Territories, and Colonies Now or Heretofore Forming the United States of America* (Washington, DC: Government Printing Office, 1909), reproduced by Avalon Project.

5. EARLY MODERN HISTORY: THE BREAK-DOWN OF THE UNIVERSAL REPUBLIC OF CHRISTENDOM

1. Lollardism took its onomatopoeic name from the habit of reading the Bible text aloud.
2. Thomas Walsingham: *Historia Anglicana*, Vol. II, *1381–1422* (London: Longman, Green etc., 1864), ed. by H.T. Riley: p. 33; my translation.
3. John Donne: *Meditation* XVII: from *Devotions upon Emergent Occasions* (1624).
4. Harald Kleinschmidt: *Geschichte des Völkerrechts in Krieg und Frieden* (s.l. Narr Franke Attempto Verlag, 2013), pp. 154f.
5. Quoted in Thomas James Dandelet: *The Renaissance of Empire in Early Modern Europe* (Cambridge University Press, 2014), p. 97.
6. '*Hispanie imperator, totius Hispanie rex et magnificus imperator, Imperator Dei gratia*', see Miguel Ángel Marzal García-Quismondo: 'El Pacto de Unión', in Vincente Ángel Álvarez Palenzuela (ed): *Historia de España de la Edad Media* (Barcelona: Ariel, 2011), p. 326.
7. Schmidt: *Spanische Universalmonarchie*, p. 127.
8. *Ordenações* of Manuel I of 1514, Book three, p. 412, digital copy in http://purl.pt/14708/1/index.html#/7/html, accessed 10 VIII 2018.
9. Quoted in Jean-Pierre Bois: *La Paix: Histoire politique et militaire* (Paris: Perrin, 2012), p. 94.
10. Andreas Osiander: 'Sovereignty, international relations, and the Westphalian myth', *International organization*, Vol. 55 No. 2 (2001), pp. 251–287.
11. Niccolò Machiavelli: *Discorsi* (Florence: Bernardo di Giunta, 1513), Book II ch. 19 trs. by Leslie J. Walker, S.J. *The Discourses* (London: Penguin, 1998), p. 336.
12. Nederman, Cary: 'Sovereignty' in Maryanne Cline Horowitz (ed.): *New Dictionary of the History of Ideas* (Detroit et al.: Thomson Gale, 2005), vol. 5, pp. 2243–2246, here p. 2243. But Philippe also posited that 'every baron is *souverains* in his barony'.
13. Catherine Secretan: 'True Freedom and the Dutch Tradition of Republicanism', *Republics of Letters* Vol. 2 No. 1 (Dec. 2010), https://arcade.stanford.edu/rofl/true-freedom-and-dutch-tradition-republicanism accessed on 3 XII 2018.

14. Edmund Burke: *Reflections on the Revolution in France* (London: J. Dodley, 1790), pp. 7, 21.

15. Andreas Osiander: S*tates System of Europe, 1640–1990: Peacemaking and the Conditions of International Stability* (Oxford: Clarendon Press, 1994), p. 28.

16. Ibid., pp. 28, 30, 38.

17. Quoted in Dupuis: *Le Principe d'Équilibre et le Concert européen de la Paix de Westphalie à l'Acte d'Algésiras*, p. 19.

18. Osiander: *States System of Europe*, pp. 80ff.

19. Quoted in Richard Devetak: 'The Fear of Universal Monarchy': Balance of Power as an Ordering Practice of Liberty, in Tim Dunne & Trine Flockhart (eds): *Liberal World Orders* (Oxford: Oxford University Press, 2013), pp. 125ff.

20. Quoted in ibid., p. 130f.

21. Brendan Simms: *Three Victories and a Defeat* (Harmondsworth: Penguin, 2007), p. 37.

22. Charles Davenant: *Essays upon I. The Ballance of Power. II. The Right of Making War, Peace, and Alliances. III. Universal monarchy* (London: Charles Knapton, 1701), pp. 3ff., and *passim*.

23. Osiander: *States System of Europe*, pp. 80f., and Andreas Osiander: 'Sovereignty, international relations, and the Westphalian myth', *International organization*, Vol. 55, No. 2 (2001), pp. 251–287.

24. Francisco de Vitoria: 'The Law of War', in Anthony Pagden and Jeremy Lawrance (eds): *Vitoria—Political Writings* (Cambridge University Press, 1991), pp. 298, 304.

25. Quoted in Beatrice Heuser: *Strategy before Clausewitz* (Abingdon: Routledge, 2017), p. 147.

26. Nikos Singalas: 'Des histoires des Sultans a l'histoire de l'État: Une enquête sur le temps du pouvoir ottoman, (XVIe–XVIIIe siècles)' in Fr. Georgeon & Fr. Hitzel (eds), *Les Ottomans et le temps* (Leiden-Boston: Brill, 2012), pp. 99–128, here p. 125.

27. Quoted in Klaus Malettke: 'Frankreich als dynamisches Element in Europa', in Peter Krüger (ed.): *Das europäische Staatensystem im Wandel* (Munich: Oldenbourg, 1996), p. 44.

28. *Reformiertr Jean Butaschi: oder frantzösischer Brillen-Reisser ... Betreffend*

die heut zu Tag verübte Frantzösishce Kriegs-Actiones in Teutsch- und andern Landen durch Wunefrid Allemann Frantzösisch und Lucretium de Pavedann ins Teutsch versetzt (s.l.: s.e., 1657).

29. Brendan Simms: *Europe: The Struggle for Supremacy, 1453 to the Present* (2013, London: Penguin, 2014), p. 39.

30. Malettke: 'Frankreich als dynamisches Element', p. 55.

31. Hervé Drévillon: *L'Individu et la Guerre—du chevalier Bayard au Soldat inconnu* (Paris: Belin, 2013), p. 78.

32. Brendan Simms: *Britain's Europe: A Thousand Years of Conflict and Cooperation* (2016, repr. Harmondsworth: Penguin, 2017), p. 43.

33. Thomas Hobbes: *Leviathan* (1651, Harmondsworth: Penguin, 1987), Chapter XIII, pp., 187ff.

34. Hobbes: *Leviathan*, Chapter XVII, p. 224. I am grateful to Dr John Stone for having brought these passages to my attention.

35. Osiander: *States System of Europe*, p. 123.

36. Quoted in Dupuis: *Le Principe d'Équilibre* p. 27.

37. Osiander: *States System of Europe*, p. 124.

38. Quoted in Simms: *Britain's Europe*, p. 44.

39. Davenant: *The Ballance of Power*, pp. 7–10, 45.

40. Quoted in Osiander: *States System of Europe*, pp. 94, 124.

41. Quoted in Simms: *Britain's Europe*, pp. 44ff.

42. A reference to the French monarchy since Clovis, the oldest in Christian Europe.

43. Quoted in Malettke: 'Frankreich als dynamisches Element', p. 43.

44. Abbé de Saint-Pierre: *Projet pour render la Paix perpetuelle en Europe*, p. 5. The proofs for his first version of the work, dating from 1712, can be found at https://gallica.bnf.fr/ark:/12148/bpt6k105087z/f1.double.shift accessed on 18 July 2018.

45. Simms: *Europe*, p. 83.

46. Ibid., p. 93.

47. Davenant: *The Ballance of Power*, pp. 40, 84, 86f., 99.

48. Frederick II of Prussia: 'Political Testament of 1762' in Richard Dietrich (ed.): *Die politischen Testamente der Hohenzollern* (Cologne and Vienna: Böhlau Verlag, 1986).

6. THE QUEST FOR A PEACE SYSTEM OR A EUROPEAN UNION, 1305–1796

1. Bruno Arcidiacono: *Cinq types de paix: Une histoire des plans de pacitication perpétuelle (XVIIe–XXe siècles)* (Paris: PUF, 2011), pp. 206–212.
2. Ibid.
3. Ibid.
4. Jiři Kejř, Václav Vaněček, Ivo Dvořak et al.: *The Universal Peace Organization of King George of Bohemia: A Fifteenth Century Plan for World Peace, 1462–1464* (Prague: Publishing House of the Czechoslovak Academy of Sciences 1964).
5. That isd a place-holder for a name to be inserted.
6. Kejř, Vaněček, Dvořak et al.: *The Universal Peace Organization*, pp. 69–78 (Latin original), 81–90 (English translation).
7. Václav Vaněček: 'Historical Background', in Kejř, Vaněček, Dvořak et al.: *The Universal Peace Organization*, pp. 11–66.
8. 'Vertrag England/Frankreich/ Aragón/Kastilien/Römisch-deutscher Kaiser/Papst u. a,' London, 2. Oktober 1518 (allgemeiner Friedensvertrag), in: Thomas Rymer (ed): *Foedera, conventiones, literae et cuiuscunque generis acta publica inter reges Angliae et alios quosvis imperatores, reges, pontifices, principes vel communitates*, Bd 13. (London 1714), pp. 624–649; also in: Jean Dumont, Baron von Careels-Cron, *Corps diplomatique universel*, Vol. 4, Pt. I (Den Haag 1726), pp. 269–275.
9. Maximilien de Béthune, Duc de Sully: *Mémoires* vol. VIII (repr. London: s.e, 1778), pp. 314–320.
10. Ibid., pp. 318ff.
11. Anja Victorine Hartmann: *Rêveurs de Paix? Friedenspläne bei Crucé, Richelieu und Sully* (Hamburg: Krämer, 1995).
12. Émeric de Crucé: *Le Nouveau Cynée, ou Discours des Occasions Et Moyens d'Establir une Paix Générale Et la Liberté du Commerce par Tout le Monde* (Paris: Iacques Villery, 1623), see particularly the preface and pp. 59–62.
13. William Penn: *An Essay towards the Present and Future Peace of Europe by the Establishment of an European Diet, Parliament, or Estates* (1693–94, second edn London: Whitlock, 1696).

14. Heinz Duchhardt: 'From the Peace of Westphalia to the Congress of Vienna', in Bardo Fassbender & Anne Peters (eds): *The History of International Law* (Oxford: Oxford University Press, 2012), p. 643.

15. Bois: *La Paix*, pp. 70ff.

16. Osiander: *States System of Europe*, pp. 278, 283.

17. Heinz Duchhardt: *Frieden im Europa der Vormoderne*, p. 71.

18. Ibid., pp. 112–120.

19. Osiander: *States System of Europe*, pp. 111–120, 125, 137.

20. Ibid., p. 133.

21. Renger Evert Bruin, Lotte Jensen, David Onnekink (eds): *Performances of Peace: Utrecht 1713* (Leiden: Brill, 2015).

22. Duchhardt: *Frieden im Europa der Vormoderne* (Paderborn: Ferdinand Schöningh, 2012), p. 71.

23. '*ad firmandam stabiliendamque Pacem ac Tranquillitatem Christiani Orbis justo Potentie Aequilibrio*' [Art I., II.], quoted in Kleinschmidt: *Geschichte des Völkerrechts in Krieg und Frieden*, p. 207.

24. Davenant: *The Ballance of Power*, pp. 1–101.

25. Quoted in Simms: *Britain's Europe*, p. 66.

26. Ibid., pp. 53ff.

27. Ibid., p. 55.

28. Ulrich Preuss: 'Equality of states—Its Meaning in a Constitutionalized Global Order', *Chicago Journal of International Law* Vol. 9 No. 1 (2008), article 3, see https://chicagounbound.uchicago.edu/cgi/viewcontent. cgi?article=1455&context=cjil, accessed on 18 VII 2018.

29. Osiander: *States System of Europe*, p. 341.

30. Abbé de Saint Pierre: *Projet pour rendre la Paix perpetuelle en Europe* (Utrecht, A. Schouten, 1712), 2 vols.

31. Loc. cit.

32. Loc. cit.

33. Jean-Jacques Rousseau: *A Lasting Peace through the Federation of Europe and the State of War*, trs. from French by C.E. Vaughan (London: Constable, 1917), p. 95.

34. Jeremy Bentham: Essay 4: 'A Plan for an Universal and Perpetual Peace' (1789), in C. John Colombus (ed): *Jeremy Bentham's Plan for an Universal and Perpetual Peace* (London: Sweet & Maxwell, 1927), pp 11–40.

35. Loc. cit.

36. Loc. cit.

37. Loc. cit.

38. Anon. [Guibert]: *General Essay de Tactique* (London: chez les libraires associés, 1772) repr. in *Comte de Guibert: Stratégiques*, with an introduction by Jean-Paul Charnay (Paris: Herne, 1977), pp. 134–150, my translation.

39. Michael W. Doyle: 'Kant, Liberal Legacies, and Foreign Affairs', *Philosophy and Public Affairs*, Vol. 12, Nos. 3 & 4 (Summer and Autumn 1983), pp. 205–235 & 323–353.

40. Immanuel Kant: *Zum Ewigen Frieden: Ein philosophischer Entwurf* (Frankfurt & Leipzig, s.e., 1796), translation by Jonathan Bennet, in http://www.earlymoderntexts.com/assets/pdfs/kant1795_1.pdf accessed on 16 Aug. 2018.

41. Loc. cit.

42. Loc. cit.

43. Loc. cit.

44. Simms: *Britain's Europe*, pp. 95ff.

45. Friedrich Gentz: 'Über den Ewigen Frieden', in *Historisches Journal* (Berlin: December 1800), pp. 711–790.

46. Ibid., p. 714.

47. Ibid., pp. 721–727.

48. Johann Gottlieb Fichte: *Der geschlossne Handelsstaat* (Tübingen: Cotta, 1800).

49. Gentz: 'Über den Ewigen Frieden', pp. 730–751.

50. Ibid., pp. 751–768

51. Ibid., pp. 728ff.

52. Bois: *La Paix*, pp. 432–453.

53. Bo Stråth: *Europe's Utopias of Peace: 1815, 1919, 1951* (London: Bloomsbury, 2016), pp. 27-34, 75-88.7.

7. FROM GREAT-POWER OLIGARCHY TO NATIONALIST COMPETITION, 1813–1918

1. Osiander: *States System of Europe*, pp. 244–247

2. Winfried Baumgart: *Vom europäischen Konzert zum Völkerbund:*

Friedensschlüsse und Friedenssicherung von Wien bis Versailles (Darmstadt: Wissenschaftliche Buchgesellschaft, 1974), p. 1.

3. Osiander: *States System of Europe*, pp. 224 ff, 237.

4. Ibid., pp. 172, 185, 187, 226.

5. Ibid., p. 221.

6. Quoted in ibid., p. 249, and see also p. 247.

7. Letter to the editor by Walter Savage Landor, *The Examiner* (13 Dec 1851), p. 789.

8. Quoted in Osiander: *States System of Europe*, p. 249, and see also p. 247.

9. The Brexit Referendum of 2016 was fought entirely with economic arguments (such as savings for the National Health System by no longer paying into the European Union's budget, with the defence of 'freedom from Brussels tutelage' thrown in for good measure.

10. Osiander: *States System of Europe*, p. 188.

11. Ibid., p. 191.

12. Text in Mehdi Ouraoui (ed): *Les Grands Discours de l'Europe* (Paris: Eds. Complexe, 2008), pp. 28–37.

13. Text in https://ihl-databases.icrc.org/applic/ihl/ihl.nsf/Article.xsp?action=openDocument&documentId=568842C2B90F4A29C12563CD0051547C, accessed 9 Aug. 2018.

14. Beatrice Heuser: European laws of war (*ius in bello*) before the Lieber Code: Ordinances and Articles of War, 866–1863, in *Yearbook of International Humanitarian Law* (forthcoming, end 2019)

15. See Chapter 2.

16. Quoted by Peter Krüger:, Das Problem der Stabilisierung Europas nach 1871', in Peter Krüger (ed.): *Das europäische Staatensystem im Wandel* (Munich: Oldenbourg, 1996), pp. 176ff.

17. Quoted in Jeremy Black: *The Tory World: Deep History and the Tory Theme in British Foreign Policy, 1679–2014* (Farnham: Ashgate, 2015), p. 217.

18. See Krüger: 'Das Problem der Stabilisierung Europas nach 1871'.

19. Winfried Baumgart: *Vom europäischen Konzert zum Völkerbund: Friedensschlüsse und Friedenssicherung von Wien bis Versailles* (Darmstadt: Wissenschaftliche Buchgesellschaft, 1974), pp. 40–42.

20. He said 'musketeer', but in translation this is usually rendered 'grenadier'.

21. Baumgart: *Vom europäischen Konzert zum Völkerbund*, pp. 52–55.

22. Bois: *La Paix*, p. 541:

23. Baumgart: *Vom europäischen Konzert zum Völkerbund*, pp. 44–46.

24. Jean Nurdin: 'Die Organisation des Europäischen Staatenvereins de Johann Caspar Bluntschli (1878)', in Michel Perrin (ed): *L'Idée de l'Europe au fil de deux millénaires* (Paris: Beauchesne, 1994), pp. 185–194.

25. Loc. cit.

26. Loc. cit.

27. Text in Harry Pross (ed.): *Die Zerstörung der deutschen Politik: Dokumente 1871–1933* (Frankfurt, 1959), pp. 29–31. After translation by Richard S. Levy.

28. Loc. cit.

29. Quoted in Dupuis: *Le Principe de l'Equilibre*, p. 156.

30. Quoted in Peter M. Stirk: *A History of European Integration since 1914* (London: Continuum, 1996), p. 2.

31. Sir Eyre Crowe, Memorandum on the Present State of British Relations with France and Germany (1 January 1907), in G.P. Gooch and H. Temperly (eds): *British Documents on the Origins of the War, 1898–1914* (London: HMSO, 1928), vol. 3, pp. 402–406 (Appendix A).

32. The Austro-Hungarian Empire continued to hold Italian-speaking cities along the Dalmatian coast, for example.

33. Quoted in Stirk: *A History of European Integration*, p. 20.

34. For various interpretations of 'Liberalism', see Chapter 2.

35. Friedrich Naumann: *Mitteleuropa* (Berlin: Georg Reimer, 1915), esp. pp. 31, 263.

36. Maximilien Robespierre: 'Premier discours contre la guerre, prononcé au club des Jacobins le 18 décembre 1791', text available on http://www.beersandpolitics.com/discursos/maximilien-robespierre/les-discours-contre-la-guerre/641 accessed on 28 August 2018.

37. Dupuis: *Le Principe d'Équilibre*, p. 75.

38. Eberhard Kolb: 'Stabilisierung ohne Konsolidierung', in Peter Krüger (ed.): *Das europäische Staatensystem im Wandel* (Munich: Oldenbourg, 1996), pp. 191–193.

39. Margaret Macmillan: *The War that Ended Peace: How Europe abandoned peace for the First World War* (London: Profile Books, 2014).

40. Christopher Clarke: *The Sleepwalkers: How Europe Went to War in 1914* (London: Allen Lane, 2012).

8. RECREATING A UNIVERSAL ORDER I: THE LEAGUE OF NATIONS

1. Text available at https://www.ourdocuments.gov/doc.php?flash=false &doc=62&page=transcript accessed on 9 VIII 2018.
2. Quoted in Simms: *Britain's Europe*, p. 153.
3. Osiander: *States System of Europe*, p. 268.
4. Margaret Macmillan: *Peacemakers Six Months that Changed the World* (London: John Murray, 2001), pp. 217–280, passim.
5. Randall Lesaffer: 'Peace treaties from Lodi to Westphalia', and Heinz Duchhardt: 'Peace treaties from Westphalia to the Revolutionary Era', both in Randall Lesaffer (ed.): *Peace Treaties and International Law in European History* (Cambridge, Cambridge University Press, 2004), p. 40 and pp. 48ff. respectively.
6. Heinhard Steiger: 'Peace treaties from Paris (1814) to Versailles', in Randall Lesaffer (ed): *Peace Treaties and International Law in European History* (Cambridge, Cambridge University Press, 2004), pp. 84–88.
7. It is not without irony that the UK's debt to the EU, payable on leaving it, is referred to popularly as 'Danegeld', the levies made by the Norsemen when they occupied parts of the British Isles, thus redefining them morally as unfair exactions.
8. Text available at https://www.ourdocuments.gov/doc.php?flash=false &doc=62&page=transcript accessed on 9 VIII 2018.
9. Oona Hathaway and Scott Shapiro: *The Internationalists: And Their Plan to Outlaw War* (New York: Simon & Schuster, 2017).
10. With the *planned* but not realised membership of the United Kingdom, France, Italy, Japan, USA.
11. Quoted in Osiander: *States System of Europe*, p. 302.
12. Ibid., p. 305.
13. Richard von Coudenhove-Kalergi: *Pan Europe* (New York: A.A. Knopf, 1926), p 55.
14. Vanessa Conze: *Richard Coudenhove-Kalergi: Umstrittener Visonär*

Europas (Zurich: Muster-Schmidt Verlag Gleichen, 2004); Bois: *La Paix*, p. 558.

15. Peter M. Stirk: *A History of European Integration since 1914* (London: Continuum, 1996), pp. 34–36.

16. Text in Peter Stirk & David Weigall (eds): *The Origins and Development of European Integration* (London: Pinter, 1999), pp. 18ff.

17. Conan Fischer: *A Vision of Europe. Franco-German Relations during the Great Depression, 1929–1932* (Oxford: Oxford University Press, 2017).

18. F.S. Northedge: *The League of Nations: Its Life and Times* (Leicester: Leicester University Press, 1985).

19. Joe Maiolo: *Cry Havoc: The Arms Race and the Second World War, 1931–41* (London: John Murray, 2010).

20. Donald Cameron Watt: *How War Came: Immediate Origins of the Second World War* (London: Heinemann, 1989).

9. RECREATING A UNIVERSAL ORDER II: THE UNITED NATIONS IN THE COLD WAR

1. Albert Resis: 'The Churchill-Stalin Secret 'Percentages' Agreement on the Balkans, Moscow, October 1944', *The American Historical Review* Vol. 83, No. 2 (Apr. 1978), pp. 368–387.

2. Beatrice Heuser & Robert O'Neill (eds): *Securing Peace in Europe* (London: Macmillan, 1992).

3. Ludolf Herbst: 'Europa nach dem Zweiten Weltkrieg', in Peter Krüger (ed.): *Das europäische Staatensystem im Wandel* (Munich: Oldenbourg, 1996), p. 201.

4. Speech of 19 September 1946, text at https://rm.coe.int/16806981f3, accessed on 31 VII 2018. But in 1951 Churchill claimed 'I have never thought that Britain ... should ... become an integral part of a European Federation.' See Young: *Britain, France*, p. 185.

5. Text at https://rm.coe.int/16806981f3, accessed on 31 VII 2018.

6. *Documents of British Policy Overseas*, henceforth DBPO, Series I, Vol. XI, pp. 528–530.

7. *Documents Diplomatiques Français* (henceforth DDF) 1948 vol. I (Brussels: Peter Lang, 2011), correspondence of early January, pp. 1–23

8. DDF 1948 vol. I, 4 Feb. 1948, pp. 189ff.

9. DBPO, I.X, p 3.

10. DBPO Series I, Vol. X, p. 15

11. Ernest Bevin to the House of Commons, 22 Jan. 1948

12. DBPO, I.X, p. 42.

13. DBPO, I.X, p. 87.

14. This was Article IV in the original treaty, and after its revision in 1954 to accommodate Italy and West Germany as new members, it became Article V. http://www.cvce.eu/en/obj/the_brussels_treaty_17_march_1948-en-3467de5e-9802–4b65–8076–778bc7d164d3.html, accessed on 19 XII 2016. It was then referred to as Article V of the revised Brussels Treaty until it was wrapped into the EU's Lisbon Treaty of 2009.

15. Article 5 of the North Atlantic Treaty leaves it up to each individual member State to decide how it will react to an attack on one of its allies. This toning down of the commitment to mutual defence was made at the insistence of the US Congress which in 1949 fully understood that the formulation of the Brussels Treaty *de facto* meant a reduction of each member State's sovereign freedom—a sacrifice made, of course, in return for greater *mutual* security.

16. Anne Applebaum: *Iron Curtain: The Crushing of Eastern Europe 1944–56* (London: Penguin, 2013).

17. Elisabeth Barker: *The British Between the Superpowers, 1945–50* (London: Macmillan, 1983).

18. Here an example of how, especially in American English, the term 'national' is used for 'of the State', to differentiate the latter ('nation')-State from the individual federal states of the USA.

19. Text in Stirk & Weigall: *The Origins*, p. 60f.

20. Young: *Britain, France and the Unity of Europe, 1945–1951*, pp. 150–166.

21. Stanley Hoffman: 'Restraints and Choices in American Foreign Policy', in Wesley Posvar (ed.): *American Defense Policy* (Baltimore, MD: Johns Hopkins University Press, 1965), p. 444.

22. Heuser: *NATO, Britain, France and the FRG*, Chapters 2, 3.

10. EUROPEAN INTEGRATION: BETWEEN CONFEDERATION AND FEDERATION

1. Altiero Spinelli in 1985, quoted in Philippe Mioche (ed): *Penser et construire l'Europe*, pp. 108–110.

2. Loc. cit.

3. Text in Mioche (ed): *Penser et Construire l'Europe*, pp. 42–44.

4. For the texts of the proposals of Robert Schuman and Jean Monnet, see Stirk & Weigall (eds): *The Origins and Development of European Integration*, pp. 75–84.

5. Quoted in Simms: *Britain's Europe*, p. 181.

6. Beatrice Heuser: 'Dunkirk, Dien Bien Phu, and Suez, or why France Doesn't Trust Allies and has learned to love the bomb', in Beatrice Heuser & Cyril Buffet (eds): *Haunted by History: Myths in International Relations* (Oxford: Berghahn, 1998), pp. 157–174.

7. Geir Lundestad: *The United States and Western Europe since 1945: from 'Empire' by Invitation to Transatlantic drift* (Oxford: Oxford University Press, 2003).

8. Paul-Henri Spaak in his memoirs, text in Stirk & Weigall: *The Origins*, p. 173.

9. Beatrice Heuser: *NATO, Britain, France and the FRG: Nuclear Strategies and Forces for Europe, 1949–2000* (London: Macmillan, and New York: St Martin's Press, hardback 1997, paperback 1999), Chapter 5.

10. Beatrice Heuser: 'Britain, France and the Bomb: The Parting of Ways between Suez and Nassau', *Storia delle Relazioni Internazionali* Vol. XIII No. 3 (Autumn 1997), pp. 75–94.

11. Text in Stirk & Weigall: *The Origins*, pp. 168–170.

12. Ibid.

13. Jean-Jacques Servan-Schreiber: *Le Défi américain* (Paris: Denoël, 1968).

14. Text in Mioche: (ed): *Penser et Construire*, pp. 75–77.

15. Beatrice Heuser: 'The European Dream of Franz Josef Strauss', *Journal of European Integration History*, Vol. 3 No. 1 (Spring 1998), pp. 75–103.

16. Text in Mioche: (ed): *Penser et Construire*, pp. 110–112.

17. Text in https://www.margaretthatcher.org/document/107332 accessed on 31 VII 2018.

11. FROM THE RENEWED UN CONCERT TO THE NEW COLD WAR

1. For an introduction to the vast debate about this subject, see Lawrence Freedman with Jeff Michaels: *The Evolution of Nuclear Strategy* (4th edn, London: Palgrave Macmillan, 2019).

2. Text in Mioche: (ed): *Penser et Construire*, pp. 133–135.

3. Frédéric Bozo: *Mitterrand, la fin de la guerre froide et l'unification allemande: De Yalta à Maastricht* (Paris: Odile Jacob, 2005).

4. https://www.bundesfinanzministerium.de/Content/DE/Downloads/schaeuble-lamers-papier-1994.pdf;jsessionid=E6E83493F73129FCA30AF0B9807EF355?__blob=publicationFile&v=1, accessed on 16 Aug. 2018.

5. Beatrice Heuser: 'European strategists and European identity in the nuclear age' in *Journal of European Integration History*, Vol. 1 No. 2 (1995), pp. 61–80.

6. https://www.consilium.europa.eu/uedocs/cmsUpload/French-British%20Summit%20Declaration,%20Saint-Malo,%201998%20-%20EN.pdf, accessed 18 III 2017; and https://www.gov.uk/government/uploads/system/uploads/attachment_data/file/238153/8174.pdf accessed on 18 III 2017.

7. http://www.presidency.ucsb.edu/ws/?pid=18820, accessed on 31 VII 2018.

8. James Gow: *Legitimacy and the Military: The Yugoslav Crisis* (Basingstoke: Macmillan, 1991).

9. Adam Garfinkle: 'Three Percent, Two or Four Percent, It Doesn't Matter Anymore', talk on 18 July 2018 at the Centre for the Study of America and the West, https://www.fpri.org/article/2018/07/three-percent-two-or-four-percent-it-doesnt-matter-anymore/ accessed on 31 VII 2018.

10. Beatrice Heuser: *Transatlantic Relations: Sharing Ideals and Costs* (London: Pinter for RIIA, 1996).

11. John W. Young: *Britain, France and the Unity of Europe, 1945–1951* (Leicester: Leicester University Press, 1984), p. 165; on 2018 trade, see file:///C:/Users/Beatrice/Downloads/CBP-7851.pdf accessed on 31 VII 2018.

12. Out of a total population of around 66 million, see https://www.ons. gov.uk/peoplepopulationandcommunity/leisureandtourism/datasets/ ukresidentsvisitsabroad accessed on 16 Aug. 2018. Even allowing for multiple trips of one person counted separately, these are big figures in relation to the total population.

13. Adam Garfinkle: 'Three Percent, Two or Four Percent, It Doesn't Matter Anymore', talk on 18 July 2018 at the Centre for the Study of America and the West, https://www.fpri.org/article/2018/07/three-percent-two-or-four-percent-it-doesnt-matter-anymore/ accessed on 31 VII 2018.

12. CONCLUSIONS

1. The historian-archaeologist Ian Morris has even deduced from this that empires in general are a good thing, see id.: *War: What is it Good For? The Role of Conflict in Civilisation, from Primates to Robots* (New York: Profile Books, 2014).

2. Frank-Lothar Kroll: *Geburt der Moderne. Politik, Gesellschaft und Kultur vor dem Ersten Weltkrieg* (Bonn: Bundeszentrale für Politische Bildung, 2013).

3. Russell Weigley: *The Age of Battles: The Quest for Decisive Warfare from Breitenfeld to Waterloo* (Bloomington, IN: Indiana University Press, 1991).

4. See Beatrice Heuser: 'Containing Uncertainty: Options for British Nuclear Strategy', *Review of International Studies* Vol. 19 No. 3 (July 1993), pp. 245–267.

5. It is worth pondering the comment to de Gaulle made by Harold Macmillan in 1956, when he was still Chancellor of the Exchequer: he claimed that the nascent Common Market which excluded Britain 'is the [Napoleonic] Continental System all over again', a system that had been aimed at destroying British commerce. And while the rest of his words did not befit the spirit in which the EEC was created, it could acquire a new relevance in some non-too distant future age of renewed collective selfishness and competition: he feared that with Britain out-side the EEC, 'we shall be embarking on a war which will doubtless be

economic at first but which runs the risk of gradually spreading into other fields.' Quoted in Simms: *Britain's Europe*, p. 181. Macmillan consequently pushed for British membership of the EEC, not least to prevent such a dangerous return to rivalry and competition in collective selfishness from materialising.

INDEX

Aachen Peace Congress (1818), 152

Achaemenid Empire (550–330 BC), 46–7

Act of Settlement (1652), 29

Addis Ababa, 34

Adenauer, Konrad, 211, 213

Adriatic Sea, 19

Aegean Sea, 19, 20, 46

Aeneid (Virgil), 55

'Age of Battles', 239

Aix-la-Chapelle Peace Congress (1818), 149, 151

Albania, 32

Albanians, 32

Albigensian Crusade (1209–29), 37

Alemanni tribe, 60

Alexander I, Emperor of Russia, 150, 153

Alexander II, Emperor of Russia, 154, 160

Alexander III 'the Great', King of Macedon, 11, 52–3

Alexander VI, Pope, 84

Alexandria, 57, 66

Alfonso I, King of Aragon, 92

Alfonso VII, King of Leon and Castile, 92

Alfonso VIII, King of Castile, 78

Algeria, 108

alliances 2, 8, 44, 47, 49, 51, 54, 79, 94, 101, 104a, 108, 112, 121, 123, 135, 142a, 145, 150, 152, 158, 167, 172a, 180a, 186a, 193a, 213f, 217, 222–224, 232a, 237

Alsace, 30, 32, 62, 112, 176

Alto Adige, 216

Amsterdam, 34

Anastasius I, Byzantine Emperor, 60

Anglicanism, 72

Anglo-Saxons, 21, 29, 72

Antarctica, 24

Antioch, 56, 66

Aquileia, 56

Arabs, 2, 107

INDEX

Arcidiacono, Bruno, 69
Arctic, 24
Aristotle, 47, 51, 74, 146, 230
Arkhangelsk, 34
Armenians, 34, 35
Arras, 79
al-Assad, Bashar, 227
Aston Tirrold, 21
Aston Upthorpe, 21
Atatürk, Mustafa Kemal, 233
Athens, 34, 47–52, 54
Attila the Hun, 53
Attlee, Clement, 194, 197, 214
Augsburg, 89, 90, 96
Augustine, Saint, 50, 68, 106
Augustus, Elector of Saxony, 79
Augustus, Roman Emperor, 14, 55, 56–7
Austerlitz, battle of (1805), 142
Austria, 26, 32, 36, 75
  Allied occupation (1945–55), 193, 218
  Austro-Hungarian Empire (1867–1918), 39, 162, 167, 168, 173, 176
  Congress System, 149, 153, 155–6, 158–9
  Empire (1804–67), 149, 153, 155–6, 158–9, 164–5, 171, 177
  and European Free Trade Area, 206
  and German 'nation-state', 32, 218
  guest workers, 29

Habsburg Austria (1526–1804), 32, 40, 63, 81, 92, 103, 110, 111, 113–16, 133, 143, 151
  Italian War of Independence, Second, (1859), 155
  and *Mitteleuropa*, 168, 169
  Napoleonic Wars (1803–15), 144
  Ottoman Wars, 94, 101, 108, 109
  Prussian War (1866), 156, 171, 177
  Roman period (c. 14 BC–395 AD), 27
  Triple Alliance (1882–1915), 167
  Vienna Peace Congress (1814–15), 149–50, 177
  World War I (1914–18), 167, 173, 176
  World War II (1939–45), 193
Austro-Hungarian Empire (1867–1918), 39, 162, 167, 168, 173, 176
autochthonous peoples, 25
Avars, 67
Avignon, 66
Azores, 84

Babylon, 43
Bahamas, 209
balance of power, 42, 75–6, 104–6, 118, 119, 129–32, 145, 157, 177, 239
  Britain and, 105–6, 114, 115,

131–2, 144, 156, 157, 160, 177, 193–4
Crimean War and, 155
France and, 94–5, 104–6, 114, 115, 144, 145, 177
German unification and, 158, 166–7
Holy Roman Empire and, 75, 94–5
League of Augsburg and, 115
Ottoman Empire and, 160
Vienna Peace Congress and, 151
Baldwin, Stanley, 23
Bâle (Basel), Switzerland, 122
Balkans, 107, 108, 158–60, 161, 218, 221
Ball, John, 88, 101
Baltic Sea, 19, 37
Baptist Church, 154
Bar, French region of, 78
Bartolo da Sassoferato, 70
Basques, 26, 29
battles—see place name
Bavaria, 118, 166, 171
Beaumanoir, Philippe de, 98–9
Bebenburg, Lupold von, 70
Becket, Thomas, 72, 73
Belgium, 20, 23, 26, 29, 36, 39, 62, 63, 176, 194, 203
Belgrade, 110, 225
Bentham, Jeremy, 8, 135–7, 146, 175, 177, 179, 181
Berbers, 2
Berlin airlift (1948–9), 24

Berlin Peace Congress (1878) 158–60
Berlin Wall, 218
Bethel, Slingsby, 105
Bethmann Hollweg, Theobald von, 168
Béthune de, Maximilien, Duke of Sully, 124–5, 137, 146, 178, 202
Bevin, Ernest, 194, 197, 214, 231
Beyen, Johan Willem, 202
Bible, 4, 43, 44, 70
Bidault, Georges, 194
Bill of Rights (1689), 102
Bismarck, Herbert von, 159
Bismarck, Prince Otto von, 32, 156, 159–60, 165, 239
Black Sea, 108
Blum, Léon, 187
Bluntschli, Johann Kaspar, 161, 196
Bodin, Jean, 99–100, 241
Bohemia, 30, 37, 87, 89, 90, 171
Bois, Jean-Pierre, 79
Bologna, 75, 92
Bonaparte, Louis-Napoleon, *see* Napoleon III
Boniface VIII, Pope, 77, 78
Book of Deeds of Arms and of Chivalry (de Pizan), 78
Borgia, Rodrigo, 84
Bosnia, 32, 108, 159
Bosniaks, 31
Bourbon, House of, 110, 111, 116, 117, 118, 150, 165, 169

INDEX

Bouvines, battle of (1214), 110

Bovet, Honoré, 66

Brabant, 78

Brandenburg, Dukes of, 152

Bretons, 29, 30

Briand-Kellogg Pact (1928), 179, 182, 241

Briand, Aristide, 179, 182–4, 202, 203

Britain, 33

  Act of Supremacy (1534), 72

  Anglo-Saxon period (c. 500–1066), 21, 29, 72

  balance of power, 75, 105–6, 114, 115, 131–2, 144, 156, 157, 160, 177, 193–4

  Celtic peoples, 21, 26, 29

  colonial empire, 15, 84–5, 135, 151, 206–7, 208, 214

  Commonwealth of Nations, 2, 198, 206, 207

  Commonwealth period (1649– 60), 14, 29, 102–3

  Congress System, 149–51, 153–8, 160

  Council of Europe, 196–7

  Declaration of Arbroath (1320), 11

  East of Suez withdrawal (1971), 214

  Entente Cordiale (1904), 166

  and 'European Affairs Commit-tee', 194

  and European Coal and Steel Community, 204

  and European Economic Com-munity, 1, 205–7, 214, 215

  and European Free Trade Area, 206

  and European Union, core of, 220–21

  and European Union, referen-dum on membership (2016), 1, 3, 230

  Glorious Revolution (1688), 114–15

  as island, 131

  Jacobite Rebellions (1688– 1746), 87

  and League of Nations, 177, 179, 181, 186

  Magna Carta (1215), 11

  Munich Conference (1938), 187

  Napoleonic Wars (1803–15), 22, 144

  non-intervention, 156

  Norman period (1066–1154), 72

  Peasants' Revolt (1381), 88, 101

  Plantagenet period (1154– 1485), 72, 78, 79, 83, 117

  Picts, 26, 57

  pre-Indo–European popula-tions, 26

  Roman period (c. 43–410), 21, 26, 27, 57

  sea, connection to, 37

  Sterling Area, 197, 210, 207, 231

Stuart period (1603–1714), 90, 114–15, 117
Suez Crisis (1956), 210, 224
Thirty Years' War intervention (1625–38), 90
Treaty of Brussels (1948), 194
Treaty of Dunkirk (1947), 193, 223
Tudor period (1485–1603), 71–2, 76, 82–3, 93, 94, 97, 101, 102, 115, 117
United States, relations with, 2, 198, 207, 208–10, 232
Utrecht Peace Congress (1712–13), 129–30
Wars of the Three Kingdoms (1639–51), 87, 90, 102, 103
and Western Union, 195
World War I (1914–18), 23, 177
World War II (1939–45), 187, 188, 189–90
Brittany, 26, 30
Brussels, 36
Budapest Memorandum on Security Assurances (1994), 227
Bulgaria, 27, 36, 37, 38, 108, 170
Burgundy, 62, 67, 74, 79, 81, 94
burka, 13
Burke, Edmund, 12, 102
Bush, George Walker, 223
Byelorussia, 193
Byzantine Empire (395–1453), 20, 35, 56, 57, 59, 60–61, 64–5, 83, 91, 107, 238

Calabria, 30
Calais, 117
Caledonia, see Scotland
Calvin, John, 89
Canada, 195
Cape Verde, 84
Caracalla, Roman Emperor, 55, 57
Carnac, 26
Carteret, John, 2nd Earl Granville, 132
Carthage (814–146 BC), 19, 34, 55
Casimir IV Jagellon, King of Poland, 123
Castel, Charles-Irénée, Abbé de Saint-Pierre, 3, 116, 132–5, 137, 142, 146, 178, 219
Castile, 78, 81
Catalans, 31
Catherine the Great, Empress of Russia, 29
Catholicism, 38, 57, 61, 68, 72, 81, 82, 83, 87, 89–90, 101, 115
Celtic peoples, 18, 21, 26, 27, 29, 55
Chamberlain, Neville, 187
Champagne, 78
Charlemagne, 15, 28, 62–4, 65, 111, 143, 164, 242
Charles I, King of England, Scotland and Ireland, 117
Charles I, King of Spain, see Charles V, Holy Roman Emperor

INDEX

Charles II, King of England, Scotland and Ireland, 112

Charles IV, Holy Roman Emperor, 70

Charles V, Holy Roman Emperor, 88, 89, 91, 92, 94–5, 109, 111, 124, 171

Charles V, King of France, 78

Charles VII, King of France, 79

Charles VIII, King of France, 75

Charles XII, King of Sweden, 114

China, 21, 84, 125, 157, 191, 231, 241, 246

Chinese diaspora, 35

Christian Commonwealth of Europe, 124–5, 238

Christianity, 14, 37, 59–85, 87–118, 234
  Anglicanism, 72
  Baptist Church, 154
  Bible, 4, 43, 44, 70
  Catholicism, 38, 57, 61, 68, 72, 81, 83, 87, 89–90, 101, 115
  Christendom, 14, 35, 42, 59, 67–9, 74, 81, 95, 104, 106–8, 111, 120, 123, 128–9, 238
  Christian Commonwealth of Europe, 124–5
  commonwealth, 14
  Counter-Reformation (c. 1545–1781), 81, 89, 101, 103
  George Podiebrad proposal and, 122–3
  and heterodoxy, 60, 61
  indulgences, sale of, 89
  International Peace Congress (1849), 154
  and just war, 45, 68, 69, 87
  Methodist Church, 154
  Papacy, see under Papacy
  Protestantism, 12, 29, 38, 82, 88–90, 94, 100–106, 111, 113
  Reformation (c. 1517–1648), 16, 45, 60, 69, 87, 88–90, 94, 95, 97, 100–106
  Rome and, 45, 56, 57, 60
  Sully proposal and, 124–5
  'turning the other cheek', 60
  Utrecht Peace Congress and, 130

Christina, Queen of Sweden, 105

Christine de Pizan, 78

Church of St Peter's, Rome, 89

Churchill, John, 1st Duke of Marlborough, 115

Churchill, Winston, 1, 189, 192–3, 201, 203, 226

Cicero, 48

cities, 35–6, 38

city states, 10, 34, 147

civil war, 10, 49, 50

Clemenceau, Georges, 177

Clement VII, Pope, 92

Clermont, 80

Clovis, King of the Franks, 60, 62, 213

coal, 23, 29, 38, 202–4

Colbert, Jean-Baptiste, 115

Cold War (1946–1990), 49, 191, 195, 198, 217–19, 221, 226–7

INDEX

collective identity, 34
collective memories, 36
Cologne, 70, 96
colonial empires, 12, 15, 83–4, 91, 92, 93, 135, 164–73, 185–6
Columbus, Christopher, 84
Commonwealth of Nations, 2, 198, 206, 207, 232
commonwealth, 14
Communism, 103, 169, 187, 193
de Commynes, Philippe, 74–5
Conference on Security and Cooperation in Europe (1973–5), 191
Confessional Wars, 37, 46, 49, 69, 87, 95, 97, 101, 106, 111, 238, 239
Congress System, 5, 148, 149–60, 173, 190, 224, 240
Constantinople, 20, 46, 56, 59, 60, 61, 66, 83, 91, 94, 108, 109, 116, 153, 160, 164
constitutions, 12
Constructivism, 17
consultation, 97
'core Europe', 220
Cornish language, 30
Corsicans, 29
Coudenhove-Kalergi, Count Richard von, 181–4, 202, 224, 232
Council of Europe, 196, 197
Counter-Reformation (c. 1545–1781), 81, 89, 101, 103
Coutumes de Beauvaisis (de Beaumanoir), 98–9

Crete, 25, 26
Crimea
    Crimean War (1853–1856), 152, 155, 156, 159
    Russian annexation (2014), 227
Croatia, 36, 225
Croats, 31, 32, 96, 188
Cromwell, Oliver, 14, 29, 102–3, 153
Crowe, Sir Eyre, 23, 166
Crucé, Emeric de, 125, 137, 178
Crusades, 37, 46, 67, 69, 80, 107
Cyprus, 37
Cyrus the Great, 40
Czech Republic, 37, 229, 233
Czechoslovakia, 33, 187, 226

Dante Alighieri, 70
Danube river, 19, 26, 64
Danzig, see Gdansk
Darfur, 27
Davenant, Charles, 118, 130
David, King of Israel, 44–5
Declaration of Arbroath (1320), 11
Deeds of God through the Franks, The (de Nogent) 45
Deeds of the Franks, The, 80
De Gasperi, Alcide, 202–3
defence co-operation, 221–2
Delian League, 47, 51
democracy, 7, 12, 41, 52, 103, 140–41
Democratic Peace Theory, 139
Denmark, 33, 79, 156, 195, 196, 206, 214, 221

INDEX

Derby, Earl of, *see* Stanley,
   Edward Henry, 15th Earl of
   Derby
despotism, 140
Deutsch, Karl, 137
Devereux, Robert, 2nd Earl of
   Essex, 82
*Dialogue on the Power of the Pope
   and the Emperor* (William of
   Ockham), 70
Diet of Augsburg (1555), 89, 90
Diet of Worms (1521), 89
Diocletian, Roman Emperor, 57
disarmament, 241, 244
*Discourses on the First Ten Books of
   Titus Livius* (Machiavelli), 97
Disraeli, Benjamin, 160, 166
Don river, 19
Donne, John, 90, 131
Dorchester, 21
Dubois, Pierre, 120–21, 178, 202,
   214
Dubrovnik, 19
Duchhardt, Heinz, 4
Dunant, Henri, 154
Dunkirk evacuation (1940), 188
Dutch Republic (1581–1795), 9,
   102, 126

earthquakes, 24
East Frankish Kingdom (843–
   962), 63, 64
East Germany (German
   Democratic Republic, 1949–
   90), 226

'Eastern Question', 159
Eastern Roman Empire, *see*
   Byzantine Empire
economic migrants, 29–30
Edict of Nantes (1698), 113
Edward III, King of England, 93
Egypt, 210, 224
Egypt, ancient, 18, 43–4, 57
Eighty Years' War (1568–1648),
   38, 90
Elizabeth I, Queen of England
   and Ireland, 82, 84–5, 93, 124
Elizabeth II, Queen of England
   (as Elizabeth I, Queen of
   Scotland), 33
Elysée Treaty (1963), 213
empire, 7, 15, 119, 142, 238–9
Encyclopaedia Britannica, 157
Engelbert of Admont, 70
Engels, Friedrich, 161, 169
England
   Act of Supremacy (1534), 72
   Anglo-Saxon period (c.
      500–1066), 21, 29, 72
   balance of power, 75, 76, 105–6
   Battle of Bouvines (1214), 110
   Becket assassination (1170), 72
   Bill of Rights (1689), 102
   Burgundy, relations with, 79
   Celtic peoples, 21, 26, 29
   Civil War (1642–51), 87, 90,
      102, 103, 153
   colonial empire, 84–5
   Commonwealth period (1649–
      60), 14, 29, 102–3, 105

Glorious Revolution (1688), 114–15

Hundred Years' War (1337–1453), 81, 98, 117

Jewish population, 35

Magna Carta (1215), 11

mediation in, 78

Norman period (1066–1154), 72

and Papacy, 71–2, 89

Peasants' Revolt (1381), 88, 101

Plantagenet period (1154–1485), 72, 78, 79, 82, 83, 117

pre-Indo-European populations, 26

Protestantism, 82

proto-nationalism, 81–2

Roman period (c. 43–410), 21, 27

sovereignty, 72–3, 74, 89, 92, 245

Stuart period (1603–1714), 90, 114–15, 117

Thirty Years' War intervention (1625–30), 90

Tudor period (1485–1603), 71–2, 76, 82–3, 93, 94, 97, 101, 102, 115, 117

War of the Spanish Succession (1701–14), 101, 115

and world rule, 93

English Channel, 22, 23, 82

Enlightenment, 137, 139, 147, 162, 172, 175, 184

Erasmus of Rotterdam, 123

Erdoğan, Recep Tayyip, 233

Essex, Earl of, see Devereux, Robert

Esslingen on the Neckar, 96

Estates, 9, 112, 129

états de droit, 196

Ethiopia, 125, 186

ethnic minorities, 29, 31

Étienne de Tournai, 71

Etruscan civilization (c. 900–100 BC), 26, 54

EURATOM, 205, 206, 213

Euro (single currency), 215, 216, 220

European Affairs Committee, 194

European Army, 204

European Bank for Investment, 205

European Central Bank, 215

European Charter of Human Rights, 39, 244

European Coal and Steel Community, 202–4, 206

European Commission, 205

European Convention of Human Rights, 197

European Court of Human Rights, 197

European Court of Justice, 203

European Economic Community, 205–7, 208, 211–15

Council of Ministers, 205

European Council, 214

Treaty of Rome (1957), 205

INDEX

Single European Act (1986), 215

UK membership bids (1961, 1967), 1, 207

European Parliament, 202, 204, 211, 213, 215

European Social Fund, 205

European Union (EU), 135, 220–21, 228–9, 232–5, 242, 244–6

   Council of Ministers, 126

   Euro, 215, 216, 220

   Qualified Majority Voting, 126

   Schengen Area, 216, 219–20

   Treaty of Lisbon (2007), 199

   UK membership referendum (2016), 1, 3, 230

   and warfare, 5

European Union of Federalists, 192

Eurotunnel, 37

Examiner, The, 152

failed states, 10

Fascism, 184–7, 195, 229

federalism, 2, 9, 14, 16, 146, 166, 182–3, 192–4, 197, 202, 220–21

Fénelon, François, 114

Ferdinand I, Holy Roman Emperor, 92, 109

Ferdinand II, Holy Roman Emperor, 90, 103

Ferdinand II, King of Aragon, 81

Fichte, Johann Gottlieb, 146

FIFA (Fédération Internationale de Football Association), 232

financial crisis

   1929–39: 184

   2008: 228–9

Finland, 206, 208

First World War, *see* World War I

Fiume, 188

Flemish language, 20, 96

Florence, Republic of (1115–1532), 75, 102

Fouchet, Christian, 213

Fourteen Points (1918), 175–6, 184

France, 63

   balance of power, 75, 76, 94–5, 104–6, 114, 115, 144, 145, 177

   Battle of Bouvines (1214), 110

   Battle of Pavia (1525), 94

   Briand-Kellogg Pact (1928), 179, 182, 241

   Burgundy, relations with, 79

   coal, 23, 29

   colonial empire, 135, 151, 164–6, 208

   Congress System, 149–51, 153–5, 159

   Council of Europe, 196–7

   Crusades, 80

   defence co-operation, 222

   Edict of Nantes (1698), 113

   Elysée Treaty (1963), 213

   Entente Cordiale (1904), 166

   and 'European Affairs Committee', 194

and European Army, 204
and European Coal and Steel Community, 202–4, 206
and European Economic Community, 205–7, 211–16
Gauls, 26
geography and, 19
George Podiebrad proposal and, 122–3
Holy Roman Empire, relations with, 2, 70, 71, 94–5, 97, 110, 111, 117, 124, 142–3
Hundred Years' War (1337–1453), 81, 98, 117
International Peace Congress (1849), 154
and Islam, 35, 36
Italian Wars, 75
Jacquerie (1358), 101
Jewish population, 35
language in, 20, 30
and League of Nations, 177, 179, 181, 186
Lumières, 14
mediation in, 78, 79
Mexico, relations with, 166
Napoleonic period (1803–15), 22, 53, 102, 142–4, 149–50, 169, 177, 213, 239
and NATO, 204, 208, 214, 222
North African population, 35
nuclear weapons, 198, 204, 207, 208, 210, 222
Ottoman Empire, relations with, 101, 108

and Papacy, 71–2, 89
Paris Peace Congress (1849), 154
Paris Peace Treaties (1918–1919), 177, 180
and *Pax Dei*, 71
Penn proposal and, 126, 128
pre-Indo-European populations, 26
President, 141
Prussian War (1870–71), 23, 154, 156, 165, 176
Religious Wars (1562–98), 90
Revolution (1789–99), *see under* French Revolution
Revolution (1848), 169
Roman period (c. 121 BC–476 AD), 27, 56
rural areas, 38
Saint-Pierre proposal and, 133
Seven Years' War (1756–63), 137–8
sovereignty, 74, 89, 92, 204, 239, 245
and Spanish Civil War (1936–9), 186–7
steel, 29
Stettin Peace Congress (1570), 79
Suez Crisis (1956), 210, 224
Sully proposal and, 125
Sweden, relations with, 103–5, 111–12, 114
Third Republic (1870–1940), 166, 170

INDEX

Thirty Years' War intervention (1635–48), 101

Treaty of Brussels (1948), 194

Treaty of Dunkirk (1947), 193, 223

Treaty of Frankfurt (1871), 177

Treaty of Madrid (1526), 94

Treaty of Paris (1814), 150

Treaty of Paris (1856), 155

Treaty of Vienna (1815), 177

Treaty of Westphalia (1648), 96, 103–4, 112, 115, 128–9

UK EEC membership bids (1961, 1967), 1, 207

United States, relations with, 208, 210, 212, 239

Utrecht Peace Congress (1712–13), 129–30

War of the Spanish Succession (1701–14), 101, 115, 116

and Western Union, 195

and world rule, 93

World War I (1914–18), 23, 173, 176, 177

World War II (1939–45), 23, 187, 188

and Yugoslav Wars (1991–2001), 225

Francis I, Holy Roman Emperor, 97

Francis I, King of France, 94–5, 97, 124

Franco-Prussian War (1870–71), 23, 154, 156, 165

Franco, Francisco, 186–7

Frankfurt on the Main, 96

Frankish Empire (481–843), 10, 21, 28, 60, 62, 65, 80

Frederick II, King of Prussia, 76, 98, 118, 136

Frederick III, Holy Roman Emperor, 81, 121

Frederick V, Elector Palatine, 90

Frederick William III, King of Prussia, 145

free trade, 12, 167

freedom, 11–13, 41, 100–106, 140, 153

French Revolution (1789–99), 34, 36, 88, 101, 102, 117, 137, 139, 142, 147, 150, 169

balance of power and, 145

Napoleon and, 142, 144

and 'nation-states' 8, 33

Robespierre and, 102, 170

Terror, 12, 139

United Kingdom and, 12, 170

Frisia, 30

Fugger family, 94

Gaelic, 30

Gallicanism, 71

Garfinkel, Adam, 230, 233

Gascoyne-Cecil, Robert, Marquess of Salisbury, 157

Gastarbeiter, 29

Gaul, 26, 56

Gaulle, Charles de, 1–2, 182, 201, 207, 210–14

Gdansk, 19

INDEX

General Council (*concilium generale*), 120–21
Geneva, 178
Genghis Khan, 53
Genoa, Republic of (1005–1797), 25, 75, 133
genocide, 13, 31, 38
Gentz, Friedrich von, 145–8, 152–3
geography, 18–25
geopolitics, 18–25, 247
George Podiebrad, King of Bohemia, 89, 121–3, 124, 178, 202, 214
Georgia, 227
geostrategy, 20
Gerlach, Leopold von, 158
Germany, 123
  anti-war sentiment, 222
  Axis alliance (1936–45), 181
  Berlin airlift (1948–9), 24
  colonial empire, 166, 167, 171
  Congress System, 156, 158–9
  and 'core Europe', 220
  East Germany (1949–90), 226
  Elysée Treaty (1963), 213
  Empire (1871–1918), 23, 32, 63, 156, 158–9, 165–9
  and European Coal and Steel Community, 202–4
  and European Economic Community, 205, 208, 211, 213, 215
  Gastarbeiter, 29
  geography and, 22
  Holocaust, 13, 34, 37, 38, 185
  and League of Nations, 180
  Liberals, 12, 168
  Locarno Treaties (1925), 182
  and *Mitteleuropa*, 167–9
  Molotov–Ribbentrop Pact (1939), 188
  Munich Conference (1938), 187
  Nazi period (1933–45), 13, 22, 32, 38, 63, 181, 185, 186, 187–8, 229
  and NATO, 195, 198
  nuclear weapons in, 198
  pan-German nationalism, 32
  Paris Peace Treaties (1918–1919), 177–8
  reunification (1990), 218–19
  Treaty of Brest-Litovsk (1918), 176
  Triple Alliance (1882–1915), 167
  Weimar period (1918–33), 226
  West Germany (1949–90), 195, 198, 202–4, 205, 206, 208, 211, 213, 215
  World War I (1914–18), 23, 176, 177–8
  World War II (1939–45), 23, 33, 34, 38, 187–8
ghettos, 36, 39
Ghibellines, 65
Gibraltar, 117, 156
Giovanni da Legnano, 70
Giscard d'Estaing, Valéry, 214

INDEX

Gladstone, William, 192

Glorious Revolution (1688), 114–15

Good Friday Agreements (1998), 33

Gorbachev, Mikhail, 217, 223

Goths, 67, 107

Granada, 81

Grand Design (Duke of Sully), 124, 126

Greece, 29, 36, 37, 38, 153, 156, 169–70, 193, 195, 196
  ancient, 2, 10, 15, 19, 34, 43, 46–53, 74, 113, 238

Greek diaspora, 35

Griko, 30

Groningen, 19

Grossraum, 22

Guelfs, 65

Guibert, Jacques Antoine Hippolyte Count de, 137–139, 181, 196, 224

Guibert de Nogent, 80Guicciardini, Francesco, 48, 75

Gustavus II Adolphus, King of Sweden, 111

Habsburg, House of, 15, 40, 83, 110, 151, 162
  Austria, rule of, 32, 40, 63, 81, 92, 103, 110, 111, 113–16, 133, 143, 151, 171
  Bourbons, rivalry with, 110, 165, 170

Counter-Reformation, 81, 89, 101

Holy Roman Empire, rule of, 71, 81, 90, 91, 94, 96, 97, 108–10, 111, 117, 192

Netherlands, rule of, 38, 82, 90, 102, 171

Ottoman Wars, 94, 101, 108–10

Spain, rule of, 38, 40, 63, 81, 82, 90, 110, 111, 115, 116, 171

Valois, rivalry with, 83, 110, 165, 170

Haile Selassie, Emperor of Ethiopia, 186

Hale, John Rigby, 74

Hamburg, 19

Hanover, 171

Hanse (1358–1862), 10, 19, 34, 147, 166, 234

Harmsworth, Alfred, 1st Viscount Northcliffe, 23

Haushofer, Karl, 22

heartland, 21

Hebrew Bible, 4, 43, 44

Heidelberg, University of, 161

Helsinki Final Agreement (1975), 13, 191

Helvetian Confederation, 161–2

Henri II, King of France, 93

Henri IV, King of France, 117, 124–5, 126

Henri, Duke of Rohan, 104

Henry I, King of England, 72

INDEX

Henry II, King of England, 72, 78
Henry the Fowler, King of the
    East Franks, 64
Henry the Seafarer, 93
Henry VI, King of England, 79
Henry VIII, King of England and
    Ireland, 71–2, 76, 94, 97
Heraclius, Byzantine Emperor, 61
Herodotus, 47
Historians for Britain', 72
History of Italy (Guicciardini), 75
Hitler, Adolf, 22, 32, 53, 184,
    185, 186, 187, 188, 239
Hittites, 43–4
Hobbes, Thomas, 48, 112, 113,
    128
Hoffman, Stanley, 198
Hohenzollern, House of, 32, 117,
    156, 165–6, 170, 192
Holocaust, 13, 34, 37, 38, 185
Holy Alliance (1815), 150, 153
Holy Roman Empire (800–1806),
    2, 15–16, 32, 42, 59, 62–6,
    69–71, 74, 88–118, 238–40,
    242
    Aulic Council, 95
    and balance of power, 75, 94–5
    Battle of Bouvines (1214), 110
    Battle of Pavia (1525), 94
    Councils, 96
    Diet of Augsburg (1555), 89,
        90
    Diet of Worms (1521), 89
    ethnicities, 30, 63
    France, relations with, 2, 70,
        71, 94–5, 97

freyheiten, 11–12
    as 'German nation', 96
    Habsburg dynasty (1273–1806),
        71, 81, 90, 91, 94, 96, 97,
        108–10, 111, 117, 192
    Hussite Wars (1419–34), 37,
        87, 89
    Imperial Diet, 96, 98
    imperium, 14–15
    Landfrieden, 69
    Napoleonic Wars (1803–15),
        142
    Ottoman Wars, 91–2, 94, 98,
        101, 108–10
    Ottonian dynasty (919–1024),
        15, 64–5
    Peasant Revolts (1524–5), 90,
        101
    proto-nationalism, 81–2, 103
    Reformation, 88–90
    Roman empire, continuity
        from, 70, 91
    Seven Years' War (1756–63),
        137
    Thirty Years' War (1618–48),
        79, 87, 88, 90, 95, 96, 97,
        100–101, 103
    Treaty of Westphalia (1648),
        96, 103–4, 112, 115
    universal jurisdiction of, 69–71,
        74, 77, 92, 111
Homer, 50
homo neanderthalensis, 25–6
homo sapiens, 25–6
Howard, Esme, 177

Hugo, Victor, 154
human rights, 12–13, 39, 169, 196, 197, 234, 242, 244–6
Hume, David, 48
Hundred Years' War (1337–1453), 81, 98, 117
Hungary, 26, 123, 169, 218, 233
    Austro-Hungarian Empire (1867–1918), 39, 162, 167, 168, 173, 176
    Crimean War (1853–1856), 159
    and George Podiebrad proposal, 123
    Habsburg Hungary (1526–1867), 152
    and Holy Roman Empire, 96, 97
    and Islam, 36, 37
    migrant crisis (2015–), 36, 229
    and *Mitteleuropa*, 168, 169
    and Ottoman Empire, 94, 108, 10, 159
    Revolution (1956), 226
    and Romania, 218
    World War I (1914–18), 173, 176
Huns, 20
Hus, Jan, 89
Hussite Wars (1419–34), 37, 87, 89
Hussites, 123

Iberian Peninsula, 26, 57, 66, 78, 80, 123
Idealism, 17, 103, 189

imagined communities, 35–6
immigration, 25–31, 39, 229, 235
imperium, 7, 14–15, 70, 92
India, 15, 18
Indian diaspora, 35, 37
Indo-Europeans, 26–7
Indonesia, 20, 25
Industrial Revolution, 38
Ingres, Jean-Auguste-Dominique, 143
Innocent III, Pope, 77
inter-state relations, 9, 10
Intermediate-Range Ballistic Missiles, 23
Intermediate-Range Nuclear Forces Treaty (1987), 217
International Charter on Human Rights (1948), 13
International Committee of the Red Cross, 154–5, 164
International Peace Congress (1849), 154
International Relations, 3–6, 7–9, 13, 16–18, 41, 50f, 85, 125, 139
International Workingmen's Association, 169
international, 7, 8–9
Internationalism, 41
Ionian Sea, 20
Iraq, 223, 226
Ireland, 38, 41, 85, 135, 196, 214, 228
    Good Friday Agreements (1998), 33'irénistes', 132–3
Isabella I, queen of Castile, 81

INDEX

Islam, 2, 13, 35, 36, 40, 57–8,
61–2, 66–7, 83, 106–10, 218,
233
and armistices, 91–2, 109–10
Dar al-Harb, 58, 109
isolationism, 132, 156, 180, 190,
209
Israelites, 44–6
Italian Wars (1494–1559), 75, 94
Italy, 10, 19, 26, 29
anti-war sentiment, 222
Axis alliance (1936–43), 181
balance of power, 75
Battle of Pavia (1525), 94
Bologna, Republic of (1115–
1506), 75
Byzantine Empire (395–1453),
20
colonial empire, 185–6
Charles VIII's invasion (1494),
75
Council of Europe, 196
Ethiopian War (1935–6), 186
Etruscan civilization (c.
900–100 BC), 26, 54
and European Coal and Steel
Community, 204
and European Economic Com-
munity, 205, 208
Fascist period (1922–43), 184,
185–6, 195
Florence, Republic of (1115–
1532), 75, 102
Genoa, Republic of (1005–
1797), 19, 25, 75

George Podiebrad proposal
and, 123
Griko, 30
and Islam, 36
Holy Roman Empire in, 14,
30, 63, 96
and League of Nations, 179
Lucca, Republic of (1160–
1805), 75
Pisa, Republic of (c. 1005–
1406), 75
soverano, 15
Ragusa, 19
refugees, 39
Restauratio Imperii, 61
Rome, ancient (753 BC–476
AD), 13–15, 26, 53–8,
59–64
Siena, Republic of (1125–
1555), 75
Treaty of Lodi (1454), 177
Treaty of Rome (1957), 205
Triple Alliance (1882–1915),
167
Venice, Republic of (697–
1797), 14, 19, 25, 34, 75, 76
War of Independence, Second
(1859), 155
and Western Union, 208
World War I (1914–18), 167,
177
Ivan III, Grand Prince of all Rus,
91, 117

Jacobite Rebellions (1688–1746),
87

INDEX

Jacquerie (1358), 101
James VI & I, King of England, Scotland and Ireland, 90
James VII & II, King of England, Scotland and Ireland, 115
Japan, 20, 25, 179, 181, 184, 186, 188, 212
Jerusalem, 46, 66, 107
Jervis, John, 1st Earl St Vincent, 22
Jesus, 45, 59–60, 66
Jewish people, 13, 34–5, 37, 46, 56, 66, 81
Johann Friedrich, Duke of Pomerania-Stettin, 79
John, King of England, 11
John II, King of Portugal, 84
John of Salisbury, 72–3, 241
Judaism, 57, 66
just war, 15, 45, 48, 68, 69, 76, 87, 106
Justinian, Byzantine Emperor, 61, 62

Kadesh, battle of (1274 BC), 44
Kaliningrad, 19
Kant, Immanuel, 12, 14, 139–42, 145, 146, 161, 176, 202, 224
Kashubians, 29
Kellogg, Frank, 179, 182
Kennedy, John Fitzgerald, 212
Kohl, Helmut, 218–19
Königsberg, 19, 139, 145
Korean War (1950–53), 191
Kosovo, 24, 32, 108, 224–6

Kostantiniyye, 20, 91, 94, 108, 109, 153, 160, 164
    see also Ottoman Empire
Kostka, Albrecht, 123
Krol, Frank-Lothar, 239
Kublai Khan, 21
Kurds, 29
Kuwait, 223

Lamers, Karl, 220
Lancaster House Treaties (2010), 223
Landfrieden, 69, 238
languages, 26, 30
Lansing, Robert, 180
Latin, 31
Law of War (de Vitoria), 106
Laws of Nature and Nations (von Pufendorf), 77
Layard, Austen Henry, 160
League of Augsburg, 115
League of Nations, 5, 151, 178–81, 184, 186, 190, 240, 241–2
Lebensraum, 22
Lechfield, battle of the (955), 64
Leipzig, battle of (1813), 149
Leo III, Pope, 62
Leopold II, Holy Roman Emperor, 117, 142
liberal interventionism, 12
Liberalism, 7, 12, 16, 41, 168
Libertäten, 100–101
liberty, 7, 11–13, 100–106
lingua franca, 21

INDEX

Lisbon Treaty (2007), 199
literacy, 10, 30–31
Lloyd George, David, 180
Locarno Treaties (1925), 182
Lollardism, 88
Lombardy, 65
Loménie, Henri-Auguste de,
    Count of Brienne, 103–4
London, 36
Lorraine, 23, 30, 32, 62, 176
Lorsch, 62
Louis IV, Holy Roman Emperor,
    70
Louis IX, King of France, 78
Louis VII, King of France, 71
Louis XI, King of France, 78, 123
Louis XIII, King of France, 111
Louis XIV, King of France, 226
Louis XIV, King of France, 97,
    112–16, 117, 129–30, 137, 142
Louis XV, King of France, 116
Louis XVI, King of France, 117
Louis XVIII, King of France, 150,
    153
Lucca, Republic of (1160–1805),
    75
Lumières, 14
Luther, Martin, 89, 91, 94
Luxembourg, 63, 78, 194, 203

Maastricht Treaty (1992), 219
Macedonia, 32, 108
Machiavelli, Niccolò, 97
Mackinder, Halford, 21
Macmillan, Harold, 205–7, 210

Madras, 34
Magna Carta (1215), 11
Magyars, 20, 64, 66, 67, 107
Mahan, Alfred Thayer, 25
Mahmud I, Ottoman Sultan,
    109–10
Mainz, 96
Mali, 222
Manuel I, King of Portugal, 93
Maria Theresa, Holy Roman
    Empress, 97, 117
Maria Theresa, Queen consort of
    France, 117
Marie Antoinette, Queen consort
    of France, 117, 142
Marie Louise, Duchess of Parma,
    143
Marini, Antoine, 123
Marlborough, Duke of, *see*
    Churchill, John
Marshall Plan, 190
Marx, Karl, 161, 169
Mary I, Queen of England and
    Ireland, 117
Mary II, Queen of England,
    Scotland and Ireland, 114–15
Matthias Corvinus, King of
    Hungary, 123
Maximilian I, Holy Roman
    Emperor, 95, 97, 124
Maximilian II, Holy Roman
    Emperor, 79, 109
Mazarin, Jules, 104
McMahon Act (1946), 209
Medes, 46

INDEX

mediation, 77–80
de' Medici, Lorenzo, 76
Meiji restoration (1868), 20
Melos, 50
Methodist Church, 154
Metternich, Prince Klemens von, 153, 165
Mexico, 166
Midianites, 45–6
Milan, 56
Mildmay, Walter, 82
Minoan civilization (c. 2700–1100 BC), 26
Mitteleuropa, 167–9
Mitterrand, François, 218–19
Mohacs, battle of (1526), 94
Mohammed, Prophet of Islam, 61
Molenbeek, Brussels, 36
Moloch, 44
Molotov–Ribbentrop Pact (1939), 188
von Moltke, Helmuth von, the Elder, 162–4, 172
monarchy, 3, 8, 10
    imperium and, 15
    Liberals and, 12
    nation-states and, 33
    republics and, 14
    sovereignty and, 15
    states and, 10
    universal, *see* universal monarchy
Mongols, 20, 53, 91, 107
Monnet, Jean, 202–3, 205, 208, 211

monopoly on use of force, 10, 72
Monroe Doctrine, 22
Morgenthau, Hans, 48
Morris, Ian, 238
Morrison, Herbert, 203
Moscow, 36
    see also Russia, USSR
Moscow Conference (1944), 226
Moses, 45–6
mountains, 24
Munich, 118
Munich Conference (1938), 187
Münster Peace Congress (1644–8), 79, 112
Mussolini, Benito, 184, 185–6, 239

Napoleon I, Emperor of the French, 239
Napoleon I, Emperor of the French, 53, 102, 142–4, 149–50, 169, 213, 239
Napoleon II, Emperor of the French, 143
Napoleon III, Emperor of the French, 159, 164, 169
Napoleonic Wars (1803–15), 22, 142–4, 149–50, 169, 177
Nassau, Bahamas, 209
nation, 7
nation-states, 2, 7, 9, 19, 30, 31–3, 40, 41, 165, 201, 211
nationalism, 25, 32, 34, 37, 39, 40, 80–83, 164, 169–73, 229
    autochthonous peoples, myth of, 25

pan-German, 32
proto-nationalism, 80–83, 103
Naumann, Friedrich, 168–9
Nazi (National-Socialist)
  Germany (1933–45), 13, 22,
  32, 38, 63, 181, 185, 186,
  187–8, 229
Neanderthals, 25–6
Netherlands, 33, 38, 62, 63, 82
  Dutch Republic (1581–1795),
    9, 102, 126
  Eighty Years' War (1568–1648),
    38, 90, 175
  Estates-General, 9, 112
  and European Coal and Steel
    Community, 204
  guest workers, 29
  Habsburg rule (1482–1794),
    38, 82, 90, 92, 102, 116, 171
  language, 20
  Ottoman Wars, 108
  Roman period (c. 55 BC–410
    AD), 27
  Treaty of Brussels (1948), 194
  Union of Utrecht (1579), 102
  Utrecht Peace Congress
    (1712–13), 80, 129–30,
    132–3, 150–51, 190, 239
Neva river, 19
Nicholas V, Pope, 83
Nicomedia, 56
Nijmegen Peace Congress (1678),
  80, 128–9
Nile river, 18
nomads, 27, 28

Normans, 72, 107
Norsemen, 19, 25, 67
North Atlantic Treaty
  Organisation (NATO), 195–6,
  217, 219–22, 224–7, 231, 233,
  235, 242
  France and, 204, 208, 214, 222
  Kosovo War (1998–9), 24, 225
  and nuclear weapons, 197–8
  United Kingdom and, 197–8,
    208
  United States and, 196
  Washington Treaty (1949), 195
  and Western Union, 199, 208
North Sea, 19, 24
Northcliffe, Lord, see
  Harmsworth, Alfred
Northern Ireland, 29, 33, 41, 220
Norway, 19, 33, 195, 196, 206,
  220
nuclear weapons, 103, 198, 204,
  208, 213, 217, 222, 227
Nuremberg, 96
Nymphenburg, 118

oil, 24
On the Recovery of the Holy Land
  (Dubois), 120
Organisation for Security and
  Cooperation in Europe
  (OSCE), 5, 191, 220, 224–6
Osiander, Andreas, 106
Osnabrück Peace Congress (1644–
  8), 79, 112
Otto I, Holy Roman Emperor,
  64, 65

Otto III, Holy Roman Emperor,
64–5
Otto IV, Holy Roman Emperor,
77
Ottoman Empire (1299–1923),
20, 35, 38, 40, 106–10, 233
balance of power and, 160
Byzantine Wars, 83, 107
Congress System, 152
Crimean War (1853–1856),
152, 155, 156, 159
Habsburg Wars, 91–2, 94–5,
98, 101, 108–10
independence movements, 151,
153, 156, 170
Russian Wars, 116–17, 156,
159, 164
Oxfordshire, 21

Pakistani diaspora, 35, 37
Palatinate, 90, 96, 112
Palmerston, Lord, *see* Temple,
Henry John
Pan-Europa, 181–4
pan-German nationalism, 32
Papacy, 14, 16, 57, 59, 60, 62,
65–7, 69–74, 76, 83
Avignon Papacy (1309–76), 66
and balance of power, 76
bicephalous order and, 69–74,
76
Charlemagne and, 62
Clovis and, 60
colonialism and, 83–4
Crusades, 67, 69, 80

Henry II and, 72
Henry VIII and, 71–2
Holy Roman Empire and,
65–6, 92
Louis IV and, 70
Louis VII and 71
mediation, 77
in Rome, 83, 89
war, sanction of, 66–7, 68,
69–70
Paris, 21, 36
see also France
Paris Peace Congress (1849), 154
Paris Peace Treaties (1918–1919),
177, 180
Pavia, battle of, (1525), 94
Pax Dei, 67–9, 71, 87, 119–20
Pax Romana, 56, 57, 67, 68, 238
peace by hegemony, 69
Peace of Lodi (1454), 177
peace treaties, 128–9
Peasant Revolts, German-
speaking lands (1524–5), 90,
101
Peasants' Revolt, England (1381),
88, 101
Peloponnesian War (431–404
BC), 11, 48–9, 74, 75, 113, 217
Penn, William, 126–9
Pentarchy of Great Powers, 3,
149–53, 240
Perceval, John, 132
Perpetual Union (*unionem perpe-
tuis temporibus duratam*), 121–3

Persia, 2, 34, 40, 43, 46–7, 52–3, 57, 61
Persian Empire, 125
Peter the Great, Emperor of Russia, 118
Peterhof, 118
Philip II, King of Spain, 82, 84, 92, 93
Philip IV, King of Spain, 93
Philip VI, King of France, 78, 120–21
Philip, Duke of Swabia, 77
Philippines, 20, 25, 84
Phoenicia (2500–539 BC), 19
Picts, 26, 57
Pisa, Republic of (c. 1005–1406), 75
Pius II, Pope, 123
Plato, 47, 50
Pleven, René, 211
Plutarch, 73
Poitiers, battle of (732), 62
Poland, 222
   and George Podiebrad proposal, 123
   guest workers, 29
   and Holy Roman Empire, 96, 108
   and Islam, 36, 37
   migrant crisis (2015–), 36, 229
   and *Mitteleuropa*, 168, 169
   October thaw (1956), 226
   and Ottoman Empire, 108
   Penn proposal and, 126
   and Russian Empire, 153

and Saint-Pierre proposal, 133
Stettin Peace Congress (1570), 79
World War I (1914–18), 176
World War II (1939–45), 33, 187, 188, 193, 194
Polaris, 209
Politics (Aristotle), 74
population transfers, 28, 29, 31
populism, 228
Portugal, 36, 75, 83–4, 92, 93, 126, 129, 133, 164, 188, 195, 206
Potsdam, 117
Prague, 96
Project to render Peace perpetual in Europe (Saint-Pierre), 133
Protestantism, 12, 29, 38, 82, 88–90, 100–106, 111, 113
Prussia (1525–1947), 14, 23, 32, 63, 76, 98, 118, 144
   Austro-Prussian War (1866), 156, 171, 177
   balance of power, 76
   Congress System, 149, 152, 154, 156
   empire, 164–5
   Franco-Prussian War (1870–71), 23, 154, 156, 165, 176
   Napoleonic Wars (1803–15), 144
   pan-German nationalism, 32
   Seven Years' War (1756–63), 98, 137
Pufendorf, Samuel von, 77

INDEX

Punic Wars (264–146 BC), 55
Putin, Vladimir, 2, 32–3, 225–7

Querela Pacis (Erasmus), 123–4

Ragusa, 19
raison d'état, 104, 110, 111
Ratisbon, 96
Reagan, Ronald, 217
Realism, 7, 10–11, 16, 17, 48,
    50–51, 103, 189
Rechtsstaaten, 196
Reconquista (722–1492), 80, 81
Red Cross, *see* International
    Committee of the Red Cross
Red Sea, 108
Reformation (c. 1517–1648), 16,
    45, 60, 69, 87, 88–90, 94, 95,
    97, 100–106, 153, 238
refugees, 24, 31, 36, 39, 54, 229,
    233
Reims, 60, 213
religious intolerance, 37–8, 39
religious tolerance, 234
Rémi, 60
Renaissance, 46, 49, 74, 219
republic, 7, 14
republicanism, 139–41
res publica, 9, 13, 59, 73
Richelieu, Cardinal (Armand Jean
    du Plessis), 111
Rijeka, 188
Rijswijk Peace Congress (1697),
    80
rimland, 21

rivers, 18–19
Robespierre, Maximilien, 102,
    170
Rochechouart, Guillaume de,
    94–5, 107
Roes, Alexander von, 70
Roma, 39
Roman Empire, 238, 242
Rome, 145–6, 186, 213
Rome, ancient (753 BC–476 AD),
    13–14, 15, 18, 21, 26, 27, 42,
    45, 54–8, 59–67, 143, 145, 170
Roosevelt, Franklin Delano, 189
Rossbach, battle of (1757), 137
Rousseau, Jean-Jacques, 135, 141
Rubens, Peter Paul, 93
Ruhr, 23
Romania, 26, 36, 38, 96, 108,
    170, 218
Russia
    and Brexit, 2
    Cold War (1946–1990), 49,
        191, 195, 198, 217–19, 221,
        226–7
    Congress System, 149, 152,
        155–6, 158–60
    Crimea, annexation (2014), 227
    Crimean War (1853–1856),
        152, 155, 156, 159
    Empire (1721–1917), 28, 29,
        152, 155–6, 158–60, 164
    Georgian War (2008), 227
    gosudarstvenniy, 9
    immigration, 29
    Kosovo War (1998–9), 225

and League of Nations, 180
missiles, 23, 198
Mackinder on, 21–2
Molotov–Ribbentrop Pact (1939), 188
Napoleonic Wars (1803–15), 142, 144, 149
and 'nation-state', 2, 32–3
and NATO, 224–8
Norsemen, settlement by, 19, 25
nuclear weapons, 217, 226, 227
and OSCE, 224, 226
Ottoman Wars, 116–17, 156, 159, 164
Poland, relations with, 37
Putin period (2000–), 2, 32–3, 225–8
Roman empire, continuity from, 91, 116–17
Soviet period (1917–91), *see under* Soviet Union
spheres-of-influence thinking, 226
and Syrian War (2011–), 227
Treaty of Brest-Litovsk (1918), 176
Ukraine crisis (2013–), 227
and United Nations, 191, 224–6
World War I (1914–18), 167, 173, 176
World War II (1939–45), 188, 189–90
and Yugoslav Wars (1991–2001), 225

Saar, 23
Sachsen, 28
Sacré Coeur, Church of, Paris, 154
Saddam Hussein, 223
Saint-Malo declaration (1998), 222
Saint-Pierre, abbé de, *see* Castel, Charles-Irénée
Salamanca, University of, 76Salvius, Johan Adler, 105
Sancho VI, King of Navarre, 78
Saracens, 66, 83
Sarmatians, 20
Sasanian Empire (224–651), 53
Sassoferrato, Bartolo da, 241
Saul, King of Israel, 44
Savoy, 129
Saxons, 28, 32
Saxon Wars (772–804), 28
Saxony, 64, 79, 96, 98, 107, 166
Seven Years' War (1756–63), 98
Scandinavia, 19
Schäuble, Wolfgang, 220
Schengen Area, 216, 219–20
Schleswig Holstein, 156
Schmidt, Helmut, 215
Schmitt, Carl, 22
Schönbrunn, 117
Schuman, Robert, 202–3, 205, 211
Schwendi, Lazarus von, 108
Scotland, 11, 26, 29, 30, 33, 57, 74, 90
Scythians, 20

INDEX

sea shores, 19–20, 25

Second War of Italian Independence (1859), 155

Second World War, *see* World War II

Seljuk Empire (1037–1194), 34, 67

Serbia, 24, 36, 108, 159, 170, 173, 225

Servan-Schreiber, Jean-Jacques, 212

Servien, Abel, 104

Seven Years' War (1756–63), 98, 137–8, 142

Shakespeare, William, 82

Sharia Law, 40

Sicily, 19, 129

Siebenbürgen (Transylvania), 29

Siena, Republic of (1125–1555), 75

Simms, Brendan, 112, 144

Single European Act (1986), 215

Six Books on the Republic (Bodin), 99–100

slavery, 11, 12, 32, 46, 50, 55

Slavs, 30, 64, 66, 67, 96, 165

Slovakia, 37, 229

Slovaks, 31

Slovenes, 31

Social Darwinism, 172, 185

Soissons, 71

Solomon, King of Israel, 44

Sorbs, 30

sovereignty, 2–3, 7, 13, 15, 31, 33, 42, 59, 69–77, 238, 239, 241, 243–5

Aristotle on, 51, 74, 243

Beaumanoir on, 98–9

Bluntschli on, 161

Bodin on, 99–100

Briande on, 183–4

European Union and, 195, 199, 208

freedom, 101

imperium, 92

Kant on, 140

layered sovereignty, 96

Penn on, 127

as 'pinnacle of development', 41

and warfare, 2–3, 5, 72, 74, 77, 98, 241

Soviet Union

Cold War (1946–1990), 49, 191, 195, 198, 217–19, 221, 226–7

collapse (1991), 32–3

and League of Nations, 180

missiles, 23, 198

Molotov–Ribbentrop Pact (1939), 188

nuclear weapons, 217, 226, 227

population transfers, 28

and United Nations, 191

and uprisings, 226

Warsaw Treaty Organisation, 198, 217–18, 220, 243

World War II (1939–45), 188, 189–90

Spaak, Paul-Henri, 202, 205, 210

Spain, 10, 15, 19, 33, 39, 222

al-Andalus (711–1492), 62, 81

INDEX

balance of power, 75, 76
Catholicism, 81, 82
Civil War (1936–9), 186–7
colonial empire, 83–4, 91, 92, 166
Eighty Years' War (1568–1648), 38, 90, 175
Habsburg Spain (1516–1700), 38, 40, 63, 81, 82, 90, 92, 102, 110, 111, 115, 116
Islam and, 36
Jewish population, 35, 81
mediation in, 78
Napoleonic Wars (1803–15), 169
Netherlands, rule of (1556–1714), 38, 82, 90, 92, 102, 116
Ottoman Wars, 108
proto-nationalism, 81
Reconquista (722–1492), 80, 81
Restauratio Imperii, 61
Roman period (218 BC–472 AD), 56
sovereignty, 74, 80, 89
Utrecht Peace Congress (1712–13), 130
War of the Spanish succession (1701–14), 101, 115, 116
and world rule, 93
Sparta, 47–52, 53, 54
Speyer, 96
St John, Henry, 1st Viscount Bolingbroke, 131
St Petersburg, 118, 154

St Petersburg Declaration (1868), 164
Stalin, Joseph, 28, 181, 187–8, 190, 226, 239
Stanley, Edward Henry, 15th Earl of Derby, 157
State, 7, 9–10
steam engine, 22, 23
steel, 29, 38, 202–4
Sterling Area, 197, 210, 207, 231
Stettin Peace Congress (1570), 79
Stockholm, 19
Stonehenge, 26
Stresemann, Gustav, 182–4
Suárez, Francisco, 77
subsidiarity, 243
Sudan, 27
Suez Crisis (1956), 210, 224
Sully, Duke of, *see* de Béthune, Maximilien
Swabia, 171
Sweden, 19, 33, 37, 79, 97, 103–5, 111–12, 114, 196, 206, 208
Switzerland, 62, 78, 162, 192, 206, 208, 220
Syria, 227
systems of states, 2–5, 9, 15f, 58, 74f, 80, 85f, 91, 107, 110, 112, 114, 118, 119–148, 149–157, 160, 172f, 177, 179, 181, 183, 190–194, 214, 219, 223–226, 228, 230, 232–234, 238–241

Taiwan, 191

de Talleyrand-Périgord, Charles-
  Maurice, 153
Tartars, 125
taxation, 10, 12, 98
Temple, Henry John, 3rd
  Viscount Palmerston, 22,
  156–7, 160
territorial states, 21, 34
Texas, United States, 9
Thames Valley, 21
Thatcher, Margaret, 215
Thebes, 52
Thessaloniki, 56
Thiers, Adolphe, 171
Thirty Years' War (1618–48), 79,
  87, 88, 90, 95, 96, 97, 100–101,
  103, 111, 125, 163
Thucydides, 48–51, 74, 75, 87,
  113
Tolbiac, battle of (c. 496), 60
Tours, 62
Transylvania, 29, 32, 39, 109
Treaty of Belgrade (1739), 110
Treaty of Brest-Litovsk (1918),
  176
Treaty of Brussels (1948), 194
Treaty of Dunkirk (1947), 193,
  223
Treaty of Frankfurt (1871), 177
Treaty of Lisbon (2007), 199
Treaty of Lodi (1454), 177
Treaty of London (1518), 124,
  128
Treaty of Madrid (1526), 94
Treaty of Paris (1814), 150

Treaty of Paris (1856), 155
Treaty of Rome (1957), 205
Treaty of Utrecht (1713–15), 106,
  129–30, 132, 150, 190
Treaty of Versailles (1919), 177–8
Treaty of Vienna (1815), 149–50,
  177
Treaty of Westphalia (1648), 96,
  101, 103, 112, 115, 128
Treuga Dei, 68, 87
Trident, 209
Trier, 56, 96
Trieste, 188
Triple Alliance (1882–1915), 167
Trojan War, 54
Truce of God, 68, 87
Trump, Donald, 2, 231
Turkey, 29, 37, 122, 127, 156,
  158, 160, 195, 196, 225, 233
  see also Ottoman Empire;
    Seljuk Empire
Tyler, Wat, 101
Tyrol, 78, 216

Ukraine, 19, 34, 96, 193, 227
Umma, 35
Union of Utrecht (1579), 102
United Kingdom, 33
  Asian population, 35, 37
  balance of power, 131–2, 144,
    156, 157, 160, 177, 193–4
  Caribbean population, 35, 37
  colonial empire, 15, 84–5, 135,
    151, 206–7, 214
  Commonwealth of Nations, 2,
    198, 206, 207, 232

INDEX

Council of Europe, 196–7

East of Suez withdrawal (1971), 214

Entente Cordiale (1904), 166

and 'European Affairs Committee', 194

and European Coal and Steel Community, 204

and European Economic Community, 1, 205–7, 214, 215

and European Free Trade Area, 206

and European Union, core of, 220–21

and European Union, referendum on membership (2016), 1, 3, 230

geography and, 22–3

immigration, 229

and League of Nations, 177, 179, 181, 186

monarchy, 33

Munich Conference (1938), 187

Napoleonic Wars (1803–15), 22, 144

and NATO, 197–8, 222, 231

non-intervention, 156, 172, 189

Northern Ireland, 33, 41, 220

nuclear weapons, 103, 198, 199, 207, 208, 209–10, 222

sea, connection to, 37

Seven Years' War (1756–63), 137

social welfare system, 234

Sterling Area, 197, 210, 207, 231

Suez Crisis (1956), 210, 224

trade, 231–2

Treaty of Brussels (1948), 194

Treaty of Dunkirk (1947), 193, 223

United States, relations with, 2, 198, 207, 208–10, 232

War of the Spanish Succession (1701–14), 115

and Western Union, 195

World War I (1914–18), 23, 177

World War II (1939–45), 187, 188, 189

United Nations (UN), 190–91

Charter, 132, 190

Security Council, 3, 132, 151, 190–91, 222, 223, 224–6

Universal Declaration on Human Rights (1948), 13, 39

and warfare, 5

United States of America, 2, 126

Bluntschli and, 161–2

Briand-Kellogg Pact (1928), 179, 182, 241

Fourteen Points (1918), 175–6, 184

France, relations with, 208, 210, 212, 239

European defence co-operation, 221–2, 230–31

isolationism, 156, 180, 209

Kennedy administration (1961–3), 212

and League of Nations, 179, 180

McMahon Act (1946), 209

Monroe Doctrine, 22

as nation-state, 9

and NATO, 196

nuclear weapons, 198, 207, 208, 209–10, 213, 222, 230, 232

President, 141

Revolutionary War (1775–83), 8, 33

'State-of-the-Nation' speech, 9

Suez Crisis (1956), 210

Trump administration (2017–), 2, 230–31

United Kingdom, relations with, 2, 198, 207, 208–10, 232

Wall Street Crash (1929), 184, 228

World War I (1917–18), 175, 180

United States of Europe, 192

Universal Declaration on Human Rights (1948), 13, 39

universal monarchy, 42, 58, 59, 164, 237, 239, 243

England and, 105–6

France and, 105, 111–12, 143, 144, 240

Gentz on, 145, 146

Habsburgs and, 116

Penn on, 128

Spain and, 82–3, 93, 105

Urban II, Pope, 67, 80

Ureinwohner, original inhabitants, 25

Urraca, Queen of Leon and Castile, 92

utopian ideas, 5

Utrecht Peace Congress (1712–13), 80, 129–30, 132–3, 150–51, 190, 239

Valla, Lorenzo, 48, 74

Valois, House of, 83, 110, 111, 118, 165, 170

Varangians, 19, 25

Vauban, Sébastien Le Prestre de, 112–13

Venice, Republic of (697–1797), 14, 19, 25, 34, 75, 76, 123

Versailles, 117

Victoria, Queen of the United Kingdom, 15, 160

Vienna, 94, 96, 101, 108, 109, 117

Vienna Peace Congress (1814–15), 149–50, 177

Vikings, 19, 25

Virgil, 55

Vitoria, Francisco de, 76–7, 106

Volga river, 19

Wales, 33

Wall Street Crash (1929), 184, 228

Wallingford, 21

Waltz, Kenneth, 48

War of the Spanish Succession (1701–14), 101, 115

warfare, 2–3, 5, 67–9

INDEX

civil war, 10, 49, 50, 68
democracy and, 52, 139
ius in bello, 76–7
just war, 15, 45, 48, 68, 69, 76, 87, 106
mediation, 77
Penn on, 127–8
private war, 68
sovereignty and, 2–3, 5, 72, 74, 77, 98, 241
Thucydides on, 48–51, 74
Vitoria on, 106
war crimes, 177
Warsaw Treaty Organisation, 198, 217–18, 220, 243
Washington, DC, United States, 9
Washington Naval Conference (1922), 185
Washington Treaty (1949), 195
Waterloo, battle of (1815), 149
Watt, Donald Cameron, 8
Weber, Max, 10
Weigley, Russell, 239
Welsh language, 30
West Frankish Kingdom (843–987), 63
West Germany (1949–90), 195, 198, 202–4, 205, 206, 208, 211, 213, 215
Western European Union, 198, 208
Western Roman Empire (395–480), 28, 55, 57, 59
Western Union, 195–9, 208
Westphalian Treaties (1648), 96, 101, 103, 112, 115, 128

Wetzlar, 96
Whig party, 131
Widukind of Corvey, 64
William I, German Emperor, 156
William II, German Emperor, 178
William III, King of England, Scotland and Ireland, 114–15
William of Ockham, 70
Wilson, Woodrow, 136, 175–6, 177, 178, 181, 184
Wittenberg, 91
World Cup (2018), 232
World War I (1914–18), 16, 23, 110, 167, 173, 175, 240
World War II (1939–45), 13, 19, 23, 31, 33, 34, 38, 187–8, 189, 225, 235, 240
Worms, 96
Wright, Moorhead, 76
Württemberg, 166
Würzburg, 102
Wycliffe, John, 88

xenophobia, 39, 172, 175, 185, 229

Yalta Conference (1945), 189
Yugoslavia (1918–2003), 19, 24, 29, 31–2, 37, 188, 221, 224–5, 227

Zadar, 19, 188
Zoë, Byzantine Empress, 64
Zurich, University of, 192
Zwingli, Huldrych, 89